NO ONE IS
COMING TO
SAVE YOU

NO ONE IS COMING TO SAVE YOU

This book resonates with the seekers, the believers, the dreamers, and those who intuitively feel there's more to life than the mundane daily grind. It's for the souls who sense another layer of existence, a deeper dimension of joy and fulfillment.

No One Is Coming To Save You

ISBN: 979-8-89109-762-9 - paperback

ISBN: 979-8-89109-763-6 - ebook

ISBN: 979-8-89109-776-6- hardcover

Table of Contents

No One Is Coming to Save You.

First things first. If you've opened this book in search of a nail-biting, edge-of-the-seat comeback story, you're in the wrong aisle. No harrowing tales of dodging death, no rags to riches transformation, no cancer warrior. By many accounts, my life probably reads like a fairly standard narrative.

Yet, the reason this book exists isn't because of the extraordinary challenges I faced but the ordinary ones. The silent battles, the subdued pain, and the subtle shifts from merely existing to truly living.

For the longest time, I believed my life wasn't significant enough, that my struggles weren't substantial enough to be etched onto these pages. A persistent voice in my head kept whispering that enduring message—you're not worthy enough. This is perhaps the most universal human sentiment, the feeling that we aren't "enough" in some way. We often feel our pain must reach cinematic proportions to be valid or that our victories must be grand to be celebrated. My journey, however, is neither of those. It's a journey from feeling "just okay" to feeling "truly extraordinary."

So, why put pen to paper? Why share my "good to great" evolution? Because I believe there's a vast expanse of uncharted territory between contentment and euphoria. I'm writing this to persuade you to venture into that territory. To dare to dream bigger, to aim higher, to strive not just for a good life but an exceptional one. To realize that regardless of the baggage of the past or the uncertainties of the future, there's a realm of possibility, purpose, and passion awaiting you.

But remember, to get there, you must make a conscious choice. Because while nobody is coming to save you, you always have the power to save yourself. Let's embark on that journey together.

As you flip through the pages of this book, my intent is to challenge and dismantle deeply held convictions. Not to rattle your core for the mere sake of it, but to help you rebuild on a foundation of authenticity, away from the conditioned beliefs and societal impositions that have held us captive for so long.

Many claim to know the "truth," but what they often mean is their truth—one that is tainted with personal experiences, biases, and inherited beliefs. Our own truths, while valuable and significant, are not always factual. They are stories, narratives, interpretations—not indisputable realities. Recognizing this is the first step to liberating ourselves.

There's an age-old saying: "Empty your cup so that it may be filled." In essence, this is about unlearning. Before we can truly grasp and embrace new wisdom, we must first make space by releasing outdated beliefs and misperceptions. This process of unlearning isn't just about forgetting; it's about liberation. Liberation from societal shackles, self-imposed boundaries, and the weight of "should" and "ought tos."

In the chapters that follow, we'll embark on a transformative expedition that transcends typical self-help jargon. Drawing from the vast realms of human psychology, the intricate dance of neurons in neuroscience, and the expansive world of metaphysics, we'll chart a course toward emotional, rather than purely logical, enlightenment. Because at the heart of a life well-lived is not just reason but deep emotion. Passion. Desire. Love.

So, as you delve deeper into this journey, I invite you to approach with an open mind and a willing heart. To question, reflect, and ultimately, to evolve.

On Empowerment, Expansion, & Enlightenment

The essence of Empowerment, Expansion, and Enlightenment weave seamlessly through this book, serving both as its grounding foundation and the ultimate destination. As readers navigate the triad journey of Self-Awareness, Self-Acceptance, and Self-Mastery, these pillars act as guiding lights, illuminating the path toward a deeper understanding and actualization of one's true self. They not only encapsulate the heart of each page but also chart the holistic evolution of one's soul through every stage of this transformative journey.

The Essence of Empowerment

Empowerment isn't just a buzzword; it's a profound shift in the way we perceive and interact with the world around us. At the core of empowerment is the understanding that our inner experience is not the byproduct of external events but, rather, the result of our interpretations, perceptions, and beliefs about those events.

From childhood, many of us are indoctrinated into a mindset that positions us as passive recipients of life's events. We're told that success, happiness, and fulfillment are contingent upon external factors—the right job, the perfect relationship, the praise and validation of others, etc. Over time, this conditioning leads us to believe that our feelings and emotions are the inevitable outcomes of external triggers.

Yet, the true essence of empowerment challenges this notion. It beckons us to realize that while we can't always control what happens to us, we have full command over how we choose to respond. It's the understanding that our emotions aren't dictated by someone else's actions but by our thoughts about those actions.

This means that the power to feel confident isn't in someone else's compliment but in our belief about ourselves. The power to feel content doesn't lie in achieving a certain milestone but in our perspective toward our journey. And the power to feel loved isn't in someone else's affection but in our own self-worth.

Stepping out of the victim mentality requires us to shift from blame to ownership, from reaction to response, and from seeking external validation to cultivating inner conviction. It's about moving from a place of "life is happening to me" to "life is happening for me."

Empowerment, then, is not about wielding power over others but about harnessing the immense power within, reclaiming our agency, and taking charge of our narratives. It's a journey toward the center, where we stand grounded in our truth, unswayed by external storms. And in this centered space, we find the freedom to craft a life that's not just a reflection of what happens to us but a testament to what we're capable of.

The Essence of Expansion

Expansion is an inner journey, a broadening of one's horizons not just in terms of experiences but in terms of awareness, understanding, and compassion. It's about embracing our infinite nature, realizing that our true essence isn't confined to the limitations we've set for ourselves or those that society may have thrust upon us.

When we talk about expansion, it's not about becoming someone "more" or "better;" it's about revealing the vastness that has always existed within us. Just as the universe continually expands, so does the human spirit, ever-evolving and always pushing the boundaries of what is known and understood.

While the societal narrative often places worth on achievements, expansion redefines this notion. It shifts our focus from external accomplishments to internal growth. It's about developing a deeper connection with oneself, cultivating an understanding of our unique gifts and capabilities, and realizing the endless potential that lies dormant within, waiting to be tapped.

This journey of expansion is fueled by curiosity, courage, and compassion. Curiosity to explore beyond the known, courage to break free from self-imposed limitations, and compassion to accept ourselves fully, imperfections and all.

Moreover, expansion is not a solitary endeavor. As we grow, we impact those around us. Our expanded consciousness influences our interactions, choices, and contributions, creating a ripple effect. We become conduits of positive change, inspiring others to embark on their own journeys of self-discovery and growth.

In essence, expansion is about returning to our true nature. It's about moving from a place of lack to abundance, from seeking to discovering, from uncertainty to clarity. It's about realizing that we are not just a small drop in the vast ocean but the entire ocean in a drop. And, as we embrace this expansive nature, we step into a world where every moment holds the promise of new possibilities, where our worth isn't defined by external metrics but recognized as an innate and unchangeable truth.

The Essence of Enlightenment

Enlightenment isn't a destination; it's a realization, a recognition of our most authentic self. It's a state of being that transcends the dichotomies and contrasts we've come to identify with. In enlightenment, we see beyond the dualities that have long governed our perceptions and interactions.

Life, with all its ups and downs, joys and sorrows, is not a series of random events but a beautifully orchestrated symphony. When we begin to see the world through the lens of enlightenment, we recognize that everything that happens is purposeful and intentional, designed for our growth and evolution.

In this state, love becomes our guiding force. Not the transactional love that demands reciprocation but an unconditional love that is pure, boundless, and all-encompassing. A love that sees no difference between the self and the other, that recognizes the divine in every being, and that celebrates the unity in diversity.

The path to enlightenment requires shedding layers of conditioning, unlearning many of the beliefs and narratives we've clung to, and allowing our true essence to emerge. It requires us to transcend the ego, the part of us that seeks to divide, label, and categorize. Instead of seeing ourselves as separate entities, we begin to understand that we are all interconnected, part of the same cosmic tapestry.

In this space of enlightenment, we are neither influenced by praise nor criticism. Our actions are not driven by the desire for reward or fear of punishment. We operate from a place of pure intent, driven by the purpose of serving the greater good.

This is where the magic happens. When we live in this enlightened space, we become channels of positive change, spreading love, joy, and peace wherever we go. We inspire others not by preaching or teaching but simply by being. Our very presence becomes a source of inspiration, radiating light and love.

Enlightenment is not about gaining new knowledge or acquiring new skills. It's about remembering who we truly are, about coming home to our true essence. It's about living in harmony with the universe, trusting its wisdom, and flowing with its rhythm. It's a state of pure being, where love reigns supreme, and all is one.

Pillars: Awareness, Acceptance, and Awakening

As we navigate the realm of personal growth and inner evolution, three distinct yet interwoven pillars emerge: Awareness, Acceptance, and Awakening. These pillars mirror these philosophies. Each represents a phase in our journey toward a deeper understanding of ourselves and the universe, a stairway leading us to higher realms of consciousness.

Awareness: The foundation of our inner journey starts with awareness. Much of our life operates from the realm of the subconscious, a vast reservoir of beliefs, memories, and patterns that influence our decisions and behaviors. Through the pillar of awareness, we aim to bring these hidden forces to the forefront of our consciousness. This illumination is like turning on a light in a previously dark room, revealing what was always there but unseen. As we shed light on these patterns and beliefs, we gain the power to change them, redirecting the course of our lives.

Acceptance: As our newfound awareness brings these hidden aspects of ourselves into the light, the next phase is acceptance. To truly evolve, mere recognition is not enough. We must embrace every facet of our being, the strengths and the flaws, with mindfulness and presence. This embrace isn't passive resignation but an active recognition of our authentic self. Through acceptance, we approach ourselves with love, compassion, and forgiveness. It is in this nurturing environment that true transformation begins, allowing us to shed layers of pretense and align more closely with our essence.

Awakening: Beyond the realms of awareness and acceptance lies the pinnacle of our inner journey—Awakening. Here, we transcend the boundaries of individual consciousness and tap into the superconscious. This state of being is characterized by profound intuition, a deep sense of interconnectedness with all that exists, and a transcendent understanding of the universe. The superconscious offers insights that are often beyond the grasp of our logical mind, guiding us toward a more harmonious existence in sync with the larger cosmos.

In essence, these three pillars represent the stages of our spiritual and emotional evolution. From uncovering hidden truths about ourselves to fully embracing them and then transcending our individual confines, the journey is one of continual growth and enlightenment. As we navigate through each pillar, we not only understand ourselves better but also our place in the grand tapestry of existence.

All these philosophies, in their essence, invite us back home. Home not as a physical space but a state of being where we are in perfect alignment with our true selves. A place where our spirits are free, our hearts are open, and our souls are at peace.

In the dance between the words and wisdom of *No One Is Coming to Save You*, we find a roadmap, not to an external treasure, but to the gold that has always glittered within our own hearts.

The Gift of Choice—Self-Awareness

Every choice begins with a spark, a moment of clarity. That spark is self-awareness.

In the vast universe of personal development, a foundational star shines the brightest: self-awareness. It is the underpinning of every transformative journey, a quiet sentinel that guides each step we take toward growth.

Self-awareness isn't just a trendy term. It's an invitation to the most profound study one can ever embark on—*the study of the self.* Dive deep, past the surface, and you'll find a world teeming with thoughts, emotions, and behaviors. It's a holistic exploration, spanning the physical realm of the body, the intricate mazes of the mind, and the boundless expanses of the soul.

Yet, for all its depth, self-awareness isn't just about introspection. It's also about acknowledging the external factors, experiences, and narratives that have shaped us. These external influences, while impactful, can sometimes cloud our self-perception, pulling us away from our authentic cores. Self-awareness, then, becomes a tool to cut through these veils, revealing the unvarnished truth of who we are.

Recognizing the need for self-awareness is the first critical step on this journey. The fact that you are here, at the precipice of this chapter, speaks volumes. You're poised, ready to embrace the illuminating power of self-awareness. Ready to unearth the treasures hidden within. Ready to make choices that truly resonate with your core.

Let's dive in and, together, rediscover the magic that's been within you all along.

Discovering the Broken Dandelion Within

At the tender age of four, the world was my oyster. Days seemed longer and brighter, and every little thing felt like a grand discovery. I recall a particularly hot day, sun blazing, and the sound of cardboard scraping on the ground as my mother and grandmother hurriedly packed boxes into our car. We were in the throes of a move. The details of where or why were fuzzy to me; my world was a lot simpler then.

In the midst of this chaos, I found joy in the simple act of picking a dandelion. Its yellow hue was my present to my mother. But, as I presented my little treasure, her gaze was elsewhere, consumed by the move. My gift, my gesture of love, was unnoticed amidst the towering boxes and to-do lists. My young heart couldn't comprehend the shift in priorities, and I felt an overwhelming sadness. The dandelion's stem broke, mirroring my fragile heart. The tape they handed to me to fix it felt like a metaphorical band-aid, a fleeting solution to a deeper pain.

Outside, while the sun bore down, a cold realization settled in me. I felt an alien emotion, a stark sense of loneliness. It was as if the world moved around me but not with me. My father was absent, and my brother, facing his own challenges, needed special care due to his health. There was no one to notice the little girl with a taped-up dandelion on the doorstep, trying to mend her own heart.

Childhood, in its essence, is the cradle of trust. We seek validation, understanding, and security from those around us. Each nod of appreciation, every word of praise, crafts our self-worth. But what happens when this trust gets shaken? When the people we seek validation from are too caught up in their own worlds?

It was in these seemingly small moments that I began to question my self-worth. A broken dandelion and an absent acknowledgment led me to believe maybe I wasn't enough. The once-secure world felt shaky, and I internalized these feelings. A narrative began to form in my mind—one of unworthiness, of not being loveable enough, of needing to hide my true feelings to avoid further pain.

Such experiences can easily mold our perception of self. They become the glasses through which we view the world, distorting our reality. This self-imposed narrative begins to dictate our actions, interactions, and decisions. We navigate life with a protective wall, fearing further hurt, further rejection.

But healing starts with recognizing these self-imposed barriers. Self-awareness isn't just about knowing your likes and dislikes; it's about understanding why you feel a certain way and the root of those feelings. It's about revisiting the hurtful moments, not to dwell in them, but to understand, heal, and grow.

Looking back, I've come to realize that we are not defined by singular experiences, no matter how impactful. We are the sum of our reactions, decisions, and interpretations. True growth lies in separating our core selves from the beliefs we've constructed around past traumas.

My journey into self-awareness began with a broken dandelion, and it led me to a path of introspection, understanding, and, ultimately, self-love. Through this journey, I've learned that the meaning we give to our experiences holds the power to shape our reality. But once we truly understand this, we reclaim the pen, becoming the authors of our own stories.

Purposeful Pathways: Journeying Toward Real Progress

In our lives, every thread we weave signifies a step, a decision, or a memory on our personal journey. But amidst the chaos of life, there's a question that often lingers—how do we direct our steps with purpose?

How do we ensure that each thread leads us toward a design that resonates with our soul's true calling?

Enter the concept of purposeful pathways—routes that guide us not just toward our goals but toward understanding, fulfillment, and growth.

What Are Purposeful Pathways?

Unlike aimless wandering, purposeful pathways are directed routes, consciously chosen, based on a deeper understanding of oneself and one's objectives. They are more than just paths leading to materialistic goals; they're about aligning our journeys with values, passions, and a sense of meaning.

The Myths We've Been Believing

There's a societal myth that paints success as a linear path, often benchmarked by possessions, titles, or societal validation. But reality and experience tell us otherwise. Not every detour is a diversion; sometimes, they lead to richer, more scenic views. Another myth is the association of speed with success. In the rush to get ahead, the joy of the journey is often lost.

Defining "Real" Progress

Real progress isn't just about moving forward but ensuring that this forward motion is aligned with one's true self. It's about personal evolution, where success isn't just measured in milestones achieved but in the wisdom gathered, relationships nurtured, and personal barriers overcome.

Myths About "Real" Progress

There's a false narrative that real progress is always tangible, always visible. This isn't true. Often, the most profound progress is silent, unseen—like overcoming a limiting belief or healing from past traumas.

Routes of Awareness

These routes aren't just physical paths but mental and emotional ones, each leading to different facets of self-discovery.

Route of Reflection: The continual practice of introspection and of understanding one's motivations, desires, and fears.

Route of Resilience: Building the capability to bounce back from setbacks and see failures as stepping stones.

Route of Relationship: Understanding that growth doesn't occur in isolation. It's about connecting deeply with others and learning from these connections.

Route of Rejuvenation: Acknowledging the need for rest and renewal to move forward with renewed vigor.

Route of Re-education: Continual learning and unlearning, understanding that knowledge and personal growth are endless pursuits.

As we navigate these routes, we realize that the journey to self-mastery isn't about a destination but about the voyage itself. It's about traveling these pathways with intent, understanding, and an open heart.

The Triad of Self: Body, Mind, and Spirit

As humans, our existence is intricate, and it's a delicate dance of physical, mental, and spiritual dimensions. To truly understand oneself, we must honor and delve into each of these realms. Ignoring one is like trying to understand the full picture with a third of the puzzle missing.

1. The Physical Canvas: The Body

Our body is not just an entity that carries us from point A to B. It is the tangible manifestation of our existence, our first interface with the world. Every scar, wrinkle, and dimple tells a story of battles won, of love lost, and of adventures undertaken.

Listening to the Body: Often, our bodies communicate with us—through aches, hunger, fatigue, etc. But in the cacophony of modern life, we sometimes forget to listen. Understanding oneself begins with tuning into these signals.

Nourishing With Intent: What we feed our bodies goes beyond mere sustenance. It's about nourishing it with what it truly needs— be it food, rest, or movement.

2. The Ever-Churning Ocean: The Mind

The human mind is a marvel, constantly processing, analyzing, and creating. It is the repository of our memories, dreams, fears, and aspirations.

Mindfulness and Mental Hygiene: Just as we clean our physical spaces, our mind, too, needs decluttering. Practices like meditation and mindfulness help us gain clarity, sifting through the mental noise.

Cognitive Patterns and Beliefs: Unraveling our thought processes and beliefs can offer deep insights into why we behave the way we do. It's a journey into understanding our mental conditioning and biases.

3. The Eternal Flame: The Spirit

Beyond the tangible body and the analytical mind lies the spirit—the essence of who we are, our soul. It's what connects us to something bigger, to the universe, to each other.

Finding Purpose: Our spirit often seeks purpose, a deeper meaning in life. Understanding this purpose can illuminate our path, making our journey more fulfilling.

Connectivity and Compassion: Our spirit thrives on connection— be it with nature, with fellow beings, or with a higher power. It's in these connections that we often find solace, strength, and love.

Embracing the Triad

It's tempting, in the age of specialization, to focus on just one dimension. But true understanding and true growth come when we honor all three aspects of ourselves. It's about aligning the Triad with the best of who we are, ensuring that our body grows strong, our mind grows wise, and our spirit enriched.

So, embark on this exploration with an open heart. Celebrate the marvel that is you. Dive deep into the realms of your body, mind, and spirit, and discover the harmonious symphony they create together.

The Four Pillars of Control

Within our life's experiences, amidst the tumult of external circumstances, lie four pillars of control that we truly hold reign over—our thoughts, our emotions, our behaviors, and the results we manifest from them.

1. Thoughts: Every journey starts with a single thought. This thought, whether positive or negative, constructive or destructive, sets the tone for our experiences. Recognizing and governing our thoughts is the bedrock of any meaningful change.

2. Emotions: Directly stemming from our thoughts, emotions are the personal barometers of our internal world. While we might not control the initial feeling that emerges from a thought or event, we have the agency to choose our emotional response and how long we hold onto it.

3. Behaviors: Our actions, born from our thoughts and emotions, are the most tangible elements of control. Through deliberate choices, we can align our behaviors with our values, dreams, and aspirations.

4. *Results:* The outcomes we achieve are direct consequences of our behaviors. Though we might not have a say in every aspect of the results due to external factors, the aspects we can influence stem from our controlled thoughts, emotions, and behaviors.

However, the quest for control can sometimes lead us astray. In our desire to shape our world, we may attempt to control the uncontrollable, from the actions of others to unpredictable events. These endeavors not only deplete our energy but can also veer us off our destined path.

By centering our focus on the four pillars, we're not limiting ourselves but rather honing in on our true power. This concentrated effort ensures that we stay on course, moving steadily toward our goals without being sidetracked by externalities.

The path to fulfillment isn't about grasping for control over everything but about mastering the domains where our power truly resides. By understanding and nurturing the interconnectedness of our thoughts, emotions, behaviors, and results, we unlock a life of purpose and joy. So, let's commit to staying in our lane, for it's in this space that our true journey unfolds.

Let's dig a little deeper into each of these pillars.

Thoughts: Navigating the Labyrinth— The Mindscape Journey

It's easy to perceive the mind as a linear space—simple, straightforward, with a clear start and endpoint. However, the reality is far more nuanced. Our minds resemble vast labyrinths, with each corridor representing a different thought, emotion, memory, or belief. Each corner we turn brings with it a new perspective, a fresh challenge, and unique revelations. Traversing this intricate maze requires not just courage but also the right set of tools and an understanding that, more often than not, the journey is as valuable as the destination.

The vast expanse of our thoughts is a domain so intricate and profound that delving into its every nuance would demand not just the remaining pages of this book but perhaps an entire series. Our mind, woven with thoughts, desires, memories, and reflections, serves as both our guiding compass and, often, our greatest challenge.

Over decades, scholars, psychologists, and thinkers have embarked on intellectual odysseys to understand this complex landscape. The insights presented here are distilled from years of rigorous exploration and contemplation.

These principles are not just theoretical musings but the culmination of lived experiences, research, and practice. They serve as guideposts, beckoning you to venture deeper, to question, and to introspect. While we touch upon the highlights, remember that each point is an invitation, a doorway into a broader world of understanding.

Consider this a starting point, a roadmap of sorts. As you journey through these principles, be open to exploration, for the realm of thoughts is as vast as it is profound. Embrace the opportunity to delve deeper, challenge assumptions, and forge your own path in understanding the true power and potential of your thoughts.

1. Thoughts: Interpretations, Not Facts

One of the first realizations to embrace is that our thoughts aren't always objective truths. They're tinted by our experiences, biases, and current emotional state. Just as two people can witness the same event and interpret it differently, our thoughts can also differ vastly from reality. Recognizing this is the first step in discerning the difference between fact and fiction within our minds.

2. The Power of Perception

Our life's trajectory is immensely influenced by our perceptions. It's not about what happens to us but how we think about what happens to us. Our reactions, decisions, and feelings stem from these perceptions, shaping our reality. Realize that reshaping our thoughts can alter our life's course dramatically.

3. The Thought Problem Paradigm

Every problem we face can be traced back to a thought. This isn't to oversimplify the complexities of life but to highlight that our perspective on a situation can magnify or diminish its impact. Recognizing that problems are often manifestations of our thoughts equips us to address the root cause, not just the symptoms. And while it's human nature to encounter problems, how we perceive and process them defines our experience.

4. Beyond Positive Thinking

The goal isn't perpetual positivity. Such a state is not only unattainable but can also be counterproductive. By suppressing negative thoughts or emotions, we risk ignoring vital signals that something needs attention or change. Instead, the aim is conscious thinking—being aware of our thoughts, understanding their origin, and choosing how to respond to them.

5. *Cultivating Conscious Thought*

Like any skill, conscious thinking requires practice. It's about pausing before reacting, introspecting before deciding, and constantly questioning our thought patterns. Over time, this deliberate approach to thinking fosters a deeper connection with oneself, enabling more meaningful decisions and enriched experiences.

The mindscape, with all its winding paths and hidden corridors, is a realm of endless exploration. Each day presents an opportunity to learn more about oneself, to challenge our boundaries, and to grow. With the right tools and perspectives, not only can we navigate this vast expanse effectively, but we can also truly cherish the journey. Remember, it's not about reaching the end of the maze but about understanding and savoring every twist and turn along the way.

Emotions: Navigating the Uncharted Waters

In our journey through life, we encounter various learning institutions—from grade school to university. But surprisingly, there's no formal "Thought School" to educate us on the intricacies of our own thinking or a "Feeling School" to guide us through the vast emotional landscape that shapes every aspect of our existence. Such vital components of our human experience, and yet, we often navigate them without a compass.

When it comes to feelings, the guidance we generally receive is minimal, even vague. "Feel your feelings," they say. But what exactly does that entail? For many, emotions become things to be sidestepped or suppressed. We sweep them under the proverbial rug, offload the responsibility onto others, or find myriad ways to distract ourselves from confronting them head-on.

Feelings, in their rawest form, are powerful indicators, painting our world with shades of joy, sadness, love, anger, and countless others. They inform our reactions, shape our memories, and dictate our decisions. Yet, the lack of understanding and awareness around emotions often leaves us reactive rather than responsive.

I am well aware that I will not be able to do them justice in the pages of this book; it is my intent to introduce to you fundamental philosophical concepts for your own awareness and personal growth. By beginning to comprehend the weight and influence of our feelings, we unlock a deeper understanding of ourselves. This is not merely an exploration but an invitation to recognize, respect, and respond to our emotions in ways that enhance, not hinder, our journey through life. Embrace this as a starting point, for understanding our feelings is a lifelong expedition full of revelations and insights.

The Symphony of the Soul: Understanding and Embracing Emotions

Emotions, those intricate rhythms of our soul, serve as the soundtrack to our life's journey. Every high and low, every triumph and setback, is punctuated by a medley of feelings, each with its own timbre and resonance. These emotions, however, are not merely passive reactions to external events. They are, in essence, a barometer of our inner world—a mirror reflecting the intricacies of our thoughts.

1. Feelings: Vibrations of Thought

Behind every emotion lies a thought or a series of thoughts. These feelings are not arbitrary but are vibrations in our body—a physical manifestation of our mental processes. Like ripples on the water's surface after a stone's toss, our thoughts send waves through our beings, translating into the feelings we experience.

2. Emotions as Guides

More than just reactions, emotions serve as indicators. They signal that there's a lesson lurking, a wound needing healing, or a truth about ourselves waiting to be uncovered. They are not nuisances to be ignored but compasses pointing us toward personal growth and self-discovery.

3. The Blame and Escape Game

One of society's gravest errors is its tendency to assign blame for our emotional states or to seek escapism. It's a paradoxical dance—on one hand, we attribute our feelings to others, believing they have the power to make us feel a certain way. On the other, we engage in overconsumption—from food to media to perpetual busyness—as a means to drown out or numb those very feelings. This cycle of blame and escape detaches us from the depths and the richness of our emotions.

4. Delegating Our Emotional Well-being

In a world that often prioritizes doing over being, many have outsourced their emotional well-being. Whether it's turning to others for validation or seeking solace in external stimuli, this delegation has made us strangers to our own emotional landscapes. Yet, the path to emotional maturity lies in taking ownership and recognizing that our feelings are our responsibility.

5. The Art of Truly Feeling

Somewhere along the line, many of us lost the inherent skill of simply feeling. We've been conditioned to categorize emotions as "good" or "bad" and to chase the former while avoiding the latter. But to live fully, we must learn to feel fully. This involves understanding each emotion, no matter how uncomfortable, as a valuable part of our human experience.

The goal is to retune our emotional instruments. It's about recognizing the profound symphony within us and learning to play each note—whether major or minor—with authenticity and grace. Remember, in the grand orchestra of life, every emotion has its place, and both understanding and embracing them is the key to producing the most harmonious and fulfilling life.

Actions: The Crucial Third Component

In our journey of self-awareness, actions stand as the third pillar of what we can control, accompanying our thoughts and emotions. But here's the catch: While knowledge is power, knowing "what" to do doesn't always translate into doing it. We've all been there, fully aware of what the "right" action is, yet finding ourselves hesitating, procrastinating, or even opting for an entirely different route.

So, what holds us back? Why do we not act upon our knowledge?

It's because our actions are not always dictated by logical reasoning or the facts in front of us. Instead, they are driven by our emotions, our feelings about the consequences of or commitment to those actions. We're not robots; we're emotionally driven beings, and our feelings often trump our logic.

Consider this: How many times have we decided against that morning jog because it felt too cold outside, even though we knew the benefits of the exercise? Or how often have we avoided having a difficult conversation because it felt uncomfortable, even though, logically speaking, it was necessary?

Understanding this, it becomes evident that the challenge isn't necessarily about discerning the right actions. It's about mastering our emotions so they can propel us toward those actions. It's about aligning our feelings with our knowledge, enabling us to move forward.

This is where the real magic happens. Because once our emotions and logic align, once we're moved not just by what we know but also by what we feel, our actions become unstoppable. We transition from living reactively, based on whims and external pressures, to living proactively, driven by intention and purpose.

Actions: The Behavior-Reaction-Inaction Trilogy

Actions, in their essence, encompass a spectrum that ranges from proactive behaviors to immediate reactions, and sometimes, even deliberate inaction. What dictates where we fall on this spectrum? Our feelings. They are the silent puppeteers pulling the strings behind every move we make.

Let's unravel this further. Think about those times you've reached for a snack, not out of hunger, but perhaps due to feelings of boredom or stress. That's a behavior prompted by an emotion. Consider those moments you've deliberately sidestepped your boss's office, not because you didn't have anything to discuss, but because anger from a previous interaction still lingered within you. That's a reaction powered by an emotion. And then, there are times when you pull away from close friends or family, not due to any tangible conflict, but out of sheer sadness or feeling overwhelmed. That's inaction, again steered by an emotion.

Our feelings serve as the internal compass guiding our actions. They whisper in our ears, nudging us toward or away from situations. While this can serve as a protective mechanism, it can also limit us, holding us back from potential growth and experiences.

To truly harness the power of actions in shaping our lives, we must first tune into our emotions. Understand them, don't merely react to them. By shifting our emotional landscape, we can drive transformative changes in our behaviors. When we choose feelings that empower, inspire, and motivate, our actions naturally align with those that foster growth and bring about incredible results in our lives.

In essence, actions are more than just what we do; they are a reflection of how we feel. Want different actions? Start with different feelings. The results will astound you.

Behavioral Insight: Aligning Actions With Aspirations

A mosaic of behaviors, actions, and reactions constitute our lives. Each tiny piece, individually shaped and chosen, collectively paints a picture of who we are. Yet, so often, we stand too close to the canvas, losing sight of the broader image. These few principles of action beckon you to step back, allowing a clearer, fuller view of your behavioral patterns and the stories they tell.

1. The Knowledge-Action Gap

As discussed above, the vast chasm between "knowing" and "doing" has perplexed thinkers, psychologists, and even the average individual for ages. How often have we berated ourselves, asking, "Why don't I do what I know?" It's a discomforting question, suggesting a conflict between our intellectual understanding and emotional drivers.

2. The Power and Pitfall of Feelings

The revelation that "people do what they feel like" is both empowering and alarming. While emotions can be potent motivators, leading us to triumphant achievements, they can also trap us in cycles of counterproductive behaviors. The fleeting nature of feelings—like the transient boost of willpower—often leaves us stranded halfway to our goals.

3. Capacity Over Ability

Our actions aren't solely a testament to our abilities. Instead, they reflect our capacity—our emotional and mental bandwidth, our resilience in the face of challenges, and our commitment to evolution. When we act from a space of growth and transformation, we transcend our current state, propelling ourselves toward the next version, even when the roadmap is unclear.

4. The Trust to Endure

Embarking on a journey without a manual, blueprint, or even a clear destination requires immense faith—in the process, in the unseen, and most importantly, in oneself. It's about embracing the intrinsic belief that we can navigate through hardships, not because it's easy, but because growth emerges from struggle.

5. Beyond Willpower: The Marathon of Consistency

Willpower is the sprint at the start, the adrenaline-fueled dash that kickstarts our endeavors. But life isn't a sprint; it's a marathon. The real champions aren't just those who begin with enthusiasm but those who maintain momentum, even when the initial rush wanes. They understand that the difference between aspiration and achievement is the consistent grind—the daily, unglamorous, relentless effort.

In decoding the intricacies of behavior, my hope is that it illuminates the path from intention to action, from aspiration to realization. It encourages introspection, challenging you to evaluate if your actions truly mirror your ambitions, and provides the insight to realign them when they don't. After all, the most authentic expression of who we are isn't found in our words but in our deeds.

Results: The Culmination of Choice

The fourth pillar, standing resolute in our realm of control, is our results. These are the tangible and intangible outcomes, the manifestations of our actions or, in some cases, our deliberate inactions. Let's unpack this.

Picture this: You find yourself struggling to button up your favorite jeans. This isn't a consequence of the jeans mysteriously shrinking in the wash. It's a result, an outcome of those times you ate out of boredom or stress rather than hunger. Or, think about the strained interactions with your boss. They didn't sprout out of thin air. They're the fallout from those times you deliberately sidestepped conversations, letting misunderstandings grow rather than addressing them.

Results, you see, are like footprints in the sand. They show where we've been, hinting at the path we chose. Every result in our life, be it the state of our health, the nature of our relationships, or the trajectory of our careers, stems from our actions. And as we've established, actions are birthed from feelings, which are, in turn, children of our thoughts.

Now, here's where it gets interesting. Many of us, in the face of unsavory results, point fingers at external circumstances. We lament, "It's not my fault; it's just how things are." But if we peel back the layers, we find that our results are seldom the byproducts of external situations. They're reflections, mirrors showcasing the internal landscape of our thoughts and feelings.

This realization, while daunting, is also incredibly empowering. Why? Because it means that the power to shape our results rests within us. If we can alter our thoughts, channel our feelings, and choose our actions wisely, then the results we desire are not just possible; they're inevitable.

So, when you stand at the crossroads of choice, remember this: Your desired results are within reach. Begin with your thoughts, for they are the compass that guides the journey to the results you seek. With awareness and intent, sculpt the life you dream of, one thought, one feeling, and one action at a time.

The Heartbeat of Self-Awareness: Trust and Authenticity

Embarking on the path of self-awareness is akin to setting sail on a vast ocean, where the compass guiding you is trust in oneself and the wind pushing your sails is authenticity. At its core, self-awareness is not just about understanding oneself but being deeply rooted in the unwavering foundation of self-trust. It's about acknowledging the whispers of your inner voice and giving them the amplification they deserve.

Yet, the beauty of this journey isn't just in recognizing who you are but in embodying that realization with raw authenticity. Authenticity is the truest expression of self-awareness. It's wearing your essence on your sleeve, undiluted and unapologetic. It's choosing to stand tall in your truth, even when the world beckons you to fit into pre-established molds.

Self-trust and authenticity go hand in hand. To trust oneself is to have faith in one's capabilities, intuitions, and decisions. And when this trust is deeply ingrained, it frees you to be your most authentic self without the shackles of doubt and second-guessing. In the dance of personal development, these two elements swirl together in a harmonious waltz, painting the canvas of life with strokes of genuine experiences and raw emotions.

In essence, the expedition of self-awareness is both an inward and outward journey. Inward, as you dive deep into the recesses of your mind and soul, unearthing layers of beliefs, emotions, and experiences. Outward, as you let the world see the authentic version of you, radiating confidence borne from the core of self-trust.

Remember, self-awareness is not a destination but a continually evolving process. And as you journey through it, let self-trust be your guiding star and authenticity your compass. For when you truly know yourself and trust in that knowledge, the world doesn't just see you; *it feels you.*

Integrity of Self:
Navigating Trust and Authenticity

In the intricacies of human relationships and self-worth, two concepts stand tall: trust and authenticity. They are the twin pillars upon which the foundation of our understanding of self and others rests. In this section, we delve into the complex matrix of trust, its origin, its betrayal, and its redemption, juxtaposed against the narrative of authenticity—our true self and the masks we wear.

1. Origins of Trust

Trust is not a lesson from textbooks; it's a lesson from life. Our earliest understanding of trust is formed in the arms of our caregivers. These foundational experiences, for better or worse, lay the groundwork for our future interactions, beliefs, and relationships.

2. When Foundations Shake

Betrayal, especially from those we hold dear, can feel like an earthquake, destabilizing the very ground we walk on. The aftershocks of these betrayals linger, causing us to question the very essence of trust. If the pillars of our childhood couldn't be unwavering, then what can?

3. The Spiral of Doubt

When trust in the external world wavers, the repercussions reverberate within. The most debilitating among these is self-doubt. "If I misjudged them, how can I trust my own judgments?" This internal dialogue becomes a self-fulfilling prophecy as our belief in ourselves diminishes, pushing authenticity into the shadows.

4. The Masks We Wear

In the quest to belong, to be accepted, and to avoid future hurt, we construct masks—personas that we believe the world wants to see. But each mask distances us further from our genuine selves, burying our authenticity beneath layers of pretense and fear.

5. Reclaiming Trust

While the journey of rediscovering trust is arduous, it's not insurmountable. By understanding the origins of our beliefs, addressing our wounds, and practicing introspection and self-compassion, we can rebuild not just our trust in others but, crucially, in ourselves.

6. The Return to Authenticity

To reconnect with our authentic selves requires courage. It means shedding the weight of expectations, past hurts, and societal dictates. It's a journey inward to rediscover and embrace the core of who we are and then to outwardly live that truth with pride.

Through the pages of this book, we undertake a transformative journey—one from shaken trust to its restoration, from hidden authentic selves to their vibrant revelation. This section is an invitation to understand, heal, and celebrate the profound relationship between trust and authenticity and to find within them a path to wholeness and self-acceptance.

The Prelude to Authenticity and Unapologetic Living

As we journey deeper into the realm of self-awareness, a recurring theme emerges, beckoning us toward its embrace—authenticity. While we've merely touched its surface in our discussion thus far, prepare to plunge into its depths in the ensuing section on self-acceptance. What does it mean to live authentically? To be unapologetically you? This is the conversation that awaits, but first, we must grapple with a foundational query: who is this "self" we seek to know and trust?

The essence of "self" is multifaceted. It's not just the reflection we glimpse in the mirror nor the titles and roles we accumulate over a lifetime. Instead, it's a complex tapestry woven from threads of experiences, beliefs, desires, fears, and dreams. This "self" is both the silent observer and the vocal participant in the theater of life.

As we delve deeper, the layers start unfolding, revealing intricacies and nuances previously overlooked. To truly know oneself is a profound endeavor, and to trust that knowledge is even more formidable. Yet, the path to such understanding and trust is paved with self-awareness.

In the upcoming section on self-acceptance, we'll explore the bold embrace of authenticity. We'll challenge the societal molds that have, at times, constrained us and learn to live in a manner that is unapologetically and unmistakably "us." But for now, let's dwell a moment longer in this space of contemplation, preparing our minds and souls for the revelations ahead. For the journey to self-acceptance, while beautiful, demands courage, vulnerability, and an open heart.

Remember, the journey to one's true self is not about finding a pre-existing entity but uncovering and creating it, layer by layer, with each moment of awareness and understanding—the gateway to acceptance.

The Art of Letting Go: Embracing Before Releasing

True awareness is akin to a mirror reflecting not only the visible but also the hidden facets of our being. And, as we delve into the depth of understanding, it's imperative to address the notion of "letting go."

Letting go is often seen as a liberation act, a gesture of freeing oneself from the shackles of the past or painful memories. But here's a profound revelation: one cannot truly release what hasn't been acknowledged or accepted. The act of letting go is intrinsically linked to the act of letting in.

Imagine trying to empty a container that was never filled or uncaging a bird that was never inside. To release, we first need to recognize, to hold, to understand. It's a delicate dance between awareness and liberation. If you find yourself struggling to let go, chances are, you've never fully embraced or allowed that experience, emotion, or memory into your conscious awareness.

Buried deep within our psyche are suppressed emotions, concealed memories, and silent stories that we've locked away, either out of shame or the misguided intention of self-preservation. We keep these elements hidden, believing that by doing so, we're shielding ourselves from pain. Yet, in this subterranean world of denied feelings and experiences, they fester, leading to internal chaos and confusion. They become silent specters casting shadows on our behaviors, reactions, and interactions, often making us question our very essence.

So, what's the way forward?

Awareness requires courage. It asks for an open-hearted dive into the depths of our being to uncover and shine a light on those long-buried aspects. By confronting them with compassion and curiosity, we offer ourselves the gift of understanding. Only then, with acknowledgment and acceptance, can we genuinely start the process of letting go. The journey might be tumultuous, but it promises a destination of genuine freedom and self-compassion, replacing the haunting questions with a profound realization of self.

The Alchemy of Release: From Shadows to Sunlight

In the great expanse of our existence, the most profound metamorphoses are born from the act of letting go. Like the shedding of a tree's old leaves to make way for the new, there lies a deep wisdom in the ebb and flow of life. This section is an ode to that transformative dance, whereby, releasing the burdens of the past, we open our arms to embrace the luminosity of the future.

Let's journey together into the heart of release.

1. The Victim's Bind

It's all too tempting to wear our wounds as badges, to allow our pain to define our narrative. But every moment immersed in victimhood is a moment lost to empowerment. The true gift? Realizing that we have the power to rewrite our stories, away from hurt and toward healing.

2. Emotions: Chains or Catalysts?

There's a deceptive allure in holding onto our anger and our resentment, believing they serve as our shield. But in truth, these emotions, when held too tightly, turn into chains that bind us. The gift lies in understanding that our feelings are ours alone, and in freeing them, we free ourselves.

3. Faith in Self: The Original Blueprint

Remember the fearless child within who dared to walk without ever having done it before? That innate courage, that deep-rooted trust in oneself, is our birthright. By releasing the doubt, we can reconnect with our essential self, rekindling the flames of self-belief.

4. The Stories We Tell Ourselves

Our minds, the master storytellers, can sometimes spin tales that limit rather than lift. By examining and rewriting these narratives, we grant ourselves the freedom to step into more expansive, empowering roles in our own life stories.

5. Forgiveness: The Self's Loving Embrace

In our attempts to make sense of a complex world, we sometimes misconstrue our experiences, leading to self-blame. But forgiveness is the balm for these wounds, allowing us to move forward with love and grace.

6. The Panoramic Perspective

Life, in all its complexity, cannot be truly understood from a single vantage point. By broadening our perspective, we allow for a richer, multi-dimensional understanding of our experiences, breaking free from the constraints of a singular lens.

In this dance of life, release is our most graceful step. Through the act of letting go, we invite newness, growth, and boundless possibilities. Join in this journey of transformation, where shadows give way to the brilliance of sunlight and where the past is released to herald the promise of tomorrow. (Invitation to the book webpage for more discovery)

As Our Path Unfolds ...

In the chapters ahead, we will embark on a deeper dive into the terrain of self-acceptance. The topics we've introduced are merely a glimpse, a beacon to beckon your curiosity and draw your attention inward. These initial musings are intended to gently provoke introspection.

Ask yourself: Where in your life are those persistent narratives of self-doubt echoing? Where are those emotions, heavy with the weight of unresolved pasts, tethering you? Where does resentment lurk in shadowed corners? Whose apology are you waiting for? What is asking to be seen?

It's essential to recognize these not as condemnations but as calls to transformation. As we traverse further into this book, these themes will re-emerge, each time more luminous, offering you not just a lens to view them but tools to master and transcend them.

The essence of this journey is not about mere identification but about liberation. It's about not only acknowledging these chains but learning how to break free, allowing you to step into the most authentic, empowered version of yourself. So, as we delve deeper, keep an open heart and an inquisitive mind, for we are about to unearth treasures that have long awaited their discovery within you.

Delving Into the Ego: The Silent Saboteur

As we delve deeper into the realm of "self," let's take a moment to acquaint ourselves with a powerful force that heavily influences our identity—the ego. This elusive entity has subtly shaped our perceptions, dictating our reactions and becoming the architect of our self-concept.

Consider emotions as the weathervane of our psyche. They point out but don't dictate our direction. They offer guidance on the winds of our internal climate, indicating whether we're living in harmony with our authentic selves or if we're being swayed by the tumultuous gusts of the ego.

When we came into this world, our slate was clean. We were embodiments of purity, untainted by ego or insecurity, brimming with trust and acceptance. But life, with its complexities of experiences, introduced uncertainty. Suddenly, the trust we had in ourselves, in our caregivers, and in the universe at large became questionable.

This insecurity germinated two pervasive fears:

1. A belief that we, at our core, were fundamentally flawed.

2. A conviction that the world around us was in disarray.

Such fears are the offspring of the ego, pushing us further from our authentic selves and into the embrace of a fabricated identity. This false self thrives in the land of "shoulds"—a place where we constantly assess and judge, setting up idealized versions of reality.

Each time we venture into the territory of "Shouldville," we reinforce the power of the ego. By saying things "should" be different, we resist the flow of life and inadvertently invite more of what we're trying to resist.

The ego-self isn't the core of who we truly are. Rather, it's a mask composed of layers of decisions and beliefs that have accumulated over time, veiling our true essence. Every judgment, every fear-induced conclusion, reinforces this façade, perpetuating patterns of self-sabotage.

But why is understanding this vital? Because as I have mentioned, self-awareness is the key to transformation. Recognizing the patterns dictated by our ego is the first step toward breaking free. To truly discover the richness of our authentic selves, we must first discern and dismantle the illusions of our ego.

In the sections that follow, we'll venture deeper into this, offering tools and insights to help peel back the layers, leading you back to your true, unadulterated essence.

The Ego's Dual Dance: The Guardian and the Gatekeeper

In the theater of our consciousness, the ego often takes center stage. While it is hailed as our protective ally, steering us through the dense forests of social acceptance and self-preservation, it can also become our most formidable roadblock, casting shadows on our true selves. Let's explore this intricate ballet of the ego: its lights and shadows and its dual role in our path to growth.

The Ego as Guardian

The ego is born out of necessity and shaped by the environment and circumstances we grow up in. It learns to wear different masks to shield us from potential harm, acting as a guardian of our perceived self-worth and identity. It wants to protect us from judgment, rejection, and vulnerability. In its protective role, the ego helps us navigate the world with a sense of identity and belonging.

The Ego as Gatekeeper

However, while it protects, the ego also restricts. It builds walls, creating boundaries that often isolate us from our truest desires, our purest emotions, and our inherent interconnectedness. It becomes the gatekeeper, often deciding what feelings are "acceptable" to express and which dreams are "realistic" to pursue. In doing so, it may prevent us from experiencing life in its fullest color, depth, and authenticity.

The Gift of Altered Reality

The ego curates a reality for us. But this reality is a mere reflection, often distorted, of who we truly are. When we recognize this altered state, we find the key to unlock a higher, more genuine state of consciousness. The gift lies not in shunning the ego but in understanding its dual role.

Feeling to Heal

One of the profound ways to transcend the confines of the ego is to dive deep into our feelings. Emotions are our compass, guiding us to the territories within that need healing, recognition, or simply to be witnessed. By giving ourselves the gift of feeling, we tap into an inner reservoir of wisdom, intuition, and healing potential.

Emotions as Teachers

Far from being mere reactions, emotions are profound lessons waiting to be unraveled. They signal unmet needs, unspoken desires, and untapped potentials. To heal, to grow, to truly understand oneself, one must feel fully, without reservation. This involves allowing each emotion, no matter how challenging, to flow through us, teaching us about our deepest selves.

Steering Toward Authenticity

By understanding the ego's dual nature and honoring our emotions, we find our way back to authenticity, away from the rigid lanes carved by the ego and toward a path that resonates with our true essence. The journey requires courage, introspection, and a deep commitment to oneself.

In this dance of self-discovery and personal growth, the ego plays its dual role, both as a protector and preventer. Recognizing this dance and learning to lead it is a significant step toward a life of genuine connection, purpose, and fulfillment.

As we peel back the layers of the ego's Dual Dance, where it alternates between the roles of The Guardian and The Gatekeeper, we begin to recognize its intricate choreography. The ego, often perceived as a singular entity, reveals itself to be multifaceted, assuming protective stances and imposing barriers with equal fervor. Yet, when we pivot our perspective and tune into a different frequency of the EGO, we encounter a profound shift. Here, the ego is not just a two-step between safeguarding and secluding but rather a distorted lens that can obscure our path to potential. By acknowledging this altered state, we move beyond the dichotomy of defense and restriction and into a realm where the ego becomes a map of misperceptions, one that, if navigated wisely, can lead us to the uncharted territories of our fullest potential

E.G.O.
The Altered State of Erroneous Gaps in Opportunity

Erroneous Assumptions

Erroneous assumptions, or "thought errors," stem from the realm of our unconscious minds. Unchallenged and deeply ingrained, these thoughts carry the power to warp our perceptions. They make us believe in a fixed reality, clouding our judgment and narrowing our horizons.

Roots of Erroneous Thinking

These thought patterns, often a residue from past experiences, can come from early conditioning, traumatic events, societal norms, or even overheard conversations from our childhood. While these thoughts may have once served a protective purpose, as we evolve, they can become limiting factors, preventing us from seizing new opportunities.

Preservation Over Progress

One of the most intricate games the ego plays is the relentless need to validate our thoughts. It's not just about having beliefs; it's about being right. The ego craves the validation that comes with having our viewpoints acknowledged as truth. It clings to these beliefs with such tenacity that it often prioritizes their preservation over our inner peace and progress.

Why does this happen? Because for the ego, its very survival hinges on the affirmation of identity and the beliefs that construct it. If a long-held belief is challenged, the ego perceives it as an existential threat. It enters a defensive mode, even if that belief is detrimental to our well-being or growth. In such moments, the ego values the safety of the known over the uncertainty of change.

This mechanism of self-preservation often manifests in our reluctance to let go of limiting beliefs, even when they hinder our progress. For instance, someone might hold onto the notion that they're "just not good at relationships" because admitting otherwise would mean confronting past pains or taking responsibility for change. The ego would rather maintain the status quo than risk the discomfort of growth.

This tug-of-war between the ego's need for validation and our soul's yearning for progress can be tumultuous. Whenever we prioritize the ego's desire for certainty over our true self's call for expansion, we trade a piece of our potential for a fleeting sense of security.

But here's the twist: While the ego's primary concern is the preservation of self, it ironically keeps us from experiencing our truest, most authentic self. It obstructs our path to genuine fulfillment, the realization of our dreams, and the profound experience of unconditional love.

Recognizing this dynamic is pivotal. By understanding the ego's motives and tendencies, we can begin to make conscious choices that favor our authentic growth over momentary comfort. It's a journey of rediscovering ourselves, unmasking the illusions, and aligning with a deeper, more genuine essence that seeks not just preservation but true flourishing.

G Gaps in Reality Perception

When our thoughts are erroneous, they create gaps—voids between what is and what we perceive. These gaps are where self-doubt breeds, where fear of the unknown lurks, and where our understanding of reality becomes skewed.

The ego, with its entangled web of perceptions, often constructs a wall, a gap that divides our authentic self from the self we present to the world. These gaps, subtle yet influential, are layers of misbelief that blur our understanding of who we genuinely are.

The ego thrives on disconnection, on the demarcations it sketches between our perceived reality and our inherent worth. These gaps arise from societal norms, childhood experiences, past traumas, and imposed labels. Over time, these labels, these descriptors, morph into a cocoon, limiting our expansiveness and rendering us disconnected from our true essence.

Here are a few of the EGO Gaps that we perceive as truth but create a false sense of both security and self:

The Prison of False Identity

Labels handed to us—sometimes gently, other times with force—find residence within our psyche. They dictate terms, often making us question our adequacy. "Am I enough?" "Do I belong here?" "Can I match up to expectations?" These questions are the echoes of the gap, a chasm that convinces us of our supposed deficiencies.

From childhood, we are often categorized by our abilities, our failures, our successes, and our quirks. We might be termed the "quiet one," the "achiever," the "troublemaker," or the "dreamer." Over time, these labels become internalized. We begin to see ourselves through these lenses and measure our worth against them. The walls of our prison take form, brick by brick, constructed by external judgments and solidified by our internal acceptance.

"Am I enough?" is a question born from a comparison to an often unrealistic or generalized standard. It reveals a doubt rooted in the fear of not living up to a labeled identity. "Do I belong here?" echoes the insecurity of not fitting neatly into predefined categories, suggesting that there might be a "right" place or a "right" mold we must fit. "Can I match up to expectations?" is the crippling weight of trying to fulfill roles and reputations that might not even resonate with our authentic selves.

The irony is these labels are often oversimplified and rarely capture the multifaceted nature of a human being. They ignore the fluidity of our growth and the ever-evolving essence of our character. When we confine ourselves to the limitations of these tags, we deny ourselves the freedom to explore, err, learn, and transform.

Breaking free from this prison of false identity requires conscious effort. It begins with questioning the authenticity of the labels we've accepted and examining the origins of our self-imposed boundaries. It's about realizing that our worth isn't determined by how well we fit a certain description but by the uniqueness of our journey, our experiences, and our personal evolution.

We are so much more than mere labels. Recognizing this truth is the first step toward dismantling the prison walls and embracing the boundless potential of our authentic selves. In the forthcoming chapters, we'll delve deeper into identities, labels, and misguided beliefs. For the moment, could you approach with an open heart and inquisitive mind? Could you surface any unconscious labels or identities you've been bearing, bringing them to the forefront of your awareness?

Ego's Loop of Dichotomies

The ego, often described as the mind's conscious mediator between the external world and our internal self, has a peculiar characteristic. It innately thrives on dualities—on binaries. It separates "us" from "them," "right" from "wrong," and "good" from "bad." While this binary thinking might have evolutionary roots in helping our ancestors quickly discern friend from foe or safety from danger, in today's intricate world, it can be more of a hindrance than a help.

One of the most profound consequences of this binary mode of operation is the sensation of separation it fosters. By continually emphasizing differences and distinctions, the ego inadvertently fuels feelings of isolation and loneliness. Instead of recognizing the myriad threads of commonality that bind all humans, the ego focuses on the disparities, often amplifying them. This skewed perspective can stifle our innate desire for connection and community, leading us to question our sense of belonging in the broader tapestry of humanity.

Furthermore, this dichotomous thinking keeps us on the periphery of experiences, never truly allowing us to delve into the rich, nuanced center of interactions. The middle ground, where understanding and compromise blossom, is often overlooked. Yet, it's in this very space that the magic happens. It's where true love isn't just a fleeting emotion but a profound understanding. It's where joy isn't just a momentary sensation but a state of being. And it's where fulfillment isn't about individual achievements but about shared successes and mutual growth.

Ironically, while the ego seeks to fortify our sense of self, its divisive tactics can distance us from the most enriching aspects of the human experience. When we allow our egos to dictate our interactions, we miss out on the deep connections and shared experiences that transcend boundaries.

The path forward, then, involves recognizing the limitations of binary thinking. It's about transcending the ego's narrow definitions and embracing the vast spectrum of human experience. By seeking the middle ground, by reaching out in understanding rather than retreating in division, we can rediscover the unity in our shared human journey, fostering true love, joy, and fulfillment in the process.

The Fantasy-Reality Gap

A particularly insidious trap the ego sets is the rift between what we desire and what is. It whispers tales of "should haves" and "could haves," magnifying our yearnings and contrasting them with the present moment's reality. This constant tug-of-war between aspiration and actuality is a source of much suffering. The ego delights in the chasm between our expectations and life's actual unfoldings, fostering discontentment.

This gap is a breeding ground for discontent. The ego capitalizes on our natural tendency to dream, magnifying every "if only" and "what could have been" and setting them against our current circumstances. The fantasies it conjures are not necessarily grandiose; they might be as simple as wishing for a different outcome in a past conversation or yearning for an alternate path in life's crossroads. Yet, the ego ensures these desires are constantly in our mental foreground, casting shadows of dissatisfaction and regret on our reality.

Within this rift, the "should haves" and "could haves" echo loudly, each one a poignant reminder of unmet expectations and unfulfilled desires. Every shortfall, every deviation from the imagined path, becomes a point of internal contention. And as the gap widens, it becomes a gorge, often filled with self-doubt, self-criticism, and lingering discontent.

This Fantasy-Reality Gap, while real in its effects, is a construct of the ego. It is a distorted lens that shifts our focus from embracing the present and its myriad possibilities to ruminating on an idealized past or an imagined future. The ego, in its quest to maintain its dominance, perpetuates this illusion, ensuring we remain ensnared in a cycle of longing and lament.

Breaking free from this trap requires an acute awareness of the ego's games. It involves grounding oneself in the present, embracing it with all its imperfections, and understanding that the beauty of life lies not in the "what could have been" but in the "what is" and the "what could be." By shifting our focus from fantasy to the actionable steps we can take in our reality, we can bridge the gap, find contentment, and truly live in the moment, unfettered by the ego's deceits.

Buddha's Insight Into Desire and Suffering

As Buddha enlightened us with the four noble truths, the root of suffering is often our desires and our attachments. More accurately, our unwavering, rigid adherence to these desires. This isn't merely the longing for material possessions or worldly pleasures. It's a deeper, ill-encompassing yearning that drives humans to cling, to attach, to demand permanence in a world that is intrinsically impermanent. Whether it's the longing for love, the insistence on certain life outcomes, or even the aversion to unfavorable situations, such desires stem from a misunderstanding of the fundamental nature of existence.

What compounds this suffering, according to Buddha, is our unwavering, rigid attachment to these desires. We cling to them, creating idealized narratives in our minds and resisting any change that challenges these narratives. This inflexible adherence sets us up for disappointment, as life, in its inherent unpredictability, often doesn't conform to our tightly held scripts.

However, Buddha's teachings weren't just a diagnosis of the human condition; they were also a prescription. He taught that the path to liberation from this cycle of desire and suffering is through understanding and acceptance. This means embracing the present moment without resistance, without the filters of our desires coloring our perceptions. It's about seeing the world not as we wish it to be but as it truly is.

In practicing mindfulness and deep meditation, one learns to observe one's desires without judgment, understanding their transient nature. By recognizing desires as mere temporary states of mind and not definitive truths, we begin to detach from them, loosening their grip on our psyche.

In essence, Buddha's wisdom guides us toward a life of balance—where desires are acknowledged but not clung to, where the present moment is valued without the weight of past regrets or future anxieties. Through understanding and awareness, we can navigate life with a sense of peace and equanimity, free from the tumultuous waves of desire-driven suffering.

Overcoming the gaps necessitates a journey inward, a pilgrimage to the heart of self-awareness. To heal the divides created by the ego, one must recognize these imposed identities, these labels. By grounding oneself in the present and accepting the current reality without judgment or resistance, one can bridge the gap between the real self and the ego's constructed self.

The gaps the ego manifests are but illusions, veils that cloud our authentic essence. By recognizing these gaps and actively working toward self-awareness, we can free ourselves from the ego's illusions and step into a reality where we are in harmony with our true nature.

Opportunity Lost or Redefined

The cumulative effect of these erroneous thoughts and perceived gaps is lost opportunities. But herein also lies a chance to redefine the narrative, to recognize these gaps for what they are, and to bridge them with truth, awareness, and conscious action.

At the intersection of our inner narratives and external stimuli, the ego establishes itself as a sentinel. Its formation was once crucial, shielding us from perceived threats and judgments. But, over time, its protective nature can inadvertently morph into barriers that stifle growth and foster self-doubt. Yet, even within these constraints, the ego offers an opportunity—a silver lining.

The Opportunity in the Ego's Constrictions

The very limitations the ego creates can become the key to unlocking our potential. Recognizing the gaps and loops the ego ensnares us in offers an invitation—a call to look inward. This awareness is a pause, a pivotal moment allowing us to introspect and decide our subsequent actions consciously. In this pause, we have the power to shift from reactive to proactive, from being driven by our ego to mastering it.

Conscious Awareness: The Observer's Seat

Transitioning from the role of a passive participant to an active observer in our life's play is transformative. Being an observer, we cultivate a certain detachment, enabling us to view situations and our reactions without judgment. This bird's eye view lends clarity and reduces emotional entanglement. It's in this state that we remember: experiences occur through us, not to us.

This observational standpoint, often referred to as "conscious awareness," is akin to watching the waves of the ocean from the shore. We acknowledge their presence, their rise and fall, but we aren't tossed about by them. Similarly, in the observer's seat, we recognize our feelings, thoughts, and reactions without becoming overwhelmed or defined by them.

Crucially, this detachment isn't about indifference or suppressing emotions. Instead, it's about understanding the transient nature of experiences and the role of the ego in magnifying or diminishing them. It offers us the grace to experience fully yet not be imprisoned by these experiences.

By embracing the role of the observer, we also come to a profound realization: experiences flow through us; they don't define our essence. We are not the anger we feel, the jealousy that arises, or the pride that swells within. These are mere states, temporary and fleeting, much like clouds passing through a vast sky. The sky remains unchanged, unperturbed.

In this conscious awareness, we find liberation. We discern the whispers of the ego from the deeper truths of our being. The dramas of life continue to unfold, but we, from our observer's seat, remain centered, understanding that we are both the play and the witness to it.

The Mind's Quest for Order

Our minds, complex and intricate, lean toward understanding and rationalizing experiences.

Our minds play a ceaseless game of connecting the dots. This tendency sometimes prioritizes seeking patterns over our well-being. To the worrier, predicting worst-case scenarios offers an illusionary sense of control—a means to navigate the uncertain terrains of life. Essentially, borrowing trouble from our future.

At the heart of this game lies an innate desire to make sense of the world around us, to impose order upon chaos, to find a predictable pattern in a sea of randomness. This is not just a function; it's a survival mechanism. By predicting patterns and outcomes, we feel more equipped to handle the uncertainties of life.

But, what if instead of being enslaved by these concoctions of the mind, we could recognize them for what they are—mere attempts at order in the vast, unpredictable expanse of life? Recognizing this is the first step in distancing ourselves from the ceaseless chatter of our thoughts. It's about understanding that not every thought pattern serves our best interest. Sometimes, our mind's quest for order leads us down paths of anxiety, fear, and doubt, all because it's trying to find a rhythm in the randomness.

However, with heightened awareness, we can discern the difference between genuine intuition and the mind's baseless narratives. We can remind ourselves of the countless times we've adapted, overcome, and thrived amidst uncertainty. Our true essence is not in the worrier that predicts the storm but in the warrior that stands firm in its midst.

The beauty lies in realizing that amidst the seeming disorder, there's a higher order at play. It's not about forcing patterns onto life but recognizing life's organic patterns. This understanding allows us to see beyond the ego's fearful tales to differentiate between reality and the stories our minds concoct.

Thus, in the dance between chaos and order, the mind and its predictions, there lies an invitation. An invitation to see beyond, to trust in our inherent resilience, and to find peace in the midst of life's unpredictable ballet.

The Power and Pitfalls of Belief

Beliefs shape our perceptions. They filter our experiences, coloring them with their hues. It's crucial to audit our beliefs periodically, ensuring they align with our authentic selves and our evolving understanding of the world. Not all beliefs are created equal. Some elevate us, driving us toward our true potential, pushing boundaries, and painting our world in shades of possibility. These empowering beliefs act as the wind beneath our wings, giving us the courage to soar to heights we never imagined.

Conversely, there are beliefs that shackle our spirits. These are the whispers of limitation that echo in our minds, painting a world filled with barriers, casting shadows of doubt, and feeding our insecurities. They stem from past traumas, societal conditioning, or even misconceptions formed during our formative years. They trap us, making us prisoners in our minds, often thwarting our own progress and happiness.

This duality of belief is where the true challenge lies. It's not about discarding all beliefs but discerning which ones truly resonate with our authentic selves and our evolving understanding of the world. Regular introspection and self-audit become essential tools in this journey, helping us shed outdated or limiting beliefs and nurturing those that uplift and empower.

But beyond this binary of empowering and limiting beliefs lies a deeper invitation—a call to discern between the beliefs of the ego and those of the higher order. The ego, with its insatiable thirst for validation and constant need for self-preservation, looks outward, operates from a space of lack, and thrives on competition. Its beliefs are often rooted in fear, scarcity, and separation.

On the other hand, the higher order seeks unity, connection, and collective growth. It operates from a space of abundance, understanding that fulfillment isn't derived from external validation but from inner alignment and purpose. This conscious entity within us recognizes that true growth isn't about competing but about elevating together.

The invitation, then, is clear: to recognize and challenge the ego-driven beliefs that keep us mired in cycles of instant gratification, comparison, and external validation. And to nurture and embrace beliefs that align with our higher consciousness—ones that foster love, compassion, unity, and a deeper understanding of our place in the grand tapestry of existence.

In understanding this distinction, we free ourselves from the pitfalls of limiting beliefs, opening our hearts and minds to a world brimming with possibilities and potential.

Navigating Emotions: The Body's Wisdom

Emotions, powerful and profound, are signals. They echo our internal states, reflecting unmet needs or unresolved conflicts. Wrestling with these emotions, we often exacerbate our distress, entering a loop where feelings intensify and cloud judgment. By shifting our approach—by feeling rather than fighting—we can channel emotions constructively.

Delving deeper into the world of metaphysics, we uncover a profound truth: the body doesn't just experience emotions—it keeps an intricate score. While metacognition speaks to the cognitive understanding of our thoughts, metaphysics dives into the body's emotional language. This realm, although vast and intricate, remains largely unexplored in mainstream dialogue. Yet, its importance is undeniable. The ability to truly "feel to heal" can transform lives.

It's a commonly accepted notion that stress, a state born from tangled thoughts and emotions, can sow the seeds of "dis-ease" within our body. Stress manifests not just mentally but physically, triggering a cascade of physiological changes, culminating in tangible health issues. If this negative emotional state can wield such power, it stands to reason that the opposite—a state of emotional balance and harmony—can foster healing.

The essence of this concept is simple yet revolutionary. While most modern medical practices focus on treating the symptoms, a metaphysical approach zeroes in on the root cause—our emotional states. By addressing and harmonizing these states, we can not only alleviate symptoms but promote genuine, lasting healing. The proposition is as empowering as it is profound—within each of us lies the innate capacity to heal, to transform, to thrive. All it requires is a deepened awareness and the courage to listen to our bodies, tapping into its vast reservoir of wisdom.

The ego, with its myriad of complexities, offers an opportunity. An opportunity to learn, to grow, and to transcend. By leveraging conscious awareness and tuning into our bodies' wisdom, we can navigate the intricate dance between the ego's challenges and our true potential. The journey may not always be linear, but every step, every realization, takes us closer to our authentic selves.

Exposing the Ego's Illusions

As we delve deeper into understanding the ego, it becomes essential to discern the misconceptions it propagates, often masquerading as truth. These seemingly benign beliefs, deeply embedded within our psyche, significantly influence our emotional landscapes and cognitive frameworks. Their pervasive nature often renders them invisible to our conscious mind, yet their grip on our life's narrative is undeniable.

Consider them as veils, obscuring the clarity of our true essence. These deceptions can range from perceptions of self-worth and definitions of success to distorted views on love and relationships. The ego thrives on them, building walls that confine us within self-imposed boundaries.

Yet, the path to liberation lies in illumination. When we courageously shine a light on these illusions, recognizing them for the fallacies they are, we begin the transformative journey from bondage to freedom. This process is not just about debunking lies; *it's about embracing the enduring truths they've concealed.*

By identifying, confronting, and dispelling these ego-driven myths, we reclaim our power. We align more authentically with our core essence, unburdened by the weight of unfounded beliefs. It's akin to wiping clean a fogged mirror, finally beholding our true reflection, unmarred and untainted.

As an example, let me share a story about a client of mine named Adam, who has been with a company for several years. Adam is proficient and capable, often receiving praise from colleagues and superiors. However, Adam harbors a strong ego, which manifests as an intense fear of failure and an overriding desire to be perceived as infallible.

Opportunity Knocks: A promotion is on the horizon, one that would require Adam to take on more responsibility and potentially expose him to new challenges and the possibility of criticism.

The Ego's Interference: Adam's ego convinces him that staying in the current role is safer. The fear of not excelling in the new position or being judged by peers leads Adam to self-sabotage, perhaps even to the point of not applying for the promotion or undermining his own interview.

Outcome: By listening to the ego's fear-driven advice, Adam misses the chance for professional growth. The ego's protectionism has created an erroneous gap in opportunity by presenting the comfort zone as the only viable option and depicting the new role as a threat rather than a chance to learn and expand.

This is a simplified scenario, but it demonstrates how the ego can limit one's potential by transforming opportunities into perceived threats. The ego's primary concern is maintaining self-identity and avoiding any risk, even at the cost of personal growth and development.

As we advance on this journey, let's commit to questioning these long-held beliefs, not as an act of rebellion but as a sacred endeavor of rediscovery. Remember, every lie the ego presents is an opportunity, a doorway, to a deeper, more profound truth about ourselves and the universe.

1. The Lie of Collective Agreement: *"If we all agree, it must be true."*

Often, we mistake collective agreement for objective truth. Just because a belief or notion is widely accepted doesn't make it accurate. Throughout history, many truths of one era became the fallacies of the next.

Truth: Critical thinking and individual discernment are essential. While societal consensus might offer a starting point, personal exploration and understanding should be the end goal.

2. The Lie of External Happiness: *"We can make other people happy."*

This lie is rooted in the belief that we hold the power to control or influence others' emotional states. It often leads to overextending oneself to please others, causing exhaustion and neglecting one's needs.

Truth: Everyone is responsible for their happiness. While we can contribute to someone's joy, it's not our responsibility, nor is it within our control, to ensure they remain in that state.

3. The Lie of Confusion: One of the most insidious lies the ego often presents to us is the statement: "I don't know." On the surface, it seems harmless, maybe even genuine. But if we dive deeper, we recognize it as a smokescreen, a barrier to progress, and a comfort zone from which we hesitate to step out.

In the digital era, where information is at our fingertips, claiming ignorance is rarely a valid excuse. Want to cook a new recipe? Google it. Want to learn a new skill? There's probably an online course for it. Want advice on an issue? Countless forums and communities can provide insights.

However, the statement "I don't know" isn't always about factual knowledge; it often represents an emotional or psychological block. It's a defense mechanism, a way to avoid the discomfort of decision-making or the vulnerability of admitting one's feelings or desires.

Truth: The truth is, deep down, we do know. The universe operates on the principle of balance, beautifully captured by the law of polarity. For every problem, an equal and opposite solution exists. For every challenge, there's an inherent answer. While we may not immediately perceive it, the counterpoint to our quandaries is always present.

4. *The Lie of Positive Thinking:* "A positive or reframed mindset alone doesn't guarantee success." Positive thinking has been heralded as a panacea for life's challenges. While beneficial, relying solely on optimism without action or planning is misguided.

Truth: While a positive mindset can provide motivation and resilience, it must be complemented with proactive strategies, plans, and actions to yield tangible results. The goal is not to think positively but rather consciously.

5. *The Web of Indulgent Lies:* There's a tangled web we often weave, filled with self-soothing indulgent lies that give us momentary relief. Yet, in the grander scheme of things, they merely serve as short-term band-aids for underlying issues.

Overwhelm: How often have you felt bogged down by the weight of tasks at hand and declared, "I'm overwhelmed!"? But in reality, claiming overwhelm is a shutdown mechanism. It's an escape hatch that gives our brains the license to avoid pushing through the discomfort.

Hardship: Saying "It's hard" feels valid when we're faced with a challenge. But does it motivate us or keep us stuck in the narrative? Often, we manifest physical symptoms like a headache or tensed shoulders. I've taught myself to bypass this thought because it's counterproductive, and quite frankly, I grew tired of the eminent headache that was sure to follow.

Fun: The concept of fun is highly subjective. When something isn't enjoyable, is it the activity itself or our mindset? As I often tell my kids, "You determine the fun; the situation doesn't." You are the creator of fun—what a great gift.

Busy Syndrome: Declaring "I'm so busy" might give a temporary ego boost, making us feel important. But is this statement factual or another energy-draining narrative? Being genuinely productive and being "busy" aren't always synonymous.

Right or Wrong: Life isn't a series of right or wrong choices but rather about the choices we make and the perspectives we adopt. In relationships, for instance, contentment doesn't primarily come from a partner's actions but from our internal narratives. Of course, boundaries are essential, but most relational issues stem from avoidable misunderstandings and internal discord.

Recognizing these indulgent lies is the first step. Once identified, we can shift our mindset and narratives, making choices that align with genuine growth, understanding, and happiness.

While lies can often provide a temporary comfort or a perceived shortcut, embracing the underlying truths offers a more authentic and fulfilling journey. By identifying these untruths, questioning them, and replacing them with genuine insights, we pave the way for a life of greater clarity and purpose.

E.G.O.—Unpacking the Threefold Path to Self-Awareness

As we conclude this deep dive into the realm of the ego, let's review its acronym to better grasp its intricacies and its impact on our lives.

E - Erroneous Thoughts: Our minds can sometimes be breeding grounds for misconceptions, for stories we tell ourselves that don't align with reality. These untruths, often shaped by past experiences and external influences, can distort our perceptions, making us prisoners within our own minds.

G - Gap: This represents the void between who we truly are and who we perceive ourselves to be due to our ego. It's the chasm that develops when we measure ourselves against societal standards or when we compare our lives to others. It's the space filled with doubts, insecurities, and the haunting question of "Am I enough?"

O - Opportunity: In every challenge, there lies an opportunity. Recognizing our ego and its plays gives us a chance to course-correct, to recalibrate our compass toward authenticity. By identifying and addressing our erroneous thoughts and bridging the gap, we find the path to genuine self-awareness and self-acceptance.

Grasping the role of the ego and its intricate games is not just an exercise in self-awareness but a journey toward liberation. By shining a light on its lies, we uncover layers of authenticity, of truth that had been obscured. Much like decluttering a space reveals its true potential, dispelling the lies and misconceptions of the ego uncovers the radiant life beneath. The life we truly desire, in all its authenticity, awaits us just beneath the clutter of everything we don't need—lies included.

The Blame-Shame Loop: The Destructive Dance

We've traversed various terrains of self-awareness, examining the many ways our ego plays its games and distorts our reality. But at the heart of it all lies perhaps the most insidious cycle of all: the blame-shame loop.

The Underlying Lie

At the heart of both blame and shame lies the belief that things should be different than they are—that someone else should be, should act differently (blame), or that we should be, should act differently (shame). This is grounded in the false premise of perfectionism, an unrealistic standard we place on ourselves and others. The truth is that everyone has their journey, replete with successes and failures, and expecting flawless behavior or results from oneself or others is both unreasonable and detrimental.

The Cycle's Nature

Blame arises when we project our internal discomfort onto others or external circumstances. "It's their fault I feel this way," we tell ourselves, abdicating responsibility for our feelings. This outward projection may seem like a short-term solution, but it sows the seeds for long-term dissatisfaction.

Shame, on the other hand, is the internalization of those external judgments. "There's something wrong with me" becomes the debilitating mantra that clouds our self-perception and our self-regard and hinders our growth. In the dance between blame and shame, we swing from finding fault outside to berating ourselves internally, never truly finding peace or resolution.

Awareness: The Solution

To truly break free from this cycle requires Awareness. Recognizing when we're engaging in the blame-shame narrative is half the battle. Once we become conscious of it, we can choose to interrupt the pattern, shifting from judgment to understanding, from criticism to compassion.

Awareness is akin to flipping a switch in a dim room. It illuminates our internal narratives, casting light on the stories we tell ourselves. When we feel the tendrils of blame wrapping around us or the weight of shame pressing down, it is this light of awareness that can help us see the situation for what it truly is. Not through the distorted lenses of judgment or self-criticism but with clarity and compassion.

With the weapon of awareness in hand, we have a choice. We can continue down the well-trodden path of blame and shame, or we can forge a new trail. This new path won't always be easy, and old habits might beckon us back, but with continued self-reflection and conscious decision-making, we can navigate toward understanding and curiosity.

Self-Reflection: As you journey through the terrain of self-awareness, take a moment to pause. Reflect on instances where blame and shame have clouded your judgment. Were these feelings truly justified? Or were they perhaps born out of an ideal that wasn't even yours to begin with? An ideal rooted in external expectations rather than your own inner truth? As you ponder on these questions, remember that with each moment of reflection, you're taking another step toward genuine self-awareness and self-compassion.

While self-reflection and discovery are tried and true empowerment tools, here are a few additional strategies to navigate out of the blame-shame loop:

Reframing Expectations: Adjust expectations to be more realistic and compassionate. Remember, everyone, including you, is human. Mistakes, misunderstandings, and imperfections are part of the journey.

Practicing Self-Compassion: Instead of spiraling into shame, remind yourself of your worth and acknowledge the effort you're putting into growing and learning.

Communication: In situations where you feel the urge to blame, engage in open communication. This can help in understanding different perspectives and can often lead to mutual understanding and growth.

Accountability Without Judgment: Recognize and own your actions without descending into self-criticism. This involves taking responsibility for your actions, understanding the reasons behind them, and taking steps to change, if necessary.

Seeking Feedback: Surround yourself with individuals who can offer constructive feedback without judgment. This can help break the cycle of self-blame and external blame.

Mindfulness and Meditation: Cultivate a practice that centers you in the present moment, helping you become more attuned to your emotional responses and triggers.

Navigating the blame-shame loop requires self-awareness, compassion, and a commitment to growth. By recognizing the cycle, questioning its foundation, and employing strategies to disrupt it, we can foster healthier relationships with ourselves and with others.

If you're still journeying with me, I commend you. This is not easy terrain. Venturing into the depths of self-awareness, confronting our patterns and shadows, demands courage. The seemingly "easy" path, the one of blame and externalization, is a mirage. It might promise relief, but it invariably leads to a labyrinth of confusion and pain. The path of self-awareness, while challenging, leads to a life that truly honors our essence, respects our boundaries, and celebrates our potential.

So, as we continue on this expedition, know that with each step, you're moving closer to a life that truly aligns with your core, a life free from the constraints of the blame-shame loop.

The Blame-Shame Loop in the Context of Judgment and Acceptance

Blame and shame are intricately tied to the act of judging—ourselves, others, and situations. Judgment, at its core, is a refusal to accept things as they are. It's an assertion that something should be different, more aligned with our subjective ideals. However, the act of judging often detracts from our inner peace and can hinder our growth. Let's delve deeper into this intricate relationship.

1. Judgment and Non-Acceptance: A Cycle of Suffering

The act of non-acceptance is a subtle and insidious one. It quietly sneaks into our perceptions, leading us down a path of judgment. What we often fail to realize is that the act of judgment is not a passive process, but rather, it's one fraught with emotional ramifications. When we resist, when we refuse to accept situations or individuals as they are, we inherently slip into a mindset of judgment.

This act of judgment is a double-edged sword, cutting deep into our well-being. Initially, we suffer as we grapple with our judgment. Feelings of superiority, bitterness, or resentment are not very motivating. Instead, they weigh heavy on our hearts, generating much unnecessary negativity. And then, as if this initial suffering wasn't enough, the universe adds its twist. By focusing our energy on what we dislike or don't want, we inadvertently draw more of the same toward us. Like a magnet, our attention, laden with judgment, pulls similar experiences and energies into our realm.

It's crucial to recognize this cyclical process of non-acceptance leading to judgment and, consequently, suffering. Because the truth is, this cycle is not inherent to our nature but rather a construct of our making. The universe operates on a principle of energy exchange; where our attention goes, energy follows. So, when our focus is anchored in judgment and resistance, we unintentionally amplify these very aspects in our lives.

By shifting from judgment to acceptance, from resistance to acknowledgment, we can alter this cycle. When we embrace situations and individuals without judgment, we not only free ourselves from the immediate suffering but also from the extended cycle of drawing unwanted energies and experiences toward us. It's a journey toward peace, one where our focus and energy are invested in harmony and love rather than conflict and judgment.

The Nuance Between Acceptance and Approval

There's a common misconception that emerges when I speak of "acceptance"— a visceral reaction that suggests I'm calling for passive resignation or even endorsement of the situation at hand. But this couldn't be further from the truth. Let's clarify: Accepting a situation does not equate to approving it. These are two distinctly separate mental and emotional processes.

When I say "accept what is," I'm advocating for a conscious acknowledgment of the present moment exactly as it unfolds. Why? Because resistance to reality serves no purpose but to create inner turmoil. Fighting against the present moment is like trying to push back the waves of the ocean with your hands—it's not only futile but exhausts your energy in the process. Yet, accepting the ebb and flow doesn't mean you're thrilled about every wave that comes your way. It simply means you recognize its existence, its inevitability.

Acceptance is about recognizing the truth of a situation, whereas approval is an emotional response, a judgment about that truth. For instance, one can accept that a storm is happening without liking or approving of the destruction it may cause. Similarly, we can accept certain painful situations or behaviors in life without endorsing them.

The beauty of practicing acceptance is that it places you in a position of empowerment. By seeing things clearly, without the clouded lens of resistance, you can discern the lessons within the challenges and make informed choices about how to proceed. Rejecting or resisting reality only robs you of the clarity and peace required to navigate complex situations.

So, as we journey deeper into self-awareness, it's crucial to delineate between these two states. Know that you can fully accept the present moment—embracing its lessons, challenges, and realities—without necessarily giving it your stamp of approval.

2. The Trap of Judgment: A Thief of Serenity

The intricacies of the human mind often lead us down pathways of judgment, a journey that invariably disrupts the serenity of our psyche. When we indulge in judgment, be it blame toward others or shame toward ourselves, we unknowingly erect barriers that block the tranquil flow of understanding and empathy. Instead of navigating the waters of compassion or seeking constructive solutions, we find ourselves in tumultuous currents, drowning in our own critical narratives.

In the fascinating realm of neuroscience, we find that our brains possess a natural propensity to seek consistency. That is to say, once we've formed a judgment or belief, our brain actively seeks out evidence to validate that very notion, even if it's detrimental to our well-being. For instance, if we internally berate ourselves with thoughts like, "Why can't I ever follow through?" not only do we plunge into a cycle of self-doubt, but our brains also look for instances to substantiate these claims. Essentially, we become our own worst critics, cherry-picking our life's events to further affirm the negative scripts we're telling ourselves.

This continual self-castigation not only steals our peace but also saps our motivation. If we're always ruminating on our perceived failures, reminding ourselves of past mistakes, the path forward becomes shrouded in a haze of negativity. We unknowingly become architects of our own self-fulfilling prophecies, reinforcing the very behaviors we condemn. Instead of being propelled by positive reinforcement, we're anchored by the weights of our own criticisms.

At the heart of it, judgment, especially when self-directed, rarely acts as a motivating force. Instead, it ties us to a past that we can't change, stealing the present's peace and the future's potential. As we journey through life, recognizing this trap and actively working to shift from judgment to compassion can be the key to regaining our lost serenity.

3. Complaining: The Invisible Shackles on Personal Growth

Complaining, while often seen as a mundane part of human interactions, holds a far more insidious power than we realize. At its core, the habitual act of finding faults in others or lamenting about their unmet potential serves as a mirror, reflecting our own stagnation. When we allow our focus to drift toward the perceived inadequacies of those around us, we inadvertently create barriers to our own growth.

Dwelling on external shortcomings is a diversion, a smoke screen that masks the vital process of introspection and self-improvement. Each moment spent lamenting the perceived flaws of others detracts from the time that could be used to better ourselves. More critically, by echoing and amplifying these complaints in our social circles, we expend energy that could be directed toward elevating our own potential. It's akin to anchoring ourselves to the ground while yearning to soar.

The act of gossiping or participating in such conversations compromises our integrity. As we engage in or endorse these low-level discourses, we inevitably diminish our own stature. The dichotomy is clear: either we can elevate ourselves through personal growth and empowerment or remain mired in the muck of trivial complaints.

To the reader of these words, the challenge is well-defined—transcend the easy allure of complaints and gossip. Make it a non-negotiable in your journey of self-discovery and growth. Commit to rising above such limiting behaviors and free yourself from the self-imposed chains of judgment. In doing so, not only will you reclaim your time and energy, but you'll also stride forward on a path to a more enlightened and empowered self.

4. The Judgment Epidemic: Social Media's Role in Global Discord

In an era where connectivity spans continents and cultures, the promise of unity has ironically birthed a wave of division, primarily fanned by the flames of judgment. Social media, while a remarkable tool for collaboration and communication, has unwittingly become the epicenter of an epidemic of micro-judgments.

Each time we engage on these platforms, we're faced with a barrage of decisions—to swipe or not, to like or scroll past, to comment positively or unleash criticism, to share or to shut down. With every digital gesture, we pass judgment, often without the full breadth of context or understanding. Over time, these tiny acts of judgment snowball into habits, and these habits seep into our real-world interactions, coloring our perceptions and decisions.

What's even more troubling is the acceptability of this new judgment-heavy norm. In a world already navigating tumultuous waters of intolerance and misunderstanding, our increasing dependency on social media platforms only amplifies our collective penchant for judgment. The rapid-fire pace of the digital age leaves little room for reflection, and the vastness of the internet makes it all too easy to broadcast our judgments without immediate consequence.

But there's a toll, albeit a silent one. Each judgment, each negative comment or disdainful share, chips away at our collective psyche. The more we engage in these acts, the worse we feel, often leading to a feedback loop of seeking more content, more engagement, more validation—an insatiable hunger that's never truly satisfied.

At its core, this unchecked culture of judgment fuels global discord, breeding mistrust, promoting stereotypes, and solidifying divisions. A world steeped in such persistent judgment inevitably drowns in its own negativity. It's essential for us to recognize the power of our digital interactions, to pause before we judge, and to strive for understanding over division. Only then can we hope to build bridges in a world that desperately needs them.

5. Mirror Neurons: A Relentless Loop

All too frequently, we find ourselves caught in a cycle of pointing fingers at others, believing that they ought to change, when in reality, we have the power to alter our own responses in those situations. How ironic is it that we often criticize others for the very behaviors we exhibit? We lament about others' complaints, become irate when someone else expresses anger, or turn defensive when faced with another's defensiveness. This mimicry, to some extent, can be attributed to our mirror neurons, which drive us to reflect the emotions and actions we observe. However, this pattern traps us in a relentless loop: while we blame others, we inadvertently mirror the behavior we're condemning. It's essential to recognize this cycle and understand that the power to break it lies within ourselves.

Concluding Thoughts: The Road From Judgment to Awareness

In this intricate dance between blame, shame, and judgment, it becomes evident that true freedom starts with awareness. At the heart of this understanding is the fundamental truth that acceptance paves the way toward the harmony we all seek. Every moment offers us a choice: to lean into judgment or to embrace acceptance. While it's natural for our minds to seek patterns and fall prey to confirmation bias, it's imperative to ensure that what we are confirming aligns with the values we hold dear.

Complaining, especially about others' potential, will rob us of ours. Further, it's essential to approach the digital age, particularly social media, with a discerning eye. While these platforms were conceived with the noble intent of bridging gaps and fostering community, their misuse can just as easily create division and foster isolation.

As we wrap up this exploration, let's be vigilant about our interactions, both online and offline. Let's commit to elevating the discourse, focusing on understanding over judgment, and fostering true connections. In doing so, we can not only reclaim our individual peace but contribute positively to the collective consciousness.

Pathways to Progress: Curiosity as the North Star

Every great journey needs a compass. In our internal exploration, that compass is curiosity. Let's intertwine this fundamental trait through our subjects, seeing how it guides and enlightens our path to self-understanding.

Interestingly, when we embrace curiosity, we tap into a realm of the brain distinct from our emotional centers. It is this very distinction that allows us to dissect thoughts without the often-blinding interference of emotions. Curiosity allows us to look at our experiences, beliefs, and judgments without the weight of past conditioning. In this light, we can examine our thought patterns not as definitive truths but as mere hypotheses open to inquiry.

Central to personal growth is the profound acknowledgment that we are the architects of our realities. The intricate dance between our thoughts, emotions, and actions crafts the world we experience. Recognizing this interplay equips us with the responsibility and power to mold a life aligned with our aspirations.

It is essential to note that wielding this power demands more than mere awareness. It requires us to muster the courage to question, to wonder, and most critically, to remain open to the possibility that some of our most deep-seated beliefs may be more fiction than fact. Curiosity is not just about seeking new information; it's about the willingness to reevaluate the old, to dismantle outdated paradigms, and to construct fresh narratives that serve our evolving selves.

As we journey through the layers of our consciousness, let's pledge allegiance to curiosity. For it is not just a trait but a beacon, urging us to look beyond, to question deeper, and to embrace the endless possibilities of who we might become.

Invoking Curiosity: A Brief Foray Into Awareness

In the myriad dialogues of awareness we've delved into, let's momentarily pause to appreciate the essence of curiosity—a subtle yet transformative force. Often overshadowed by louder sentiments, like conviction or skepticism, curiosity remains a quiet influencer, gently nudging us to explore beyond the horizons of our known.

Every insight we've discussed, every revelation we've encountered, holds its root in an initial spark of curiosity. While awareness helps us recognize patterns, behaviors, and beliefs, it is curiosity that propels us to dig deeper and question the "whys" and "hows" behind these observations. Why do we hold certain beliefs? How did certain patterns become ingrained in our behavior? It's the inquisitive nature of curiosity that prompts such introspection.

This invaluable trait has the unique power to strip us of our defensive armor, allowing us to approach our inner world without judgment or resistance. It encourages a sense of wonderment, where instead of rigidly holding onto our beliefs or resisting change, we become open to possibilities, eager to learn, and willing to evolve.

So, as we reflect upon our conversations on awareness, let us be profoundly thankful for the gift of curiosity. It's this unassuming guide that makes the journey of self-discovery not just enlightening but truly enchanting.

Curiosity is the journey of enchantment.

What are the thoughts that you resist thinking?

What are the feelings that you resist feeling?

What are the actions you resist taking?

What identity are you not willing to let go of? Why? If you were not that identity, who would you BE?

What are you not willing to try because of fear? Fear of rejection? Embarrassment? Being seen starting small? Failure?

What outcome are you too scared of that you won't even try?

What are you not willing to do to get what you want?

Who do you fear you might lose along the way?

Curiosity is the space for enlightenment.

How often do you need to be right?

How often do you think you are doing it wrong?

How often do you find yourself doubting your worth?

How often do you find yourself doubting your life and how it played out?

How often do you need someone else's approval?

How often do you find yourself waiting for permission?

How often are you needing the how to the goal?

How often do you give yourself permission to believe the impossible?

How often do you find yourself blaming other people, your situation, or the past for your current results?

As we approach the conclusion of this segment on awareness, allow me to intertwine the profound essence of curiosity with the philosophical paradigms we've navigated. Envision curiosity as the lane markers on the highway of our journey. They're omnipresent, often subtle, yet crucial in their function.

These markings aren't loud or imposing; they don't command or control. Yet, just like curiosity, they play an indispensable role in ensuring we stay our course, veer neither too left nor too right, and progress steadily toward our destination. They keep us safe, remind us of our paths, and, most importantly, embolden us to drive forward even through unfamiliar terrains.

In the vastness of self-discovery, where awareness throws light on the contours and terrains, it's curiosity that ensures we don't just observe but also explore. Like those unassuming lane markers, curiosity keeps us engaged, propels us to question, and fosters a continual state of learning.

So, as we recapitulate our discussions, the many turns, stops, and accelerations, let's remember and revere curiosity. It's this gentle yet compelling force that has kept us anchored, ensuring that in our quest for understanding, we always stay aligned, inquisitive, and ever-forward-moving in pursuit of our dreams.

Comprehensive Self-Insight

Before understanding the world, we must understand ourselves. Curiosity prompts us to ask, "Why do I think this way? What events have shaped my beliefs?" By questioning our foundational beliefs, we start uncovering deeper layers of our psyche.

Navigating the Mindscape

The mind is a labyrinth. But with curiosity as our guide, we can navigate its intricate pathways, seeking clarity amidst its complexities.

Every thought, memory, or dream becomes a point of interest waiting to be explored. When we move from being spectators of others' imagined thoughts to being active participants in understanding our own minds, there we discover the intricacies of our personal "mattering" and the power to transform our lives from the inside out.

Tuning Into Feelings

Feelings aren't just spontaneous reactions; they're messages. A curious heart asks, "Why do I feel this way? What's this emotion trying to tell me?" "Leah, Love, what do you need?" By delving into our emotional responses, we can decipher their underlying causes.

Actions Under the Microscope

Curiosity helps us scrutinize our behaviors. "Why did I react that way? What patterns can I observe in my actions?" It prompts us to assess our decisions critically, leading to refined choices in the future.

Authentic Bonds and Genuine Self

Being curious about others allows us to form deeper, more meaningful connections. "What makes this person tick? How do they perceive the world?" Simultaneously, curiosity about our true selves ensures authenticity in these bonds.

The Art of Letting Go

When we're curious about our attachments, we better understand their roots. "Why am I clinging to this? What fear is behind this attachment?" This inquisitiveness aids in releasing what no longer serves us.

Ego's Dual Dance

Curiosity turns the spotlight onto our ego. "When does my ego serve me, and when does it hinder?" Understanding this dance allows us to harness the ego's strengths while mitigating its overreaches.

The Cycle of Self-Judgment

Curiosity breaks this cycle by inserting a moment of reflection. Instead of automatic self-blame or shame, we start asking, "Why am I judging myself? Is this judgment valid or an old narrative?"

Journey to the Inner Frontier

The ultimate adventure is the journey within. Curiosity equips us with the tools to delve deep and to brave the unknown recesses of our souls. Every discovery, every revelation, is a step further into this vast frontier.

Curiosity isn't just a trait—it's a beacon. It illuminates the shadows, unveils mysteries, and transforms passive existence into an active quest for understanding. By embedding curiosity into every facet of self-awareness, we not only enrich our knowledge of ourselves but also elevate the quality of our lives. As we tread the intricate pathways of our being, let curiosity be our unwavering guide, shedding light on the darkest corners and revealing the wonders within.

The Dawn of Understanding; The Door to Acceptance

As I bring this section on self-awareness to a close, I recognize the depths of memories and reflections that I've ventured into. While the nuances of such experiences may not have been discernible to my younger self, the onus lies upon my present being to sift through, untangle, and uncover the truths that have always been present, waiting to be acknowledged.

There, on that stoop under the blazing sun, with a withering dandelion clutched in my tiny hands, were sown the first seeds of my quest for self-awareness. It was a day of many "firsts"—the first pang of solitude I felt, the first echoing silence where my voice went unheard, the first realization that people, including those closest to me, might not always align with the pedestals I placed them on. In that poignant moment, surrounded by shifting cardboard boxes and the hum of life moving on, I felt my diminutive existence fading into the background. The decisions I made in that fragile moment—that I was unimportant, that I was merely a shadow in a world full of vibrant hues—began to shape my identity.

What I didn't recognize then, and what took me years to understand, is that these decisions weren't the essence of "me." They were defense mechanisms, tools I crafted to navigate the intricate maze of my emotions and experiences. They were the lens through which I viewed the world, tinted by the hurt and confusion of that moment. These decisions were not my identity; they were constructs, built brick by brick, as a sanctuary against the harsh winds of vulnerability.

Realization is the first step to healing. Recognizing that I am not my past decisions but rather the sum of my experiences, my resilience, and my potential illuminates the path forward. It's about forgiving those early misconceptions, shedding the protective layers that once seemed essential, and re-embracing a sense of self-trust, self-acceptance, and self-love. These are not mere concepts; they are my inherent rights, my birthright.

I've come to see that every situation, every emotion, every twist and turn in my life's journey is not a test but a gift. It's an opportunity, tailored by the universe, God, for growth, understanding, and evolution. Accepting this, I embrace the entirety of my being, flaws and all, with gratitude, curiosity, and open arms. For the story is not of a broken child and her wilted dandelion but of an ever-evolving soul navigating the vast cosmos of self-awareness.

PILLAR 2

The Gift of LOVE—Self-Acceptance

From Seeking Validation to Finding Self-Love

My world crumbled when my dad walked out when I was eight years old. His absence imprinted upon me a painful narrative: I wasn't enough. I began to think, "If my own father couldn't find it within him to stay and love me, then surely there was something fundamentally flawed about me." This sentiment, though unbeknownst to my young self, would set the stage for the next several decades of my life.

In a bid to fill that gaping void, I embarked on an exhaustive quest for validation. I thought if I could just be a tad prettier, excel a little more in school, or be the kind-hearted daughter everyone praised, maybe he'd return. Maybe his reappearance would be the testament to my worthiness I so deeply yearned for. Ironically, my pursuit of growth, masked by the countless personal development books lining my shelves, was less about genuine self-improvement and more a desperate search for a defect, a confirmation of my inherent inadequacy.

This pursuit came at a cost, a hefty one. Relationships strained under the weight of my incessant need for validation. Opportunities slipped through fingers clenched in anxiety. Dreams faded as I constantly molded myself to be anything but who I genuinely was, believing my true self wasn't worthy of my father's love, or anyone else's for that matter.

While this tale might seem intensely personal and unique to my experiences, the essence of it finds resonance in many of our stories. The next leg of our journey delves into the realm of self-acceptance. While the theories are enlightening, it's their application that is truly transformative. Embracing these philosophies promises a renaissance of self-worth and love.

If you're ready to move past the shadows of past narratives and step into the embrace of self-love, let's embark on this transformative voyage together.

The Gift of Love: Embracing Reality

In today's hyper-curated, filters-first world, there's an ever-growing chasm between the actual and the ideal, the genuine and the glossed-over. It's become all too easy to get caught up in the digital riptide, clinging to modified images and enhanced narratives. But true personal growth is anchored in understanding and embracing reality. Here's why:

The Power of Acceptance

No journey can begin without first acknowledging the starting point. Similarly, no transformation, no matter how profound, can happen without accepting the reality of the present moment. As mentioned in pages prior, acceptance isn't synonymous with resignation. Instead, it's a conscious, empowered choice to see the world and ourselves with clarity and compassion. Judging our starting point or denying it only hampers our growth. Acceptance, on the other hand, propels us forward, laying a sturdy foundation for what lies ahead.

The Futility of Resisting Reality

We teased this out prior, but it is worth repeating. Resisting reality is akin to trying to hold back the waves of the ocean with mere hands. It's not only exhausting but futile. Resisting reality saps our energy and denies us the opportunity to effectively engage with the world. Every moment spent in denial or wishful thinking is a moment lost from making tangible progress.

Understanding Life's 50/50 Rule

Life is, in many ways, a delicate balance of opposites: joy and sorrow, highs and lows, triumphs and defeats. By expecting life to be a constant high or an uninterrupted joyride, we set ourselves up for disappointment and disillusionment. Embracing the 50/50 rule—recognizing that life will be 50% positive and 50% negative—frees us from the unending chase for perpetual happiness. It allows us to fully experience the range of human emotions and, in doing so, enriches our understanding of ourselves and the world around us.

The Trap of "Should-ing"

The notion of how things "should" be can be a debilitating frame of mind. It leads us into a quagmire of judgment, guilt, and missed opportunities. By constantly should-ing over situations or people, we impose unfair expectations and, in the process, rob ourselves of the chance to experience things as they genuinely are. More often than not, it's this very "should-ing" that prevents us from seeing the beauty and potential in the present.

Unlocking the Potential of the Present

By truly understanding the rules of the game, especially the 50/50 rule, we equip ourselves to navigate life with agility and grace. Instead of shrinking from challenges or getting mired in the fear of the unknown, we're better poised to face them head-on. Embracing reality, with all its imperfections, becomes our greatest strength. It allows us to harness the present, mold it, learn from it, and use it as a stepping stone to a brighter, more authentic future.

The path to self-love and growth is paved with the bricks of reality. Only by accepting and understanding where we currently stand can we hope to reach the pinnacle of our potential. As we peel back the layers of illusions and step into the raw, unfiltered world, we're not just confronting reality; we're embracing ourselves. And in that embrace lies the profound promise of transformation.

Layers of Self: The Journey to Authentic Identity

Our identity is akin to an onion, built layer upon layer over the years, with each layer shaped by experiences, beliefs, and encounters. Understanding these layers can help unravel the mystery of who we truly are, how society and upbringing have molded us, and how we can choose which layers to shed or embrace as we move forward.

Let's delve deeper.

The Construct of Identity

Identity, at its simplest, is our understanding of who we are. But, it is neither static nor straightforward. It's an intricate tapestry woven from the threads of personal experiences, society's labels, familial expectations, and our innermost beliefs. This is why the quest for understanding identity is so pivotal. It's not just about introspection; it's about deconstruction and, subsequently, reconstruction.

Interpreting Reality: The Making of "You"

Each individual's reality is a unique blend of personal experiences and external influences. From a young age, we're fed stories of what success looks like, how love should feel, what's "right" and what's "wrong." Our parents, teachers, peers, media, and culture all have a say in the narrative of our lives. These tales, these beliefs, become our reality. They form a lens through which we see the world and, more importantly, how we see ourselves.

The Borrowed Layers

We often adopt layers that aren't intrinsically ours. We wear masks to fit in, to be loved, or simply because we believe that's who we're supposed to be. Over time, these borrowed layers become so intertwined with our being that distinguishing between the authentic self and the adopted self becomes a challenge.

Programming: The Dual Nature

The human experience is a dance between polarities: love and fear, thriving and surviving, soul and ego. Our minds have been programmed to oscillate between these dualities. But understanding this is only half the battle. When we acknowledge the 50/50 nature of our existence, we gain clarity. It's like lighting a torch in a dim room—suddenly, all the choices and all the potential paths become visible.

Understanding our identity isn't just about knowing oneself; it's about choosing oneself. When we recognize that our identity is malleable and that we have the power to choose who we want to be, it becomes an act of liberation. By shedding the layers that no longer serve us and embracing those that resonate with our cores, we step into a space of authentic living.

The layers of our self are both a testament to our past and a canvas for our future. By understanding and navigating these layers with curiosity, self-acceptance, and intention, we not only discover who we truly are but also unleash the potential of who we could be.

Decoding Identity: Navigating the Duality of Our Being

The Making of "I AM"

Our identity, the essence of our self-concept, is intrinsically linked to our internal dialogue. The words that follow "I AM" are incredibly potent. They frame our worldview and how we perceive our position within it.

When we proclaim, "I AM capable," it's more than just a declaration; it's a manifestation. The statement itself, stemming from a place of abundance, acts as a bridge to the realities we create for ourselves. Conversely, an "I AM incapable" belief, born from scarcity, acts as a barrier, limiting the horizon of possibilities.

The Dichotomy of Unconscious Default and Conscious Choice

Picture a board split down the middle. On the left, you have the unconscious, default realm rooted in scarcity and disempowerment. On the right, you have the conscious, chosen realm rooted in abundance and empowerment. The side from which we operate significantly influences our identity.

UNCONSCIOUS DEFAULT: SCARCITY THINKING & DISEMPOWERMENT	CONSCIOUS CHOICE : ABUNDANT THINKING & EMPOWERMENT
➤ I am incapable.	➤ I am capable.
➤ I am not worthy.	➤ I am worthy.
➤ I am not like her.	➤ I am enough.
➤ I am not as pretty as her.	➤ I am ready.
➤ I could never do that.	➤ I am complete.

The Mechanism of Thought and Feeling

Thoughts aren't mere ephemeral entities; they're powerful shapers of our reality. Our thoughts, especially when amplified by emotion, set the tone for our experiences. Thoughts rooted in scarcity lead us down a path of feeling "less than," while those rooted in abundance uplift us, making us feel "more than enough."

Scarcity's Disempowerment

This mindset traps us in a vortex of negative emotions:

Shame, where we internalize the narrative that we are fundamentally flawed.

Blame, projecting our insecurities and failures onto others.

Confusion, leading to inaction and stagnation.

Loneliness, the belief that we're misunderstood or unrelatable.

Anger and resentment, the fiery guards that keep us imprisoned in our self-made cages.

Worry, the shadow that clouds our potential and dims our light.

Victimhood, where life's challenges are perceived as targeted assaults against us.

Each of these emotions stems from falsehoods—misinterpretations of our experiences or borrowed beliefs that don't serve our growth.

Abundance's Empowerment

From a place of abundance, our emotional palette is vibrant and uplifting:

Confidence, assurance in our abilities.

Control, not externally but over our emotional states.

Curiosity, an eagerness to learn and grow.

Compassion, for ourselves and others, recognizing shared human experiences.

Connection, a deep sense of belonging and understanding.

Decisiveness, a clarity in purpose and direction.

Agency, where life isn't just happening to us but for us, each event a lesson or a blessing.

In essence, our identity isn't just who we believe we are, but it's also shaped by how we feel about who we are. Recognizing the malleability of our identity and understanding that we have the power to reshape it is the first step toward a life of purpose, meaning, and fulfillment.

FEELING DISEMPOWERED	FEELING EMPOWERED
▶ Feels shame. (*Something is wrong with me*)	▶ Feels confident, competent, and enough.
▶ Feels blame. (*Something is wrong with them*)	▶ Feels in control of emotions.
▶ Feels confused. (*I don't know*)	▶ Feels curious and compassionate.
▶ Feels alone. (*No one gets me*)	▶ Feels connected to themselves and others.
▶ Feels angry, defensive, and resentful.	▶ Feels decisive and assured.
▶ Feels worried.	▶ Feels as if life is happening for them.
▶ Feels as if life is happening to them.	
*All **disempowered** feelings are riddled on false pretenses.* **LIES**.	*Abundant identities show up in some version of more than enough, feeling empowered.*

Scarcity: The Behaviors Driven by Fear

When we adopt a scarcity mindset, our behaviors are born out of fear. Fear pushes us toward instant gratification, leading us to buffer our discomfort and pain through distractions. These buffering behaviors—be it indulging in food, alcohol, shopping, or seeking external validation—offer a momentary reprieve from our internal distress but perpetuate a cycle of dependency.

Defensive postures, where we guard ourselves against perceived threats, even when none exist.

Judgment and gossip, as we project our insecurities onto others.

A reactive state, where others' actions and words have power over our emotional well-being.

Operating on the notion of "shoulds," placing unrealistic expectations on ourselves and others.

Recruiting allies to our perspectives, seeking validation in numbers.

Inability to access problem-solving and creativity.

Abundance: The Behaviors Inspired by Love

On the contrary, when our identity is rooted in abundance, love takes the driver's seat. Love invites exploration, understanding, and acceptance. It prompts us to view life as an adventure, replete with possibilities and opportunities.

Agency, recognizing and respecting everyone's autonomy and choices.

Dropping expectations and accepting people as they are, understanding that our well-being doesn't hinge on their actions.

Curiosity, about ourselves and the world around us, fostering deeper connections and insights.

A stance of self-sufficiency, where validation, permission, or approval from external sources isn't sought or required.

(Scarcity & Disempowerment): Here lies the realm of involuntary reactions. These reactions arise from deep-seated beliefs, often acquired over years of conditioning. They're the knee-jerk responses to life's stimuli, rarely questioned, often accepted.

(Abundance & Empowerment): This is the realm of choice. When we "STEAR" to this side, we actively choose how we define ourselves, aligning with our highest values and aspirations.

Choice: Our Superpower

Choice is our true superpower. Each day, we're presented with countless opportunities to either succumb to our default programming or make intentional decisions that reflect our authentic selves. We can either get trapped in the quagmire of fear or soar with the wings of love.

Our identity isn't a fixed blueprint handed down by our genetics. While our DNA provides a starting point, it doesn't script our destiny. The science of neuroplasticity underscores this by highlighting our brain's dynamic ability to change and adapt. Our experiences, choices, and beliefs shape our neural pathways, reinforcing the idea that our identity, and consequently our life, is a masterpiece of our making.

To truly harness this power, we must recognize that our identities are not a destination but a journey. A journey that's navigated through the choices we make, each step either echoing fear or resonating with love.

As we navigate the winding paths of self-discovery and change, the power of "I am" statements cannot be overstated. These simple declarations are the architects of our identity, constructing the framework of our thoughts, feelings, and, ultimately, the actions we take. They are the whispers that become roars in the chambers of our minds, shaping our internal narratives and projecting their echoes into the external world.

When we say "I am capable," we step into a state of readiness to face challenges; "I am learning" becomes a shield against the fear of failure, transforming it into an opportunity for growth. Each statement is a choice—a conscious selection of the bricks that build the foundation of who we are and who we aspire to become.

Yet, amidst this construction of self, we must be vigilant. For just as positive affirmations can elevate us, so too can a misguided adherence to societal "false formulas." These formulas, often rooted in collective misconception, suggest there is a singular path to fulfillment and achievement—a one-size-fits-all solution to the complex equations of our lives.

As we transition to the next chapter, we will unravel these deceptive formulas. Like mirages in the desert, they promise water but leave us thirsty. They are the seductive math that doesn't add up, insisting that certain behaviors, acquisitions, and accolades equate to success. Yet, this illusion ignores the individual uniqueness of our dreams and the authenticity of our paths.

We must challenge these false formulas, for they can impede our progress as surely as a misguided "I am" statement. By consciously choosing who we want to be and recognizing the diversity of success, we can break free from these constraints. We will explore how to deconstruct these formulas, not to discard structure, but to rebuild it in alignment with our truest selves, and in doing so, author our own definitions of success.

In the upcoming chapter, "The Deceptive Formulas of the Mind," we will dissect these pervasive myths and reclaim the narrative. Join me as we step beyond the allure of universal solutions and into the empowering embrace of personalized authenticity.

The Deceptive Formulas of the Mind

Life has its own mathematical intricacies, equations we subconsciously conjure up to make sense of our experiences. These formulas, however, are often based on long-held beliefs rather than tangible truths. But let's be clear—a belief is not inherently a fact. Rather, it is a thought we've chosen to validate time and again, gathering evidence to reinforce its authenticity in our minds.

Such deceptive formulas don't add up in the realms of science or math, but in the psyche of the believer, they become irrefutable laws. And herein lies the dilemma: these equations operate in the background, unconsciously steering the course of our decisions, relationships, and dreams. Without even realizing, we can become ensnared in a web of self-sabotage, all due to unexamined beliefs that simply "don't compute."

Awareness and acceptance become our greatest allies in this journey. By acknowledging these hidden formulas, we can decipher their patterns, understand their origins, and ultimately rewrite the equations that shape our lives. With this newfound clarity, we are empowered to construct formulas aligned with our true desires, ushering in the health, wealth, and relationships we've always yearned for.

Where might these formulas be playing out in your life?

Failing = Failure

Failing, be it in a task, relationship, or venture, is often equated to being a failure. This equation doesn't account for the inherent value of experience and learning. Failing is a natural part of growth. It is a sign of trying, of risking, and of stepping out of one's comfort zone. A failure is just an event, not a person's identity.

Overweight = Unlovable

Society's obsession with physical appearance has propagated the idea that anyone who is overweight is less deserving of love. This couldn't be further from the truth. Love isn't contingent upon one's physique but upon the essence of who they are.

Being Rich = Worthy

Wealth is often perceived as a validation of one's worth. True worth is the unshakeable core of our being. It is the part of us that doesn't diminish when we fail or amplify when we succeed. It is a steadfast presence that simply is free from the fluctuations of fortune and the judgments of others. This form of worth does not demand that we become anything other than what we inherently are; it asks only that we recognize and honor the intrinsic dignity we all possess.

College Degree = Smart

Education is undoubtedly valuable, but intelligence isn't solely dependent on formal degrees. Many brilliant minds have thrived without conventional education. Smart is a spectrum, and a degree is just one point on it.

Beauty = Success

Physical beauty might open some doors, but it doesn't define success. Success is a measure of one's accomplishments, their impact, and the lives they touch. Beauty is subjective and fleeting; success built solely on it is on shaky ground.

Skinny = Loveable

Much like the equation of being overweight and unlovable, the converse is equally flawed. Being skinny doesn't guarantee love or acceptance. Real love goes beyond physical appearance, seeing and valuing the person beneath.

Size 6 = Happy

Dress sizes don't come with a happiness tag. Basing contentment on a number is to overlook the multitude of factors that contribute to genuine joy. True happiness is internal and not defined by external measurements.

Right = Worthy

A person's worth isn't determined by how often they are right. Mistakes and misjudgments don't devalue someone. Often, the pursuit of always being right stems from insecurity and the fear of judgment. Worthiness is innate and not subject to external validations.

Joy = Irresponsible

Somewhere along the way, many came to believe that constantly exuding joy or seeking pleasure is a sign of irresponsibility. However, joy is a testament to one's ability to appreciate life and find beauty in moments. It isn't a measure of one's commitment to duty or responsibilities.

These are just a few of the formulas that have been governing our lives—it's enlightening to acknowledge their immense impact on our paths. Whether it's navigating my own journey or guiding others through theirs, the influence of these formulas is undeniable. But here lies the most empowering revelation: these formulas are not set in stone. They are malleable, adaptable, and entirely within our grasp to redefine.

The pages that have unfolded before us are more than just stories or strategies; they are testimonies to the plasticity of our beliefs and the transformative power we hold. The "shoulds" and "musts" that once seemed like insurmountable truths are, in fact, open to reinterpretation. We are not bound to live by legacy codes or inherited equations that do not serve our highest good.

Embracing this, we stand at the precipice of possibility, ready to sculpt our guiding philosophies with intention and insight. The best news ever is that this creative license is ours for the taking. Our lives are our canvases, and the brushes—with bristles dipped in the vibrant hues of experience, wisdom, and personal truth—are in our hands.

As we transition from the old paradigms to the new, let us do so with the knowledge that the power of redefinition is one of the most profound freedoms we possess. We can recalibrate our compasses, redraw our maps, and embark on a journey that resonates with the core of who we are and aspire to be. This is not just change; this is evolution—our evolution—crafted by our choices, our dreams, and our unyielding courage to author our own lives.

Redefining Life's Equations

Throughout my journey, I've realized that many of the equations I was using to navigate life were simply off the mark. They weren't inherently wrong or malicious, but they were based on beliefs and patterns that didn't serve my highest potential. These were the false formulas I unwittingly allowed to dictate my choices, emotions, and outcomes. Essentially, I was living unconsciously, from the left side of the board.

It's a bit like attempting complex mathematical problems with a flawed formula—you can put in all the effort, time, and energy, but the results will always be skewed. No matter how hard I tried, using these deceptive equations always led to answers that didn't resonate with my authentic self or the life I aspired to lead.

Recognizing these inaccuracies was the first crucial step. It required introspection, vulnerability, and a willingness to challenge long-held notions. But once I began to discern the patterns and understand where they originated, a transformative shift occurred. I was able to deconstruct these old formulas and create new math for myself— equations that were aligned with my true desires and aspirations.

In redefining my life's equations, I found clarity, purpose, and direction. My actions started producing results that felt right, fulfilling, and in sync with who I truly was—shifting in consciousness to the "right" side of the board. It's a continuous process, one of unlearning and relearning, but the journey is worth every recalculated step.

So, if you ever find yourself stuck in repetitive patterns or outcomes that don't seem to align with your heart's desire, consider examining your life's formulas. You have the power to redefine them, creating a path that truly resonates with your essence. Your life's math is yours to determine. Ensure your equations lead you toward your most cherished outcomes.

The Power of Belief: Beyond Science and Math

At its core, a belief is a powerful tool our minds use to make sense of the world. It's the scaffold on which we hang our experiences, the lens through which we interpret our reality. However, unlike the definitive nature of science or the unwavering logic of math, beliefs aren't necessarily universal truths.

Belief Versus Fact

A fact, be it in science or math, is consistent. Water boils at 100°C at sea level. Two plus two always equals four. These statements are verifiable and consistent across various conditions and contexts. But a belief? It's more malleable. For instance, someone might believe that "rain on your wedding day is a sign of future tears." Yet, this isn't a universal fact; it's a sentiment, a superstition, and it varies across cultures and individuals.

The Making of a Belief

How do beliefs come to be? Often, they are shaped by our upbringing, society, experiences, and even the media we consume. They might start as simple thoughts, which, when repeated and reinforced, solidify into beliefs. For instance, if a child is continuously told that they are "clumsy," they might grow up believing it, even if they aren't inherently accident-prone.

The Self-Fulfilling Prophecy of Beliefs

The danger (and power) of beliefs lies in their ability to shape our reality. A person, let's just say this author, who believed she was unworthy of love, might act in ways that push people away, thus "proving" her belief right. In psychology, this is termed as the "self-fulfilling prophecy." Our beliefs influence our actions, which, in turn, can shape our experiences.

Challenging Our Beliefs

It's crucial to periodically examine our beliefs, to differentiate between what's a deeply held conviction and what's merely an unverified thought we've clung onto. Asking ourselves, "Is this a universal truth, or is it a personal belief?" can lead to profound transformation. By understanding the origin of our beliefs, we can choose which ones to hold onto and which to let go.

The Freedom in Flexibility

While some beliefs can provide comfort and a sense of identity, it's liberating to remember that many of our beliefs are optional. Just as we can adopt new beliefs, we can also discard those that no longer serve us. Life isn't static, and neither are we. As we evolve, it's only natural that some of our beliefs will too.

In our human existence, beliefs play a pivotal role. But by distinguishing them from irrefutable facts, we grant ourselves the freedom to navigate life with an open mind, continuously learning, growing, and reshaping our understanding of the world and our place in it.

I hope you are encouraged to deconstruct these formulas and beliefs and find their truths. By challenging these ingrained equations, one can build a life based on personal values rather than live under the weight of societal misconceptions.

Unbinding the Self-Imposed Chains

There's a subtle, often unseen, architect of our lives, one that we ourselves have inadvertently designed over the years. This architect doesn't shape structures or cities but constructs the intricate maze of our mind—self-imposed rules and impositions. They are the silent guidelines, the invisible barriers, that often determine our choices, reactions, and interactions.

We all have them. These unwritten scripts that tell us how to behave, what to believe, and even how to feel. They are shaped by years of experiences and influenced by societal norms, familial expectations, past failures, or seemingly innocent comments that left indelible marks. Over time, these rules solidify, often running in the background like outdated software, influencing our every move.

The most perilous aspect of these self-imposed directives is their covert nature. Many of us aren't even aware that we're living within these confines. We might wonder why certain aspirations feel out of reach, why specific patterns keep repeating, or why certain relationships feel stifling. More often than not, it's because of these unspoken, internalized doctrines that we've allowed to govern our lives.

These regulations aren't inherently evil. In fact, many might have been formulated as protective mechanisms meant to shield us from past pains or perceived threats. But as we evolve, grow, and change, these once protective guidelines can become stifling prisons, holding us back from realizing our fullest potential.

Shattering these self-imposed chains is essential for authentic living. It requires introspection, bravery, and, above all, a commitment to challenging and rewriting these hidden commandments. It's about distinguishing between what truly serves us and what merely confines us.

In the quest for a life that feels truly ours, it's crucial to recognize and redefine these boundaries. Only by consciously choosing which rules to uphold and which to discard can we craft a life that's congruent with our deepest desires and highest aspirations. Are you ready? We are going to explore the seven impositions that stall our progress and limit our potential. Let's go!

1.Self-Imposed Potential

The concept of potential is a double-edged sword. While it carries the promise of what could be, it also shoulders the weight of what hasn't been or might never be. It's a vast horizon, but like any vast expanse, it comes with terrains that are challenging to navigate. Let's delve deeper.

The Landscape of Potential

When we talk of potential, we often visualize a continuous stretch of open, inviting space. It's a canvas waiting to be painted. But not all canvases are blank, and not all brushes are easy to maneuver. Some canvases come with textures and patterns, and some brushes have bristles that are hard to control. These are the limits and impositions that color our potential, and they're as much a part of us as the potential itself.

The Myth of the Unlimited

While self-help literature and motivational talks often focus on the "limitless" aspect of potential, it's crucial to remember that everyone has created their own set of limits. These limits aren't just physical or external but often are internal and rooted deeply within our psyche. Statements like "I can't do that" or "This won't work for me" are manifestations of these internalized limits.

Where Do These Limits Come From?

Several factors play a role. Past experiences, particularly failures or traumatic events, can impose limits. Societal norms and expectations can also confine us within boxes, creating a bounded understanding of our potential. However, among the most potent limiters are the narratives we tell ourselves, the inner dialogues that reinforce what we can and cannot achieve.

Reframing Limits as Guideposts

Rather than viewing these self-imposed capabilities as barriers, we can choose to see them as indicators or signposts on our journey. They can be signals pointing us to areas that need healing or growth. For example, the belief "I need someone to support me" might highlight a deep-seated fear of loneliness or abandonment, which, when addressed, can unlock a new realm of potential.

The Power of Reflection and Exploration

To navigate this landscape, reflection is paramount. Why do I believe I can't achieve this? Where does this belief stem from? Who needs to believe this? By asking ourselves these questions, we engage in a dialogue with our internal limits. We get to know them, understand them, and ultimately decide whether they serve our journey or deter us from it.

Exploration is equally vital. Venturing beyond our comfort zone and trying new things, even if they scare us, can lead to revelations about our potential. This isn't about ignoring our limits but understanding that they aren't as rigid or definitive as we might believe.

Potential is not just about limitless horizons but also about understanding and navigating the terrain. By reframing our limits, engaging in reflection, and exploring new paths, we can journey toward a more authentic, fulfilling realization of our potential.

2. Self-Imposed Scarcity

Self-Imposed Scarcity: Living in the Shadow of "Enough"

Scarcity, at its core, revolves around the idea of insufficiency. In the realm of economics, it pertains to the basic imbalance between limited resources and unlimited wants. But when projected onto the self, scarcity manifests as self-doubt, self-devaluation, and a persistent feeling of never being "enough." This self-imposed scarcity is not rooted in the external world but in the intricate web of our internal narratives.

The Origins of "Not Enough"

From a young age, many of us receive mixed messages about our worth. While we might be told that we're unique and valuable, societal standards and peer comparisons often send the opposite message. These external signals can plant seeds of doubt that, over time, grow into deep-rooted beliefs. Phrases like "I am not smart enough" or

"I am not pretty enough" become the lens through which we view ourselves.

The Echo Chamber of Scarcity

These self-deprecating beliefs are often reinforced in our day-to-day experiences. Every setback, every rejection, every perceived failure echoes the narrative of "not enough." This voice, while often unnoticed, has profound implications on our self-worth, aspirations, and interactions with the world around us. Over time, this forms a feedback loop. The internal narrative of scarcity influences our behavior, which in turn shapes our experiences, further cementing the belief.

The Silent Stories We Tell Ourselves

Scarcity doesn't scream; it whispers. Its language isn't overt, but its message is clear: "You are lacking." Although hidden, it is pervasive. It operates in the background, casting shadows over our achievements and highlighting what we perceive as shortcomings. It amplifies our flaws and diminishes our strengths. This skewed self-view makes us focus more on what we believe we lack than on our accomplishments and capabilities.

The Domino Effect of Self-Imposed Scarcity

One area of self-imposed scarcity often bleeds into another. Someone who feels "I am not skinny enough" might also start to feel they aren't attractive enough, leading them to believe they aren't worthy of love or attention. This spiraling effect can be debilitating, casting a shadow over multiple facets of an individual's life.

Where does scarcity show up?

Unearthing Scarcity in Daily Dialogues: The most telling signs of a scarcity mindset aren't always in the blatant self-deprecating remarks but in the subtler cues of our day-to-day conversations.

The Comparison Trap: One of the clearest indicators is when we measure our worth relative to others. Thoughts like "If only I had her charisma, then I'd be more liked" or "If I had his intelligence, I'd be more successful" are manifestations of this mindset.

Judgments as Mirrors: Sometimes, the harshest judgments we cast on others are projections of our insecurities. Criticizing someone else's success or choices often stems from our internal feelings of inadequacy.

Conditional Aspirations: The scarcity mindset often makes our aspirations conditional. We tell ourselves, "I'll pursue this dream when I'm more confident," or "I'll take that step when I feel ready." But these conditions, rooted in scarcity, can keep us perennially on the sidelines.

Breaking the Cycle: From Scarcity to Abundance

While self-imposed scarcity is a formidable adversary, it's not unbeatable. The first step toward breaking free is recognizing these internal narratives for what they are—mere beliefs, not truths. Reframe the narrative. Instead of focusing on what you believe you lack, concentrate on what you have. For every "I am not ..." there's an "I am ..." For instance, "I am not outgoing" can be reframed to "I am introspective and thoughtful."

Embrace the 4 S Framework: Shift Out of Scarcity and Step Confidently Into Your Life

Self-compassion: Remember that everyone has insecurities. It's okay to have doubts, but it's essential to treat yourself with the same kindness and understanding as you would treat a friend. Treat failures as lessons, not reflections of worth.

Search for External Perspectives: Sometimes, getting an external opinion can help break the internal echo chamber. Trusted friends, family, coaches, or therapists can offer a more objective perspective on your beliefs.

Small Wins: Celebrate them. Recognize and celebrate your achievements, no matter how minor they might seem. These positive affirmations can help counterbalance the weight of self-imposed scarcity.

Seek Authenticity: Embracing our unique journey without the need for comparison can be liberating. Each of us has a unique blend of strengths, experiences, and values that define our path.

Every thought we nurture, every belief we hold, shapes our world. By recognizing and reshaping the subtle yet powerful narrative of scarcity, we can step into a life of greater self-assurance, potential, and abundance. We can step over the gap into the realm of consciousness. The journey from scarcity to abundance begins with a "right" shift.

3. Self-Imposed Fear: The Chains of Shoulds" and "What Ifs"

Fear, while a basic human emotion designed to protect us from threats, has evolved in modern society into a complex maze of doubts, insecurities, and self-imposed limitations. This advanced form of fear doesn't just alert us to physical dangers but delves into the emotional and psychological realms, challenging our perceptions and actions. Let's dive deeper into the intricacies of self-imposed fear and how it manifests.

At the heart of our self-imposed fears lie two fundamental insecurities. First, there's the unsettling belief that our life should have taken a different trajectory than it did. This is often accompanied by a barrage of "what ifs" and "if onlys," leading us to question our past choices, circumstances, and even fate itself.

The second deep-seated fear is the corrosive notion that we, in our very essence, are flawed. We wrestle with the belief that we should be different, better, or more than what we are now. This can manifest as self-deprecation, constantly comparing ourselves to others, or seeking relentless external validation. In my own journey of introspection, I've observed that most of my anxieties and apprehensions can be traced back to these two foundational fears. So, let's delve deeper into understanding how they shape our perceptions and behaviors.

The Weight of "Shoulds"

The term "should" can be one of the heaviest words in our vocabulary. Wrapped up in this seemingly innocuous word is a lifetime of societal expectations, personal pressures, and unmet goals.

My life should be different: This belief suggests a dissatisfaction with the current state of life and the circumstances surrounding it. It sets an idealized version of life that often isn't rooted in reality but in societal expectations or fictionalized life standards presented in media.

I should be different: This phrase reveals a deep-seated discomfort with one's true self. It implies that there is a "better version" of oneself that should have been achieved, discounting personal growth, experiences, and achievements.

The Paralysis of "What Ifs" and "Buts"

These phrases highlight the anxiety of potential outcomes, constantly holding us in the liminal space between action and inaction.

What if: The phrase "What if" often functions as a gateway to the vast realm of possibilities but not always the positive kind. For many, it's a lens that magnifies fears and exaggerates concerns. It's as though the mind, in its bid to protect us, projects the most dramatic outcomes, usually skewing toward the negative. This can tether us to a life of caution, preventing us from venturing into the unknown or taking meaningful risks.

At its core, "What if" embodies the human tendency to seek safety and predictability. While this instinct has evolutionary roots meant to shield us from danger, in today's world, it often acts as a self-imposed boundary. Each time we're on the cusp of trying something new, these two words can pull us back, painting vivid pictures of failure, embarrassment, or loss.

However, this narrative can be shifted. This reframe is most likely one of the most popular but nonetheless effective. By consciously reframing our "What if" scenarios, we can tap into its constructive potential. Instead of "What if I fail?" we can ask, "What if I succeed?" This shifts the energy from fear-based speculation to aspirational anticipation. In recognizing and harnessing the dual nature of "What if," we can choose to use it as a tool for growth rather than a harbinger of hesitation.

One of the most effective ways that I have found to navigate the treacherous "What if" pathway is to come to terms with the worst-case scenario. Our brains, naturally inclined toward self-preservation, will inevitably drift to those dreaded "worst possible outcomes." So, instead of fighting this natural inclination, we can strategically harness it to serve our mental well-being.

Making peace with the worst-case scenario involves confronting it head-on. By envisioning the most unfavorable outcome and then recognizing that, at its root, the deepest fear is often just an uncomfortable feeling or emotion, we can strip away much of its intimidating power. Feelings, no matter how overwhelming, are transient and manageable.

For example, if you're anxious about a big presentation, delve into the depths of that anxiety. Ask yourself, "What if I forget my lines?" The worst thing? Perhaps a moment of embarrassment or awkwardness. But will you be okay? Absolutely. The sun will still rise the next day, and life will go on.

By actively engaging in this thought exercise, we effectively tell our brains, "I've been there, I've thought it through, and I've made peace with it." This preemptive reassurance can prevent our minds from spiraling and instead ground them in reality. It's like preparing for the rain with an umbrella—the rain might still come, but you're ready for it. The next time your brain drifts into the "What if" territory, remind it gently, "Hey, we've considered this. We're prepared, and no matter what, we'll be okay."

But ...: This is the counter-argument to our aspirations, the reason we give ourselves to not proceed. It's the internal skeptic, always finding reasons for inaction. The word "but" often acts as a mental speed bump in our narratives. Whenever I hear phrases like "I love my husband, but ..." or "I love my job, but ...," I am instantly reminded that everything following that "but" is usually a manifestation of uncertainty or fear. While "but" serves to introduce a contrasting point, it frequently diminishes the sentiment expressed before it. It's as if we're giving ourselves permission to indulge in doubt or to let our apprehensions overshadow our affirmations. More often than not, what follows "but" isn't a genuine, objective concern; it's the echo of internal fear, limiting beliefs, or unresolved emotions. If we're striving for clarity and honesty in our self-expression, it might be worth reconsidering how often and why we use that seemingly innocuous conjunction.

Fear of Perception

One of the most potent fears in our modern era is the fear of how others perceive us.

Scared to be seen starting small: In a world that often glorifies "overnight successes" and "viral sensations," there's an underlying pressure to appear successful from the outset. This fear disregards the fact that every success story often has years of hard work behind it. It's imperative to understand that those who've forged the path ahead, who've faced the challenges and emerged victorious, are seldom the critics. They understand the journey's trials and are more likely to extend a hand than point a finger. Surrounding ourselves with individuals who've walked the path can provide not just guidance but reassurance. Their understanding and empathy are priceless.

Scared to feel like an imposter: The Imposter Syndrome is that nagging doubt that makes us question our accomplishments and internalize the fear of being "found out" or seen as a fraud. Impostor Syndrome isn't always about doubting our abilities. Sometimes, it's the dissonance between who we believe we should be and who we think we are. It's the fear that others will see through the facade and realize that we're not as competent or deserving as we project. Often, individuals with impostor feelings are indeed competent, but they mistake their lack of unyielding confidence as a sign of ineptitude.

Scared of what other people think: This thought highlights the weight we give to societal opinion, often prioritizing it over personal happiness or authenticity. One of the most debilitating aspects of this fear is the belief that there's a vast audience scrutinizing our every move. But in reality, most people are too engrossed in their narratives to pay undue attention to ours.

How often have we held back from pursuing our passions or our projects or voicing our opinions due to the looming presence of "all the people"? In truth, "all the people" is a mirage. Most are preoccupied with their lives, dreams, and fears. The overwhelming chorus of critics we anticipate is, in reality, a small handful, and even then, they're often projections of our insecurities.

Navigating the treacherous waters of perception can be challenging in our hyper-connected, opinionated world. We often expend enormous amounts of energy trying to manage or manipulate how others see us. However, one transformative approach is to simply make peace with the inevitability of judgment.

It's true; we are wired in many ways to judge—it's a survival mechanism, a way our ancestors categorized threats and rewards. In our modern society, this instinct has manifested in less life-threatening ways, like forming opinions about one another based on appearances, beliefs, or actions. So yes, people will judge—and that's okay.

Some might view us in a positive light, admiring our choices or values, while others might not understand or agree with our path. And nothing has gone wrong. Instead of getting tangled in the exhausting endeavor of trying to please everyone, we can liberate ourselves by allowing others their perceptions, regardless of whether they're "right" or "wrong" about us. By doing so, we're essentially giving people permission to be wrong about us. How nice of us.

Embracing this mindset is not only freeing but also empowering. It shifts the locus of control back to us. We no longer become puppets to the whims and views of others but remain steadfast in our own self-worth and self-perception.

In the end, the only opinion about ourselves that truly matters is our own. And by making peace with the inevitable judgments of others, we make space for authenticity, growth, and self-assuredness.

Fear of Decisions

For most, making decisions is daunting. Every choice we make opens up a pathway to a new reality while simultaneously closing the door to countless others. The anxiety associated with this is compounded by the fear of judgment. What if we make the "wrong" choice? What if others perceive our decisions as flawed? What if we ourselves regret the path taken?

Our early years in school train us to believe in the binary of "right" and "wrong." This binary system, however, does not mirror the real world. Life isn't a neatly organized math problem with a singular solution. It's a mosaic of experiences, where every piece—no matter how seemingly incongruous—contributes to the overall picture. It's essential to understand that decisions aren't about right or wrong but about choices and experiences. When we don't realize this, we tend to live in the "Land of Maybe." The Land of Maybe is a realm where decisions go to languish. It's a place of indecision, of waiting for the perfect moment, the perfect conditions. It's a place where we surrender our power, avoiding the act of deciding so as not to confront the resultant feelings. But power isn't just about control. It's about agency, the ability to shape our narrative and the direction of our lives.

To continually defer decisions due to fear of feelings is to rob oneself of authentic experiences. Fear, adversity, joy, satisfaction—these are the spectrum of emotions that paint the canvas of life in vibrant hues. Avoiding them is akin to viewing the world in grayscale.

In the quest to avoid potential negative outcomes, we might think we're keeping ourselves safe. In reality, we're keeping ourselves stagnant. Embracing decisions, with all their potential pitfalls and triumphs, is a testament to embracing life itself. Each decision, regardless of its outcome, is an opportunity for growth, learning, and progress.

Decisions are doorways to experiences, and experiences are the threads from which the tapestry of life is woven. To fear decisions is to fear life itself. So, let's embrace decisions, feel our feelings fully, and step into the fullness of life. After all, it's not about making the "right" decision but about making right by the decision that is made.

The Illusion of "There" in Decision-Making

It's a common belief that once we make a decision, everything will align, and life will be better on the "other side." This perspective fuels our impatience. We hurry toward that elusive "there," convinced that our current dissatisfaction or discomfort will evaporate once we've traversed to the other side of a decision.

However, this belief is rooted in the illusion that our external circumstances dictate our internal well-being. We think that the grass will definitely be greener, the skies bluer, and our days brighter once we've made that choice. In our quest for better tomorrows, we often overlook the inherent value of our todays.

The truth is, life is made up of a series of moments, each with its blend of good and bad, joy and sorrow, peace and turmoil. This 50/50 mix doesn't magically skew toward 100% happiness when we move from one decision to the next. "There" will have its challenges, just as "here" does. The landscapes change, but the balance of experiences remains.

What does shift, however, is our perspective and personal growth. With every decision, we gather new experiences, insights, and wisdom. We don't necessarily move from discomfort to comfort but from one set of learnings to another, each molding and refining us in different ways.

In our rush to get "there," we must remember that impatience robs us of the journey's richness. It's not about reaching a destination where everything is perfect but about evolving and growing along the way, savoring the lessons and moments that come with each step.

Instead of looking at decisions as gateways to better realities, see them as opportunities for growth, understanding, and deepening of one's journey. When we realize that the promise of "there" is not about escaping the now but about embracing the journey, we find contentment and depth in our present, making each decision a stepping stone rather than an escape route.

Speaking of fearing feelings … Let's take a closer look.

Fear of Emotions

The fear of experiencing negative emotions is paralyzing for many. Emotions like embarrassment, rejection, discomfort, and failure, although natural, are often seen as things to be avoided at all costs. This avoidance can limit experiences, risks, and opportunities for growth.

The Ancient Brain in the Modern World: Running from Bears and Burning Desires

Throughout the evolution of humanity, our brains have been finely tuned to respond to threats to ensure our survival. The primitive parts of our brains, most notably the amygdala, played a pivotal role in this. When our ancestors roamed the prehistoric world, their primary concerns were very immediate and physical. The snarl of a saber-toothed tiger, the rustling of a hidden predator in the bushes, or the unmistakable growl of a bear required instantaneous reaction—typically the choice of fight or flight.

Physical Danger: The Legacy of the Ancients

In the primal world, these immediate and tangible threats were a matter of life and death. The amygdala's function was to instantly assess these situations. When a threat was perceived, it would send rapid signals to prepare the body for action. Adrenaline would surge, heart rates would increase, and all non-essential functions would momentarily shut down to allow for maximum physical performance. In essence, the amygdala was our early warning system, keeping us alert and alive in a world full of tangible dangers.

Emotional Danger: The Challenge of the Modern Mind

Fast forward to our contemporary world, where most of us are free from the daily threats of wild predators. Yet, the amygdala remains ever vigilant. The challenge arises from the fact that this primitive part of our brain does not particularly differentiate between the tangible threat of a bear and the intangible threat of, say, public speaking, rejection, or failing to achieve our dreams.

This inability to discern between physical and emotional dangers means that the same intense reactions triggered by a charging predator can be activated by the prospect of a difficult conversation or the fear of failure. Such an overly protective response can hinder our personal growth and exploration in a world where the risks are more about bruised egos than physical harm.

From Burning Houses to Burning Desires

Just as our ancestors might have fled from a burning dwelling, our internal mechanisms can make us flee from our burning desires. The fear of judgment, the potential for rejection, or the sting of failure can light up our amygdala as if we're facing a genuine life-threatening scenario. This can be seen in phenomena such as stage fright, where the mere act of standing in front of an audience can elicit a response comparable to facing a mortal threat.

Taming the Primitive Brain: The Powerhouse to Unlocking Your Potential

Imagine that inside you, there's a primal force, a prehistoric version of yourself, that still runs on survival instincts: always chasing pleasure, avoiding pain, and conserving energy. This is your primitive brain, and while it served our ancestors well when evading predators, it can pose challenges in our modern world. If left unchecked, this primitive mindset can hijack your potential, keeping you stagnant in your comfort zone and impeding your growth.

Let's break it down. The primitive brain operates on the motivational triad:

Seek Pleasure: This isn't about enjoying a good book or a sunset but about immediate gratification—like binge-watching a show instead of finishing a task or grabbing that extra slice of cake when we're not even hungry.

Avoid Pain: This doesn't just mean physical pain. The primitive brain shies away from emotional discomfort, too. Fear of rejection or failure? It'll whisper, "Better not try at all."

Save Energy: Why take risks or put in effort when staying in the comfort zone feels ... well, comfortable? It means missed opportunities and untapped potential.

In the vast landscapes of our minds, the primitive brain is like a powerful but outdated software. It's always scanning the horizon for threats and rewards, focusing on the immediate, never the long-term. And while this might have been vital for our ancestors trying to survive in the wilderness, it can be limiting in a world where our challenges are different.

Here's the empowering part. We're not just our primitive brains. We also have the most advanced, high-functioning part of our brain—the prefrontal cortex. This is where intention, logic, and reasoning reside. This is where we dream, plan, and create. This is the realm of potential, where we can visualize a goal and chart a course toward it, even if it's challenging or uncertain.

It's crucial to recognize when the primitive brain is steering our actions. Are we avoiding a task because of the effort it requires or the fear of failure? Are we opting for short-term pleasures at the expense of long-term goals?

By understanding the dichotomy within us—the primitive desires versus the higher aspirations—we can consciously choose which part of our brains we let take the driver's seat. Do we want to remain in a cycle of instant gratifications and missed opportunities, or do we wish to challenge ourselves, set ambitious goals, and truly unlock our potential?

Every worthwhile goal comes with its own emotional invoice. As we strive for our ambitions, we're often faced with discomfort, doubt, fear, or uncertainty. These feelings, however unwelcome, are the hidden costs of progress and transformation. But why do such aspirations come with emotional tolls? And why is paying this price crucial for our growth?

The very essence of setting a goal requires us to step outside of our comfort zones. It demands that we confront the unfamiliar, challenge our own boundaries, and sometimes even grapple with our deeply held beliefs. In this journey, negative emotions are inevitable. They arise not as barriers but as checkpoints, testing our commitment and resilience.

However, herein lies the secret—our capacity to achieve is directly proportional to our ability to endure these emotions. The more adept we become at processing and navigating our feelings, the more expansive our life becomes. Just as a muscle grows stronger with resistance, our emotional resilience strengthens when faced with adversity.

By understanding that negative emotions are an integral part of the journey and not impediments, we can approach them differently. Instead of avoiding discomfort, we can lean into it. Instead of fearing failure, we can embrace it as a stepping stone. By allowing ourselves to fully experience these feelings without judgment, we give them less power over our actions.

Moreover, feeling our emotions in their entirety offers another gift: clarity. By acknowledging and understanding our feelings, we gain insights into what truly matters to us, refining our goals and our paths to reach them.

So, the next time you set a goal and negative emotions surface, welcome them. Recognize them as the price of admission to a life of growth and fulfillment. Remember, every pang of discomfort, every twinge of doubt, is a testament to your progress. The better you become at handling these emotions, the more expansive and enriched your life journey will be. Embrace the emotions, for they are the unsung markers of your growth.

In essence, taking charge of our lives means supervising our primitive brain, understanding its motivations, but not being enslaved by them. Embrace the incredible capabilities of your evolved mind, welcome the negative emotions, chart your course, and embark on a journey of limitless potential.

The journey to silence self-imposed fears isn't about reaching a destination where fear doesn't exist but rather learning to navigate its presence. Recognizing the whispers of these fears for what they are—echoes of our insecurities—and choosing to listen to the more empowering voices, both internal and external, can be the key to unlocking our fullest potential. Remember, the most significant critics and champions reside within us; it's a matter of choosing which one to amplify.

Reconditioning the Modern Brain

Understanding our primitive brain, the motivational triad, and the misfiring of our ancient alarm system is crucial. By recognizing that our acute stress responses in non-threatening situations are echoes from our evolutionary past, we can begin to retrain our reactions.

4. Self-Imposed Righteousness

In our quest to navigate the complexities of life, it's easy to fall into the trap of believing we hold all the answers. This belief, fueled by our experiences, knowledge, and perhaps even our egos, can lead us down the path of self-imposed righteousness. It's a mindset where we elevate our perspectives above all others, believing that our way is not just the right way but the only way.

The Cloak of Righteousness

Self-imposed righteousness is one of those cloaked adversaries, often masquerading as humility or open-mindedness. It's a complex trait that lingers in the shadows of our psyche, convincing us of its absence even as it dictates our responses.

For many, the very idea of self-righteousness conjures images of loud, dogmatic individuals steadfast in their beliefs and dismissive of others. However, in its subtler forms, self-righteousness doesn't always appear so overt. It's the silent smirk when someone shares an unfamiliar perspective, the quick dismissal of an idea that doesn't align with our worldview, or the quiet belief that our approach is inherently superior.

Many of us genuinely believe we embrace open-mindedness. We celebrate diversity of thought, affirm the value of varied perspectives, and profess a willingness to be proven wrong. Yet, buried deep within is a latent urge to be "right'," to have our beliefs affirmed, and to find solace in the validation of our perspectives.

The danger of this subtle self-righteousness is that it limits our potential for growth. When ensnared by its grasp, we become less receptive to learning and more resistant to change. Our convictions, no matter how well-intentioned, can become cages that stifle our understanding and growth.

Breaking free from this requires introspection and an unflinching honesty with oneself. It means acknowledging our biases, confronting our need for validation, and actively seeking out perspectives that challenge our comfort zones. Only by doing so can we genuinely open the doors to enlightenment.

In a world that is vast and diverse in its thoughts, cultures, and beliefs, humility is our greatest ally. Recognizing the sneakiness of self-imposed righteousness is the first step toward truly embodying it. After all, true enlightenment doesn't come from being "right;" it emerges from the understanding that there's always more to learn and that every person, every perspective holds a piece of the puzzle we're all trying to solve.

The Cost of Always Being Right

While the need to be right might give a momentary sense of validation, it comes at significant costs.

Forfeiting Genuine Connection

In our human relationships, one of the most elusive yet fundamental elements is genuine connection. This bond, though fragile, forms the core of our interactions, and yet, it's often the first to be sacrificed at the altar of self-righteousness.

Being "right" can sometimes feel so vital that we inadvertently place it above everything else, even at the cost of real connection. But in this fervor to defend our point of view, what are we truly gaining? And more importantly, what are we losing?

When we prioritize our need to be "right," we erect walls around ourselves. We turn interactions into debates and conversations into contests. Defensive behavior, rather than fostering understanding, acts as a barricade.

Ironically, in our quest to be "right," we might ruminate over someone else's perceived need to be right, blind to our own mirror image in the reflection of the argument. This cycle disrupts genuine communication. Instead of listening to understand, we listen to counter, preparing our response even before the other person has finished their sentence.

This righteousness not only leads to us dismissing what's being presented but also to a counter-productive cycle of taking offense and then deflecting. Instead of a space of mutual respect, conversations turn into battlegrounds where every statement is seen as an attack or defense, leaving no room for genuine understanding.

Beneath this lies a deeper issue: the mistaken conflation of admitting a mistake with admitting unworthiness. In our minds, conceding a point becomes equated with diminishing our value. But true strength lies in recognizing that our humanity isn't tethered to always being right. It's tethered to our capacity for empathy, understanding, and growth.

If we wish to nurture our relationships, we must be willing to set aside our armor of righteousness. To embrace vulnerability, to truly hear and be heard, and to understand that sometimes, the beauty of connection lies not in asserting our perspective but in celebrating the kaleidoscope of human experience that every interaction brings.

The Illusion of Infallibility: Embracing Relative Truths

In our pursuit of righteousness, we often shoulder the weight of being infallible. Imagine a life where every step, every decision, every word spoken is tinged with the looming dread of error. Such is the life when one feels they always have to be right. It's an existence shrouded in constant pressure, demanding perpetual perfection, leaving no room for the simple human experience of learning through errors.

But here's a freeing thought: what if we didn't always have to be right? What if, instead of contending with different views, we allowed everyone their perception of right? After all, the ultimate, absolute Truth is so vast and intricate that our human definitions can never encapsulate it fully. Our versions of it are mere reflections, clouded by our experiences, beliefs, and individual paths.

Take the parable of the three blind men and the elephant. Each man, limited by his touch, described the massive creature based on the part he felt. To the man feeling the trunk, the elephant was like a snake. To the one feeling its leg, the elephant resembled a tree trunk. And for the man who touched its ear, the elephant was like a large fan. Who among them was truly right? Or were they all just narrating their slice of reality?

Arguing over the "right" perspective here is futile. Each is valid in its own right, much like the myriad beliefs and truths we all hold. In attempting to deem one perception as the sole truth, we disregard the richness of diverse experiences that paint our collective reality.

This book doesn't aim to define morality or provide stringent guidelines on right and wrong. Instead, it's an invitation to explore. To understand that while we all inhabit the same universe, each of us navigates through it on our unique trajectory. Our perceptions, our truths, stem from our distinct encounters and experiences.

So, who among us can release the shackles of always being "right"? Because understanding the relativity of truth is not about conceding defeat but about celebrating the multitude of perspectives that make our world unique with diverse stories and beliefs.

While it's natural to want confirmation and validation from those around us, the deepest insights often come from our inner selves. Learning to balance our knowledge with humility and our intuition with openness ensures we *don't just strive to be right but to be wise.* The journey from self-imposed righteousness to self-aware openness is one of growth, connection, and profound understanding.

Re-orienting From Righteousness to Openness

Many of us have fallen into the righteousness trap at one point or another, driven by a desire for validation or a fear of vulnerability. The journey out of it involves:

Active Listening: Instead of formulating our responses while someone else is talking, truly listen to understand.

Seeking to Understand, Not Just to Be Understood: It's a principle that reminds us of the importance of empathy and compassion in our interactions.

Self-reflection: Regularly check in with ourselves. Ask: Am I genuinely open to other perspectives? Am I listening to respond or to understand?

Celebrating Others' Expertise: Recognizing and celebrating when others know more about a subject is not a sign of weakness but of strength. It shows humility, wisdom, and a desire for continuous learning.

Fostering Intuition in Others: By creating spaces for others to share and explore their feelings and thoughts without judgment, we inspire them to trust their intuition. This approach not only empowers them but strengthens our relationships.

5. Self-Imposed Glass Ceilings

In the vast skyscrapers of our aspirations, every floor has a ceiling. While these ceilings can be a barrier to our progress, what's truly confounding is when we discover that some of these barriers are of our own making. These are our self-imposed glass ceilings, invisible but palpable constraints that keep us from reaching our highest potential. The irony? They're not set in stone; they're forged from beliefs we can choose to unmake.

These ceilings represent the limitations we unconsciously (or sometimes consciously) set for ourselves based on internalized beliefs, past experiences, or societal conditioning. They are the "I can'ts," the "I'm not worthys," and the "It's just not possibles" of our internal dialogue.

Perceived as Truth

These self-impositions often feel like undeniable facts. They've been reinforced, perhaps by repeated experiences or societal messages, to a point where questioning them seems absurd. Here's the twist—these beliefs, as steadfast as they might seem, are optional.

I find myself circling back to this pivotal concept time and again: thoughts are optional. Yes, I harp on about it. Yes, I might sound like a broken record. But there's a reason for my insistence.

In my journey, understanding the malleability of thoughts wasn't just an "aha!" moment—it was a life-altering revelation. For so long, I believed that thoughts were fixed entities, unchangeable and deeply embedded in who I am. But once I grasped that I have the power to choose my thoughts, my entire world shifted. And this didn't happen overnight.

I had to hear it repeatedly, ruminate on it, and put it into practice day in and day out. It was an endeavor, a consistent act of mindfulness, until one day, it wasn't. It became a part of my very being. The realization that I wasn't enslaved to every thought that crossed my mind, that I could pick and choose which ones to entertain and which ones to let go, was liberating.

You might be quicker on the uptake than I was, but I emphasize this point not to be repetitive but to underscore its significance. It's not just a footnote in the story of personal development; it's a whole chapter. Recognizing that thoughts are optional is like discovering you've had wings all along.

So, bear with me as I hammer this point home because if there's one thing I want you to carry forward, it's the profound empowerment that comes from understanding that your thoughts, those seemingly uncontrollable entities, are, in fact, optional. And when you truly grasp that, the possibilities for your life become boundless.

We have to know that every belief, at its core, is a repeated thought we've chosen to agree with. Recognizing this gives us the power to question, challenge, and ultimately change them.

Shattering our self-imposed glass ceilings requires introspection, courage, and persistence. By continually challenging our limiting beliefs and redefining what's possible for ourselves, we pave the way for a future unbounded by invisible barriers. As we break through each ceiling, we don't just elevate ourselves but set a precedent for others to do the same.

6. Self-Imposed Burnout

The Double-Edged Sword of Limitlessness

The world often lauds those who push boundaries, those who refuse to be confined by any perceived limitations. The "sky's the limit" mentality is celebrated, especially in our era of entrepreneurship and relentless hustle. But, here's an unpopular truth that many high-achievers come face-to-face with—sometimes, the very absence of a ceiling is what brings us crashing down.

For many driven individuals, ambition knows no bounds. We are taught to break the glass ceiling, to shatter the barriers placed upon us by society. Yet, in doing so, some of us forget to set a new ceiling, a safety net for our well-being. This lack of a self-imposed ceiling can be as detrimental as any external limitation.

Unbridled ambition can often be a treacherous path. It's akin to a car with no speed limits, going faster and faster until the inevitable crash. You may have the prowess to run marathons back-to-back, but should you? The absence of constraints leads to exhaustion, both mental and physical. It's the culprit behind the dark circles under a CEO's eyes, the burnout of a startup founder, or the weariness of an over-achieving student.

When every hour becomes an opportunity to do more and achieve more, the very essence of life starts slipping through our fingers. The laughter of loved ones, the tranquility of a quiet morning, the joy of doing absolutely nothing—these moments become rare. It's no wonder that despite accomplishments, a void begins to form, leading to questions like, "Is this all there is?"

The irony is that the same tenacity that drives success can also drive disconnection from what truly matters. Setting a ceiling isn't about limiting potential. It's about preserving the essence of life, ensuring there's room for joy, rest, love, and self-care. It's about recognizing that while the universe might be limitless, our time and energy aren't.

Holistic success isn't just about accolades and achievements. It's about balance, contentment, and cherishing the journey as much as the destination. It's time to recalibrate and ask the crucial question—"What is my 'enough' point?" By setting our own ceilings, we're not confining ourselves but rather ensuring that in our quest for greatness, we don't lose the greatness of life itself.

The Double-Edged Sword of Limitlessness: When Freedom Becomes Overwhelming

Human psychology is complex, shaped by a constant interplay between our desires, fears, and external influences. One moment, we crave to break free from our self-imposed limitations, and the next, we're daunted by the vast expanse of endless possibilities. But why does the absence of ceilings sometimes feel scarier than their imposing presence?

Endless Possibilities, Endless Stress: It's called the paradox of choice. Barry Schwartz, in his book of the same name, discusses how having too many options can lead to analysis paralysis and a decreased level of satisfaction. In the context of life aspirations, when we remove our self-imposed ceilings, the multitude of directions and possibilities can be paralyzing.

The Paradox of Limitations: A Guide to Conscious Navigation

The very term "limitations" evokes a sense of confinement, a barrier holding us back from our potential. Yet, limitations can serve a contrasting purpose—they can anchor us, providing clarity amidst the vast sea of life's possibilities.

Imagine standing at the edge of an endless horizon with infinite paths stretching out in all directions. The sheer vastness can be paralyzing. Which way to go? How far to travel? Without some form of limitation, the choices are overwhelming, leading to inertia or, even worse, a frenzied pace that lacks true direction.

Limitations, when consciously imposed, act as a compass. They create a sense of structure, allowing us to channel our energy efficiently. They become our safe markers in the expansive map of life, ensuring we don't get lost in the wilderness of overextension. The ceiling becomes our north star, guiding us while preventing the descent into the abyss of burnout.

But here's where the balance comes into play … these ceilings shouldn't be confused with the walls that our mind sometimes builds, walls created from fear, past failures, or societal expectations. These are the constraints that hold us back. The ceiling we advocate for is different. It's not about setting a cap on our potential but about knowing when it's time to rest, reflect, and recharge.

The challenge, then, is discerning between the two. Consciousness becomes our greatest tool. With introspection, we can dissect our limitations and understand their origins. Are they borne out of genuine self-awareness or merely reflections of deep-seated insecurities?

Clarity of values plays an instrumental role. When we're clear about what truly matters, it becomes easier to set meaningful boundaries. It's about acknowledging the difference between "Can I?" and "Should I?"

Finally, knowing our "enough" point is the culmination of this self-exploration. It's the point where ambition meets contentment. It's the acknowledgment that while the universe's possibilities might be limitless, our well-being has its boundaries. Recognizing this balance ensures we chase our dreams with vigor but without the cost of our peace.

In our lives, limitations can be our most unexpected allies. When consciously chosen, they don't restrict; they refine, ensuring that in our boundless journey, we always have a direction, a sense of purpose, and, most importantly, a sense of self.

Before we move on to the next (seventh and final) imposition, I wanted to briefly explore two additional ways that "limitless" can lead to feeling "lifeless."

The Overworker's Dilemma: When faced with a horizon of limitless potential, one common reaction is to overextend. Without clear boundaries, it's easy to take on too much, say "yes" to every opportunity, and work tirelessly in the hopes of capitalizing on every possible outcome.

Perpetual Motion, Diminishing Returns: This ceaseless action often becomes counterproductive. As the law of diminishing returns posits, there comes a point when every additional hour of work, every added responsibility, starts yielding lesser value. In fact, it can become detrimental to both mental and physical health.

The Joyful Transition: From FOMO to JOMO

In today's hyper-connected world, FOMO has evolved into a near-universal experience. The ceaseless buzz of notifications, the parade of social media highlights, and the perpetual agenda of events have ensnared us into a trap of constant longing. We are haunted by the specter of missed experiences, conversations, or milestones. But amidst this frenzy, a contrasting philosophy emerges—JOMO, or the Joy of Missing Out.

JOMO is not just an antonym to FOMO; it's an antidote. It's about recognizing that every moment spent trying to be everywhere is a moment missed being truly present somewhere. Every "yes" to a non-priority means a "no" to something that might genuinely matter to us.

Embracing JOMO is a deliberate act of self-care. It's understanding that our energy, attention, and time are finite resources. When we guard them, rather than squandering them in pursuits of fleeting satisfaction, we find richer, deeper joy in experiences that align with our core values and desires.

Overcommitting stems from the fear of being left out, but the irony is that in overextending ourselves, we leave ourselves out of the essence of life. The quality of our engagements suffers. Our presence becomes fragmented. Instead of absorbing the joy from one experience, we find ourselves hopping from one thing to another, never truly settling, never truly savoring.

JOMO is about cherishing simplicity, celebrating stillness, and relishing the pleasure of purposefully chosen engagements. It's about understanding that sometimes the most meaningful moments come not from being everywhere but from being in one place fully, immersed and engaged.

So, the next time FOMO tries to lure you into the whirlwind of endless activities, take a step back. Evaluate, introspect, and ask yourself: Is this in harmony with my priorities? Will this bring genuine joy or just momentary satisfaction?

Remember, every time you consciously choose JOMO over FOMO, you're not missing out; you're making space. Space for genuine experiences, deeper connections, and, most importantly, for the profound joy that comes from truly living in the moment.

Limitlessness, while liberating, can also be a source of distress. The key lies in striking a balance. While it's crucial to challenge our self-imposed limitations, it's equally important to ensure we don't become victims of our own ambitions. By setting conscious boundaries, we can navigate the vast ocean of possibilities without feeling adrift.

Setting Healthy Boundaries

Acknowledging Limitations: While we don't want to be hindered by self-imposed ceilings, it's essential to recognize that we have physiological and psychological limits. Continuous overwork and lack of rest can lead to burnout, impacting both well-being and the quality of work.

Prioritizing & Setting Non-Negotiables: Even in a limitless space, prioritization is crucial. It's impossible to chase every opportunity or master every skill. Establishing non-negotiables—things that one won't compromise on, like health, family time, and mental well-being—can provide some structure.

Learning to Say "No": The art of refusal is vital. By declining opportunities that don't align with our core values or long-term goals, we create space for those that truly matter.

Mindful Engagement: Being present in whatever we choose to do ensures quality over quantity. It also enhances satisfaction and reduces feelings of being overwhelmed.

7. Self-Imposed Adversity

Self-Imposed Shadows of the Past

The human mind is like a vast museum, cataloging experiences from our pasts. But unlike a museum where artifacts remain passive, our mental archives can actively influence our present. One of the potent forces in this museum is self-imposed adversity, especially the one emanating from unresolved past events. These dormant specters have a knack for casting long shadows on our present.

Past events, especially those colored by pain, regret, or trauma, can feel like chains holding us back from moving forward. Perhaps it's a past failure, an ended relationship, a lost opportunity, or even childhood trauma. When these events are not processed and resolved, they tend to create narratives. "I'm not good enough," "I always mess things up," or "I can't trust people" might be some recurring scripts.

Rather than serving as lessons, these unresolved events haunt our daily lives. They cloud judgments, induce anxiety, and stifle growth. We might find ourselves repeatedly drawn into similar situations or experiencing similar pains, *almost as if* history is determined to repeat itself. This is the baggage of self-imposed adversity, and it's a weight many unknowingly carry.

Interestingly, to address this adversity, one doesn't have to delve deep into the past. Instead, recognizing its manifestation in the present is the key. What are the patterns you see today that might have roots in the past? What thoughts, feelings, or actions seem to have a recurring theme?

Once identified, it's time for transformation. While the past events are unchangeable, our interpretations are fluid. The narratives can be rewritten. For instance, a past failure can transform from "I am a failure" to "I learned something valuable." By changing the narrative, we strip the event of its adverse power.

Recognizing and accepting is half the battle. When we pinpoint these past adversities affecting our present, it's like shining a light on a shadow. It dissipates. The mere act of acknowledgment can be incredibly liberating.

Self-Imposed Future Adversity: Anticipating Tomorrow's Storms Today

Amid life's many challenges, a unique kind arises not from the past or present but from a future we've not yet met. This self-inflicted adversity comes from our propensity to anticipate, or rather, dread, what lies ahead. Humans, with our evolved brains, have the unique capability to project into the future. This ability has been key to our survival, allowing us to plan and prepare. However, the very same skill, when intertwined with our fears and insecurities, can result in creating adverse scenarios that might never materialize.

These aren't mere concerns about tangible future events, like an impending exam or job interview. Instead, they're often amorphous, exaggerated "what ifs." What if I end up alone? What if I never achieve my dreams? What if all my efforts are in vain? These imagined challenges haven't occurred, and there's no certainty they ever will. Yet, their mere possibility casts a shadow on our present.

By anticipating adversity, we essentially "borrow trouble" from the future, paying a toll in the form of present stress, anxiety, and paralysis. This forward-focused anxiety doesn't just rob us of present joy but also diminishes our capacity to address real challenges. The irony of future-focused adversity is that it's entirely a product of our imagination. The future remains a blank canvas, yet we sometimes paint it with the dark hues of our worst fears. Our projections, no matter how vivid, are not prophecies. They're constructs, influenced more by our present mindset than any concrete knowledge of tomorrow.

Life is inherently uncertain. While preparation has its place, excessive anticipation creates needless burdens. By focusing on the present and taking actionable steps, we can shape a future aligned with our aspirations rather than being held captive by imagined adversities.

While it's natural to ponder what lies ahead, it's crucial to discern between constructive planning and debilitating dread. The future remains unwritten, and it's up to us to pen its chapters with hope, resilience, and an open heart, free from the shackles of self-imposed adversity.

Self-Imposed Internal Adversity: Battles Within the Mind

Life presents us with a myriad of challenges, but not all battles are external. Some of the most enduring struggles are waged within the confines of our own minds. This internal, self-imposed adversity often manifests as a web of negative beliefs and self-doubts that entangle our thoughts and shape our behaviors.

The genesis of these internal conflicts can be diverse, but they aren't concrete issues but rather phantoms of our imagination. These imagined adversaries can be even more potent than tangible challenges because they're deeply ingrained in our psyche.

Manifestations of Self-Imposed Internal Adversity

Fear and Doubt: Doubting one's abilities or fearing potential outcomes can paralyze us. This paralysis often inhibits us from venturing outside our comfort zones or pursuing our true passions.

Optional Mistakes: These include procrastination, where we delay tasks due to dread or laziness; self-sabotage, where we undermine our own success, often subconsciously; and preemptive failure, where we give up on endeavors even before they begin, anticipating defeat.

Self-Worth and Validation: A deeply felt lack of worthiness can stem from internalizing past criticisms or failures. We might constantly seek external validation, tying our self-worth to external accolades.

Self-Perception: Our mental self-portrait can become tainted by beliefs about our capacity, capability, and intrinsic value. This distorted self-view can lead us to act out of alignment with our true selves.

The Ripple Effect: While these adversities might be internal, their effects ripple outward. They shape our interactions, choices, and even our potential. They can affect our relationships, careers, and overall well-being.

The mind is a powerful tool. While it can create internal landscapes of doubt and fear, it also possesses the capacity for transformation. Recognizing, challenging, and reshaping our self-imposed adversities can pave the way for a life led by clarity, confidence, and authenticity.

And finally ...

Growth Through Opposition

Our journey through life is often filled with opposition, roadblocks, and internal battles. Certainly, there are more than the seven I outlined for you to consider. But rather than viewing these as obstacles, what if we considered them vital signposts guiding our path to growth? The very essence of personal development lies in the recognition and acceptance of these oppositions as intrinsic components of our growth journey.

1. The Role of Awareness and Acceptance

The first step to breaking through barriers is recognizing they exist. Awareness allows us to identify these self-imposed limitations. Acceptance, on the other hand, is about acknowledging these impositions without judgment. By accepting, we're not resigning ourselves to them; we're positioning ourselves to change them. You can't be curious in judgment. This dual act of awareness and acceptance is the gateway to transformation and unlocking our next growth phase.

2. The Emotional Motivator

Our actions and decisions are often driven by a desire to feel a particular emotion or to avoid feeling another. It's important to understand this emotional motivator. Are our actions being influenced by fear of experiencing negative emotions? By addressing this, we can shift our behaviors to ones that genuinely align with our goals and desires rather than ones simply meant to shield us from discomfort.

3. Paying the Emotional Price

Achieving any goal often comes with its share of emotional costs. Whether it's the fear of failure, the discomfort of stepping out of our comfort zone, or the vulnerability of exposing our true selves, each goal has an emotional price tag attached. The question is, are we willing to pay it? Recognizing that there's a cost involved—often in the form of negative emotions—can empower us to face these feelings head-on. Consider, *anything you want in your life is available if you are willing to feel everything.*

4. The Dual Purpose of Self-Impositions

While self-impositions may seem detrimental, they also serve a protective function. These mental barriers often stem from deep-seated instincts to seek pleasure, avoid pain, and maintain the status quo. They have kept us safe, even if they've also held us back. Understanding this dual nature—how these impositions both serve and limit us—can help us approach them with compassion and a clear strategy for change.

5. Creating Solutions From Problems

Every problem inherently holds its solution. They exist as two sides of the same coin. When we understand that our self-impositions and limitations are self-created problems, it empowers us to find the corresponding solutions. It's a shift in perspective—from being trapped by our limitations to being empowered by the possibilities of change.

6. The 4 Byproducts of Failure: Embracing the Silver Linings

Wisdom: Every failed attempt is a lesson in disguise. It offers insights that textbooks and lectures often can't. Wisdom isn't just the accumulation of knowledge but the application of it. And failure, in all its bitterness, provides real-world scenarios where this knowledge can be applied and re-tested.

Tolerance: With each setback, our threshold for adversity increases. We develop a stronger stomach for disappointments and become more resilient in the face of challenges. This tolerance isn't about passive acceptance but about developing a tenacious spirit that refuses to be subdued.

Experience: Experience isn't just about what we achieve but also about what we endure. While successes contribute to our resume, *failures contribute to our character.* They offer firsthand experience of what doesn't work, sharpening our decision-making for the future.

Self-knowing: Failures force introspection. They push us to confront our weaknesses, acknowledge our blind spots, and understand our motivations better. This heightened self-awareness paves the way for personal growth and transformation.

7. The Depths of Urge Resistance: A Journey Within

Often, we blame external factors for our urges. We point fingers at the tantalizing dessert, the addictive nature of social media, or the thrill of gambling. However, these are mere triggers. The real urge comes from within, from our own reactions to these stimuli. At the heart of every urge is a desire to escape discomfort. Whether it's boredom, loneliness, stress, or sadness, we often seek solace in food, drink, or distractions. Recognizing this discomfort is the first step to understanding the urges it births.

Here's the irony. The very discomfort we're trying to escape is often self-created. For example, the stress that leads us to binge eat might be due to our own procrastination. Thus, the urge to eat is a direct consequence of our own actions. The way out isn't to suppress or avoid the urge but to feel it fully. When we sit with our discomfort without giving in to the urge, we strip it of its power. By acknowledging and understanding our feelings, we embark on a journey of healing. It's about recognizing that *the real problem isn't the urge itself but our ignorance of its origins.*

Both failure and urge resistance offer invaluable insights. While the former reveals the hidden treasures in setbacks, the latter shines a light on our inner worlds. Both push us to confront and understand ourselves better, driving personal growth and empowerment.

In the end, our growth journey is about embracing the entire spectrum of human emotions. It's about understanding that while negative emotions are uncomfortable, they're also inevitable and, more importantly, navigable. By acknowledging and addressing our self-impositions, we can craft a life where these barriers become the very stepping stones to our next achievement.

The Power of The Model: An Integration of Great Minds

Over the years, I've been blessed with the opportunity to sit and learn from some of the industry's brightest minds. From Joe Dispenza's deep dives into neuroscience to Bruce Lipton's pioneering work in epigenetics, from Gary Zukov's spiritual insights to Brendon Burchard's high-performance strategies, each of these thought leaders has contributed immensely to my understanding of the human psyche and potential.

Among these luminaries, Brooke Castillo stands out for her creation of "The Model."[1] While my journey with other leaders like Amit Goswami played a vital role in blending Quantum concepts into my coaching, it's "The Model" that offers a robust foundation. The brilliance of Castillo's work is its simplicity. It breaks down complex emotions, reactions, and outcomes into comprehensible segments, making the process of introspection and self-improvement more accessible.

In essence, "The Model" demystifies the chain reaction that starts with a thought and culminates in a result, emphasizing our control and responsibility in shaping our reality. What makes this tool exceptionally potent in my practice is how I've been able to weave in the Quantum principles. The integration elevates "The Model" from being not just a tool for self-awareness but a bridge to understanding the interconnectedness of our thoughts with the universe.

---

1   Brooke Castillo, Self-Coaching Model, 2016, https://thelifecoachschool, The Life Coach School.

As we delve into "The Model," you'll recognize its elegance. It's a roadmap, a compass, guiding us through the maze of our mental constructs. While the foundation remains rooted in Castillo's original teaching, the added layers of Quantum understanding enrich the journey, offering a more holistic view of our place in the cosmos.

Remember, tools and models are just facilitators. Their true power is unlocked when we, as individuals, commit to the process, embody the teachings, and apply them in our daily lives. Through "The Model" and the wisdom of the greats who've illuminated my path, I aim to light the way for others, hoping that the synthesis of these teachings can transform lives just as they transformed mine.

By placing our self-imposed beliefs into this model, we can observe:

Situations: These are the external facts of our experience, devoid of any personal interpretation or emotional charge.

Thoughts: These are our interpretations of the situation. It's here we can locate our self-imposed beliefs and scrutinize them.

Emotions: Stemming from our thoughts, our feelings can either empower or hinder us. They are key indicators of whether our thoughts are serving our aspirations.

Actions: Driven by our emotions, actions (or inactions) are the tangible manifestations of our internal narratives. They're where we can see the direct impact of our self-imposed glass ceilings.

Results: The outcome of our actions. Proof of our thoughts. If the results aren't aligning with our goals, it's time to trace back and identify which part of the model is off-kilter.

Breaking Through

Awareness: Recognize and accept the presence of these impositions without judgment. Understand that they have been created over time and can be uncreated just the same.

Questioning: For every self-imposed belief, ask: "Is this thought serving my growth? What evidence do I have for and against this belief? What would I believe in its absence?"

Replacement: Swap out limiting beliefs with empowering ones. It's not about blind optimism but finding a more constructive perspective that aligns with our goals.

Consistent Check-ins: Regularly check in with your thoughts. That being said, the model is a self-coaching tool I teach where we separate out the situation from the thoughts of the situation to see what we are creating for ourselves emotionally and behaviorally to check if old impositions are creeping back in or if new ones are forming. Adjust as necessary.

Navigating Real-Life Adversity: Facing Life's Toughest Challenges

After exploring the maze of self-imposed adversities, it's essential to differentiate them from the genuine challenges life inevitably presents. While internal struggles are largely born from our perceptions, real-life adversities don't rely on our acknowledgment or perspective. They're tangible and present and often demand immediate attention.

Whether it's a distressing diagnosis, the painful end of a cherished relationship, sudden unemployment, or an unexpected conflict, real adversities can shake our worlds. These aren't figments of our imagination or negative spirals of our thinking. They're events that happen, irrespective of our mental landscape.

The Wisdom Within the Struggle: Delving Deeper Into Adversity

Every challenge, setback, or struggle carries hidden wisdom. Instead of asking, "Why me?" this section encourages a deeper inquiry into the underlying lessons adversity brings. By understanding the cause, nature, and message of our struggles, we turn obstacles into stepping stones.

Adversity isn't a mere obstacle; it's a teacher with lessons crafted just for us. By seeing it in this light, we shift from being victims of circumstances to students of life.

Strategies for Navigating Adversity: Turning Trials Into Triumphs

The mere understanding of why we struggle can serve as a compass, guiding us through the murkiness of life's challenges. But how do we transform this understanding into action? How do we not just survive adversity but use it as a catalyst for growth? Let's delve into strategies that can help us navigate adversity with strength, grace, and purpose.

1. Expect Adversity: Welcoming It as a Teacher

Embrace the Inevitability: Realize that life is replete with ups and downs, joys and challenges. Rather than fearing or denying adversity, anticipate it. Expecting adversity doesn't mean living in constant dread but acknowledging that it's a natural part of the human experience.

Adversity strengthens us in ways comfort never can. Like muscles growing stronger under resistance, our character, resilience, and capabilities expand when tested. Embrace adversity as an opportunity for growth, wisdom, and self-discovery.

Each challenge offers a chance to improve our emotional intelligence. Instead of running from discomfort, lean into it. Develop a richer emotional vocabulary, pinpoint what you're feeling, and get better at processing and expressing those emotions.

2. Perception Is Everything: Reframing Adversity

From liability to asset, consider every adverse situation or emotion as raw material. With creativity and perspective, you can mold it into something valuable. Failed business? It's a wealth of lessons for the next venture. A broken relationship? It's a mirror reflecting areas for personal growth. Every cloud, no matter how dark, has a silver lining. It's not about being naively optimistic but about looking for lessons, opportunities, or blessings hidden within challenges.

Don't let adversity define you, but let it refine you. Incorporate it into your life's story as a pivotal chapter that leads to transformation, not as a tragic endpoint.

3. Activate Resilience: Building Back Stronger

Embrace failures and setbacks as opportunities to learn, evolve, and come back stronger. This mindset, as researched by Dr. Carol Dweck, allows us to view challenges as malleable and within our control to change.

Surround yourself with positive, supportive, and forward-thinking individuals. They will not only help you navigate adversity but also provide different perspectives, reminding you of your strength and potential. In the face of adversity, celebrate every small victory. This boosts morale, reminds you of your capability, and builds momentum toward overcoming larger challenges.

Adversity isn't a signal to retreat but an invitation to rise. By understanding our struggles, reframing our perspective, and actively building resilience, we can navigate any challenge that comes our way, turning trials into triumphs.

Recognizing the difference between self-imposed adversity and real-life challenges is pivotal. By cleaning up the mental clutter of self-imposed struggles, we equip ourselves better to handle actual adversities.

Roots of Rejection:
Navigating the Triple Threat

At the very core of our being, there lies an intrinsic need to belong, to be accepted, and to matter. These primal instincts, driven by our evolutionary journey as social creatures, can become a double-edged sword. On one side, they bind us together, building communities and fostering relationships. On the other, they plant the seeds of what we'll come to know as the roots of rejection.

When we talk about rejection, we often envision it as an external force—others pushing us away, society not understanding us, or circumstances preventing our assimilation. But what's far more profound and, unfortunately, damaging is the rejection we administer upon ourselves.

Beneath the facade we often present to the world lie deeply ingrained tendencies that can sometimes be our own worst enemies. They work subtly, eroding our confidence, authenticity, and sense of self-worth. They are the roots of self-rejection, and they manifest prominently in the form of a "triple threat": perfectionism, people-pleasing, and pretending.

1. *Perfectionism:* It's the voice that whispers, "It's never good enough." It's the drive that pushes us to work tirelessly, not for the joy of the process or the learning but out of fear of making a mistake. Perfectionism convinces us that any slight flaw or error is a reflection of our worth, leading us to reject ourselves for the simple human act of being imperfect.

2. *People-Pleasing:* This is the insatiable need to be liked and accepted by everyone. It makes us suppress our desires, needs, and feelings in favor of others. Over time, chronic people-pleasing makes us lose touch with who we truly are. It makes us reject our genuine selves in exchange for fleeting moments of validation from others.

3. *Pretending:* Whether it's wearing a mask to fit into a certain group or hiding behind a constructed identity online, pretending denies our true self its rightful place in the world. It's a tacit statement saying, "Who I truly am isn't worthy enough."

Ironically, these roots of rejection that we believe will make us "matter" often render us invisible.

As we delve deeper into these roots, we must remember that while they might be deeply embedded, they're not permanent. With awareness, reflection, and a strong sense of self-belief, we can untangle ourselves from these roots, reclaim our authenticity, and truly matter—not for the world, but for ourselves.

Triad of Triumph: Shifting From Threats to Thriving—The ABC's

A. Awareness

Dive deep into understanding why you're drawn to perfectionism, people-pleasing, or pretending. Often, these behaviors stem from underlying fears, past traumas, or learned behaviors. Recognizing them is the first step toward breaking free.

B. Being Honest

Allow yourself the freedom to be true to who you are, irrespective of external pressures. This means acknowledging your feelings, aspirations, and even your fears without judgment.

C. Consistently Taking Aligned Action

Set goals that resonate with your authentic self, not what you think you "should" be doing.

Fear is natural. However, taking steps despite these fears is the hallmark of growth. Over time, as you act in alignment with your true self, confidence builds, and the old patterns of the triple threat lose their grip.

In essence, moving from the Triple Threat to the Triad of Triumph is a journey from external validation to inner realization. This triad isn't just a formula for success; it's a blueprint for a fulfilling and impactful life.

Let's dig a little deeper into how each of these plays out both practically and philosophically.

Triple Threat #1: Perfectionism

The Perilous Path to Perfection—A Personal Odyssey

When my father walked out of our lives, I was left with an inexplicable void. That gaping hole, over time, became filled with an overwhelming compulsion to prove him wrong. I bandaged my hurt with layers of pretense, hoping that perfection would be the remedy.

In my young, impressionable mind, his absence became a loud, echoing affirmation that I was flawed, perhaps deeply so. I deduced that if I could just erase all imperfections, he'd see the error of his ways and come back. This hypothesis became the foundation of my existence.

Every single aspect of my life became a theater of perfection. From acing every exam to participating in "all" the things, from being the "ideal" friend and daughter to upholding an unwavering faith—the pressure was relentless. Some might have perceived me as a paragon of discipline and dedication, but deep down, it was fear—*the fear of being inadequate*—that drove me.

Real ambition arises from a desire to push boundaries, to grow, to challenge oneself. In contrast, my relentless pursuit of perfection was a defense mechanism, a protective shield I'd constructed to prevent further rejection. I lived in the paradoxical fear of both standing out too much, not standing out enough, and forever standing too tall. (I am 5'12".)

The cost of this charade was high. Real, deep connections eluded me, for how could anyone connect with a facade? Authenticity was replaced with a meticulously constructed image, leaving little room for vulnerability. Potential opportunities were foregone in fear of tarnishing my "perfect" record, stifling my growth. Every feedback, instead of being a tool for self-improvement, became an affront to my constructed identity. I became impervious to genuine advice, holding onto my "perfection" as a lifeline.

The sad irony is that in this fervent quest for perfection to draw my father back, I lost myself. The vibrant, real me was submerged beneath layers of pretense. The energy it took to maintain this facade was staggering. Each night, I'd lay in bed, mentally replaying my actions, ensuring they aligned with my "perfect" narrative, praying that tomorrow, maybe, my father would see my perfection and return.

But as days turned into months and months into years, I started to question this exhausting charade. Was it worth it? Was I living for myself or a distorted memory of my father? Slowly, I began to understand that true value isn't derived from others' perceptions but from authentic self-awareness and self-acceptance. And perhaps, it was time for me to rediscover and embrace the real, imperfectly perfect me.

Perfectionism: The Illusion of Flawlessness

Perfectionism is, at its heart, a quest for love, belonging, and worthiness. Yet, paradoxically, it can push those very things further away.

Origins of the Perfection Pursuit

Childhood Conditioning: Sometimes, praise in childhood is associated with achievements. "Good grades" might be synonymous with "good child," causing children to internalize that they're only worthy of love when they perform flawlessly.

Societal Pressures: Social media, peer groups, and certain cultural norms can propagate an image of a "perfect life"—one that looks impeccable from the outside but is often devoid of genuine happiness or fulfillment.

Fear of Vulnerability: To admit flaws is to be vulnerable. For some, vulnerability equates to weakness, so they shield themselves behind a wall of perceived perfection.

The Cost of Perfectionism

Lost Authenticity: In the pursuit of perfection, one's true self is often suppressed or altered. Over time, this can create a disconnect, making it hard to discern one's genuine desires and aspirations from those they think they should have.

Unattainable Standards: No human can achieve absolute perfection. By setting such unattainable standards, individuals set themselves up for consistent disappointment.

Fear of Rejection: The need to be perfect often arises from a fear of rejection. If I'm flawless, the thought goes, I cannot be rejected. Yet, this mindset prevents true connection, as people connect with authenticity, not facades.

Embracing Imperfection

Self-Acceptance: Begin by accepting yourself, flaws and all. This doesn't mean complacency; it means recognizing that while you strive to improve and grow, you're already enough as you are, and from that place, you become inspired by potential, not perfection.

Vulnerability as Strength: Being open about our imperfections, fears, and failures can be a source of strength. It allows for genuine connections and shows courage in facing and sharing one's true self.

Re-define Success: Instead of viewing success as an end state of perfection, see it as a journey of continuous growth, learning, and evolving.

Seek Genuine Connections: Form relationships based on mutual respect and authenticity rather than ones based on appearances or achievements.

The desire to be perfect is rooted in a longing to be loved and accepted. However, true acceptance—by others and, most importantly, by ourselves—comes when we embrace our imperfections, recognize our inherent worth, and understand that we are, and always have been, enough.

The Illusion of Perfection and the Gift of Failure

The relentless pursuit of perfection is a trap that many of us fall into. We become so ensnared by the illusion of flawlessness that we begin to equate our self-worth with our ability to meet impossible standards. But when we delve deeper, we must ask ourselves, what would the world look like if we were all perfect?

The Void of Perfection

Imagine a world where everyone was perfect. There would be no challenges, no room for growth, no variance, and, most importantly, no way to understand and appreciate the beauty in our differences and imperfections. The journey, with all its ups and downs, teaches us more about ourselves and the world than any destination ever could.

The True Essence of Growth

The essence of human evolution, both personally and as a species, lies in our ability to learn, adapt, and grow. Every stumble, mistake, or perceived failure is an opportunity in disguise. It provides insights into areas that need attention, understanding, and transformation.

The Misconception of Failure

We've been conditioned to fear failure, to see it as a mark of inadequacy. But when we step back, we see that the most innovative minds in history often failed many times before achieving success. Failure isn't a statement about our self-worth; it's feedback guiding us toward our true path.

Embracing a Growth Mindset

By cultivating a growth mindset, we can reframe how we view setbacks. Instead of seeing them as insurmountable obstacles, we can recognize them as essential components of our learning process. When we do, we free ourselves from the shackles of perfectionism and step into a world brimming with possibilities.

Re-Defining Success

Success isn't about avoiding failure; it's about how we respond when faced with adversity. The true mark of success is the resilience to stand up, dust oneself off, learn from the experience, and continue moving forward with renewed clarity and purpose.

The Liberation in Understanding

When we liberate ourselves from the false identity of being a flawed person, we open ourselves to the vastness of our potential. We begin to understand that our worth isn't determined by external markers but by our inner resilience and our ability to learn, adapt, and evolve.

While the allure of perfection can be tempting, it's a mirage that keeps us from embracing the richness of our authentic selves. As we embrace our imperfections and understand the value of failure, we tap into an inner reservoir of strength, wisdom, and potential that fuels our journey toward becoming the best versions of ourselves.

Triple Threat #2: People Pleasing

Lost in the Halls of Life: A Tale of Silence and Conformity

In the quaint town I grew up in, the school stretched from K-12, resembling a never-ending path of learning. Technically, there was a separate kindergarten unit, making the main building a hub for grades one through twelve. My school years painted a cheerful picture. The corridors echoed my laughter, friends surrounded me, and teachers acknowledged my diligence. I walked the line between rules and conformity, never stepping out, always eager to fit in.

I wasn't rebellious or controversial. I adhered to the unwritten codes of the classroom: always raise your hand, ask for permission, respect authority. This adherence wasn't merely a ritual; it was my shield, my way of blending in, of avoiding conflict. I wasn't the kind to challenge the status quo or defend the underdog—that courage I'd discover much later in college.

But one day, the quiet corridors of my sanctuary became the backdrop for an incident that would haunt my thoughts for years. Walking past the younger classrooms, the library, and toward the art room, I found myself unexpectedly and violently punched in the stomach by a classmate. What provoked him remains a mystery. My vision blurred, and pain coursed through me as I crashed against the wall, sliding to the ground, gasping for air.

The world dimmed. Moments stretched into an eternity. How could a hallway so often bustling with activity suddenly be devoid of any witnesses? My mind raced, expecting someone to rush to my aid, but there was only silence. The stark absence of intervention felt as painful as the punch itself.

It wasn't long before a teacher's voice snapped me back to reality, questioning my presence on the floor. A mix of shock, fear, and an odd sense of shame led me to weave a story of a simple trip and fall. A lie came easier than confronting the painful truth. As the teacher left, doubt lingered in my mind, amplifying my feelings of vulnerability. Did others witness the incident and choose to remain silent? Why was I conditioned to shield my assaulter? These questions plagued me, marking the beginning of a pattern I'd replicate throughout life.

Time and again, I'd find myself prioritizing the comfort of others over my truth. A simple incident in a school hallway set in motion a lifelong tendency to mask pain and gloss over unfairness, all in a bid to "fit in." This pattern wasn't just about people-pleasing; it was a continuous act of self-betrayal.

People-pleasing is, in essence, a form of lying. It's wearing a mask, a facade, that hides the real you from the world. And every time you wear that mask, you distance yourself a little more from who you truly are.

So, reflect and ask yourself: where do you wear your mask? What patterns do you see in your own life? Is it time to remove the facade and step into your authentic self?

The act of people-pleasing is a manifestation of one's desire for external validation. It's a dangerous game we play when we shift the responsibility of our self-worth onto others. At its core, people-pleasing is a form of deception. By bending our will, suppressing our desires, and masking our emotions to appease others, we are essentially lying about who we are and what we believe in.

For my beautiful reader to know:

1. Your Likeability Is Not About You

It's a sobering thought to realize that whether or not someone likes you rarely has anything to do with your actual character or actions. Instead, their perception of you is filtered through their own beliefs, experiences, biases, and current circumstances. This association has nothing to do with you, and yet, you may bear the brunt of their displaced emotions.

2. People's Opinions Are More About Them Than You

Every individual is a culmination of their past experiences, upbringing, cultural background, and current circumstances. So, when someone forms an opinion about you, it's often based on these factors rather than who you truly are. Their judgments, good or bad, are colored by their own stories and challenges.

3. Authenticity Lies in Pleasing Yourself

Gaining genuine self-approval is empowering. When you live according to your values and not the values of others, there's an inner harmony that develops. This doesn't mean being selfish or inconsiderate. Instead, it's about understanding your worth and not compromising on your core beliefs for the sake of external validation.

4. Losing Yourself to Please Everyone

In the constant effort to fit into different molds for different people, we risk losing our true selves. By not setting boundaries, not only do we undermine our own feelings and beliefs, but we also become a chameleon, forever changing colors based on the environment and having no true color of our own.

5. The Disservice of Covering for Others

By constantly stepping in to shield others from the consequences of their actions or emotions, we deprive them of growth opportunities. Life is filled with lessons, many of which come from facing challenges head-on. By preventing others from experiencing these challenges, we rob them of essential life lessons and the emotional growth that comes with them.

The pattern of people-pleasing is toxic for both the pleaser and the ones they aim to please. It's essential to recognize this behavior within oneself and actively work toward authentic interactions. When you value and respect yourself, you pave the way for genuine relationships based on mutual respect, not appeasement.

Triple Threat #3: Pretending

Lost Along the Highway: Journey Through Pretense

The silver screen always has a way of evoking memories, but for me, the most vivid memory isn't about the cinematic magic but rather the haunting drive that followed. The first film I ever witnessed was *Ghostbusters*. I was 10—the world still a vast mystery, each experience a lesson.

My sister, six years older than me, had the maturity and responsibilities most wouldn't comprehend. We shared more than rooms; we shared silent struggles. From the incessant questions I'd ask to my uncontrollable silliness, I knew I could be bothersome. She wore patience like a stretched-out rubber band, and on that fateful night, it snapped, she snapped: "Get out." The highway was dark, save for the passing headlights, and there I was, abandoned and scared. My pleas fell on deaf ears, and Shara, my friend, could only watch in horrified silence.

Hwy 58 stretched before me, an endless road of uncertainties. The weight of regret pressed heavily on my young shoulders, each step a reminder of my follies. The familiar dark silhouettes of passing cars forced me into ditches time and time again, tears streaming down my face. Every echo of a revving engine sent shivers down my spine, pushing me to run faster, to hide deeper.

For four miles, I battled my fears, each stride a mix of anger, confusion, and determination. The pattern of run-hide-cry became a painful dance I'd engage in for much of my life.

Upon my late return, I painted a fabricated tale for my concerned mother. The story of a fallout with Shara felt easier to narrate than the bitter truth. How could I reveal my sister's action without making her the villain? Pretending everything was alright was less painful than facing the reality.

We often wear masks, pretending to fit into roles, to be characters we think the world desires. We mask our pain, our discontent, and our true selves. Pretending becomes second nature and a defense mechanism to avoid confrontations or disappointments. How many times have we forsaken our truths to maintain peace? How often do we compromise our essence for mere existence?

As I reflect on that night, I realize it wasn't my father, the bully, or my sister I resented. The true enemy was the stranger in the mirror. How can one harbor love for an identity that's foreign or unknown?

The Facade of Pretense

In a world that's increasingly influenced by curated social media posts, societal expectations, and an unspoken code of conforming to fit into various roles, the act of pretending has become an integral part of our daily lives. The lines between our true selves and the facades we wear have blurred, and, at times, we're left wondering which is which.

Pretending as a Defense Mechanism

Many times, the act of pretending isn't just about fitting in; it's a defense mechanism. By masquerading as someone else, we shield our vulnerabilities from the world, ensuring we don't get hurt. This could range from feigning interest in a popular hobby because your group of friends love it to pretending to be okay with something you're not, just to avoid confrontation.

Sacrificing Authenticity for Acceptance

Every time we suppress our true feelings or opinions to fit into a mold, we're trading a piece of our authenticity for temporary acceptance. But at what cost? The more we do this, the more detached we become from our core selves, leading to a profound sense of emptiness and disconnection.

Existence at the Expense of Essence

Conceding for peace might seem like the easy way out. No confrontations, no hard feelings. But when we constantly do this, we're not just compromising; we're sacrificing our essence for existence. We exist, but without authenticity, without the vibrant colors of our personality shining through. Run. Cry. Hide. This is what I spent the majority of my life doing.

Self-Alienation: The True Cost of Pretending

My profound realization, "It wasn't my dad, the bully, or my sister that I didn't like, it was me," resonates deeply. Because when we constantly pretend, we begin to alienate ourselves from our true identities. We don't recognize the person staring back at us in the mirror because we've layered on so many masks.

Reconnecting With the Self

How can we genuinely appreciate or love ourselves if we don't even recognize who we are beneath all the pretenses?

To reconnect, we need to introspect. We must ask ourselves:

Why am I pretending? Is it fear of judgment, rejection, or conflict?

What am I sacrificing in the process? Is it my values, beliefs, or peace of mind?

How do I feel when I am not pretending? Liberated? Vulnerable? Authentic?

To thrive in life, it's essential to find a balance between adapting to societal norms and staying true to oneself. It's alright to compromise in certain situations for aligned harmony. However, constantly suppressing one's identity for the sake of fitting in is a path to self-discontentment. Trust me, I know.

Recognize the moments of pretense, understand why they exist, and work toward embracing your authentic self. Only by accepting and loving our true selves can we hope to be genuinely happy and content.

Therein lies the triple threat I've come to understand:

Perfectionism: The endless chase to mold oneself into an ideal image.

People Pleasing: Sacrificing personal values and beliefs for the sake of others' happiness.

Pretending: Living a life that isn't truly ours.

These roots of rejection rob us of authenticity. But recognizing them is the first step toward embracing our genuine selves. It's about shedding the masks and standing in our truth, however uncomfortable or raw it may be.

In the prior sections, we dipped our toes into understanding the impact of such labels through the lens of awareness. This foundational knowledge is essential, but mere recognition isn't enough. To truly transcend these labels and tap into our most authentic selves, a deeper dive is crucial.

The irony of labels is that while they might provide a fleeting sense of identity or even a feeling of belonging, they often subtly dictate our life's trajectory, limiting our horizons. Think about it. How many times have you held back from doing something because it didn't fit the "responsible adult," "dedicated parent," or "ambitious professional" label? How often have you denied yourself an experience because it didn't align with societal expectations of your gender, age, or status? These labels, which we often wear proudly, can act as silent jailers, making us prisoners of our own creation.

However, as with most things in life, it's not black and white. Some labels can indeed be empowering, serving as a beacon of strength and resilience. A label like "survivor" or "fighter" can evoke a sense of pride and signify overcoming adversity. The key is discernment. It's crucial to sift through these labels, hold them up to the light, and see if they truly serve our highest self or merely keep us tethered to a version of ourselves we've outgrown.

Growth begins with acknowledgment. By recognizing where we've allowed labels to limit us, we take the first step toward breaking free. In acceptance, we find the strength to redefine or discard labels that no longer serve us.

In this sacred space of acceptance, we find peace. We begin to free ourselves from the weight of external expectations, embracing a life of authenticity. As we shed these layers, we realize that beneath them lies our truest self, unburdened and free, ready to soar to new horizons.

The Awakening of the "Responsible One": The Paradox of Labels

In the orchestra of family dynamics, I played the instrument of responsibility. Whether explicitly said or just subtly understood, I had unknowingly been cast in this role. Each member of my family seemed to have their own unique parts: my sister, the audacious boundary pusher, and my brother, the one who was the center of attention in desperate need of nurturing.

I don't recall exactly when I accepted the mantle of the "responsible one," but over time, it seemed like the most harmonious note I could strike. I grew into a person who seldom disrupted the rhythm. My words and actions became punctuated by "yes, ma'am" and "yes, sir." It was my tacit agreement to not add more turmoil to an already tumultuous household.

In our home, where the air was thick with unspoken threats and imagined fears, there was one particular memory that haunted me. After a minor disagreement, my sister would hang me from a hook in our basement just out of sheer mischief. Each time, she'd release me mere moments before our mother's return. It was a silent understanding between us. I never mustered the courage to voice out against her antics. After all, voicing out meant possible retaliation and, in my young mind, perhaps even "grave" danger. Instead, I bore the brunt of my mother's ire for incomplete chores, always silent about my "hanging around" escapades.

In my quest to escape these troubles, I embarked on a myriad of after-school activities. If there was a club, group, or team, I was on it. These activities became my sanctuary, my excuse. I believed that in doing so, I would evade the threats at home, earn my mother's approval, and maybe, just maybe, draw my estranged father back into my life.

But these endless pursuits came at a cost. In my world, equations were simple:

Responsibility equaled drudgery. Recklessness meant freedom. And familiarity was the safety net that prevented me from toppling over.

The paradigm I built for myself was that fun and responsibility stood at opposite poles. Choosing fun would mean neglecting my responsibilities, and who would pick up the slack then? So, I trudged along, letting life happen to me rather than living it. Decades passed, and the weight of my perceived duty nearly crushed my spirit.

It was only when I delved deeper into self-reflection and understanding that a revelation dawned on me. Responsibility didn't mean forsaking happiness or experiences. The tag of the "responsible one" was just that—a tag. Not my identity, not my destiny.

And as I navigated through my 40s, I began the transformative journey of rewriting my story. It wasn't about shirking responsibilities; it was about finding a balance and discovering that joy and duty could coexist. I could be responsible and still relish the beauty and fun that life had to offer. After all, we aren't confined to the roles we're assigned; we have the power to redefine them.

The Paradox of Labels

Human beings have a natural inclination to categorize and simplify complex information to make it more comprehensible. In our social interactions, this often manifests in the act of labeling individuals based on observable traits, behaviors, or even fleeting incidents. As helpful as this might seem on the surface, it becomes a double-edged sword. While some find solace or even pride in their labels, for others, these designations become invisible cages.

Seeking Validation Through Labels

When we're labeled, particularly at a young age, it can create a road-map of behavior for us. If we assume the role of "The Responsible One," like I did, we might feel an undue burden to always be reliable, even at the cost of our own well-being or desires. We may start seeking out situations where we can be responsible to reinforce this label, hoping it brings us validation and acceptance from our peers and loved ones, and when it doesn't, and because we take it on as an "identity," we will be on a never-ending search to "fix" ourselves.

Conforming to these labels can be comforting. It gives us a pre-defined role in the complex play of life. If we act according to our label, we believe it guarantees certain reactions or treatments from others. "The Funny One" might feel pressured to always be the life of the party, even when they're going through tough times, because that's the role everyone expects them to play, discounting their own struggle.

The Ruinous Label of the "Peacemaker"

In our society, we often celebrate the "Peacemaker," the one who constantly maintains harmony, the "Agreeable One" who avoids conflict and confrontation. At first glance, these labels seem virtuous and noble. But on closer examination, it may be the most detrimental label one could wear.

Being a peacemaker can sometimes mean never asserting oneself, never standing up for one's beliefs, and constantly suppressing one's desires and needs for the sake of keeping the peace. This constant act of self-negation can lead to deep-seated resentment, a sense of lost identity, and the simmering frustration of unexpressed feelings.

More importantly, the external peace that a peacemaker maintains is often a façade. Beneath the calm surface, there can be a tempest of emotions: from anger to sadness, from frustration to disillusionment. Ironically, in their quest to avoid conflict, they internalize it, leading to inner chaos.

The most tangible manifestation of this inner turmoil is the inability to say "no." By always saying "yes," even when every fiber of their being wants to disagree, they slowly lose touch with their true self. They get caught in a cycle of pleasing others, sacrificing their needs, and mistaking self-neglect for selflessness.

But saying "no" is powerful. It establishes boundaries, asserts one's individuality, and, most importantly, gives one the space to prioritize their well-being. It's a declaration that one's feelings, beliefs, and desires matter.

While it's important to maintain harmony and build bridges, it should not come at the cost of one's peace of mind. Being agreeable should never mean agreeing at the expense of one's authenticity.

In essence, the label of the "Peacemaker" might seem like a path to harmonious living, but it's a double-edged sword. To truly keep the peace, one must first find it within oneself, and that begins with honoring one's feelings, needs, and beliefs. Only then can one truly live in harmony, both internally and externally.

Most labels, even if initially given in admiration or jest, can be limiting. They inadvertently tell us that there's only a particular aspect of our personality that's valued or acceptable. Over time, it becomes an identity, pushing us into a repetitive pattern where we might dismiss, neglect, or suppress other parts of our character.

Finding Freedom Beyond Labels

As you've probably realized by now, awareness of the labels we carry is the crucial first step toward the freedom you seek. You can't let go of something you don't know exists. But awareness alone is not enough. The next vital step is acceptance. Acceptance doesn't mean surrendering to these labels; rather, it's the process of embracing them with compassion and understanding. It's acknowledging that these labels have shaped our experiences but do not define our entire beings.

Acceptance is the path out of judgment. When we accept our labels, we free ourselves from the weight of self-criticism and harsh judgments. It allows us to see these labels as aspects of our identity, not as restrictive definitions. We can begin to explore which labels empower us and which ones limit us.

By consciously choosing which labels serve us and to what degree, we gain the power to shape our identities in a way that aligns with our true selves. We can leverage the positive aspects of our labels, using them as tools for growth and connection while letting go of those that hold us back or perpetuate stereotypes.

You can't leverage what you judge, and you can't grow beyond what you deny. Embrace your labels as part of your unique journey, and in doing so, you'll find the path to greater self-awareness, personal empowerment, and authentic living. It's in this process that we truly break free from the limitations of labels and discover the boundless potential within ourselves.

In life, it's essential to remember that we are multifaceted beings capable of growth, change, and evolution. While labels might provide a comfortable niche, they shouldn't become our prisons. Embrace your entirety, defend your "Yes" with your "No," and remember that you are more than just a label. You are a continuous story of transformation and potential.

These roles might have been our armor, our defense mechanisms against a world that at times seemed overwhelming. As children or even young adults, these roles might have been adaptive (a way to navigate familial dynamics or societal pressures). Yet, as protective as they might have been then, these very roles can morph into cages that limit our true potential and authentic selves as adults.

It's ironic, isn't it? What was once our shield becomes our shackles.

Dr. Joe Dispenza's wisdom rings particularly true here: breaking the mold is challenging precisely because it involves shedding familiar habits and roles.[2] It means waking up and choosing not to be the character you've played for years, if not decades.

The most liberating realization in this journey is understanding that we are not bound by the roles we've assumed or that were thrust upon us. We are not mere products of our past or prisoners to outdated patterns. Instead, we are dynamic beings with the capacity for change and growth. We must become curious investigators of our lives, sifting through the layers of roles and identities, acknowledging

---

2   Joe Dispenza, Breaking the Habit of Being Yourself: How to Lose Your Mind and Create a New One, Hay House, 2012.

them, and then deciding which ones to retain, modify, or discard entirely.

True transformation is not a single leap but a series of consistent, mindful steps. The process involves deep introspection, breaking away from deeply ingrained habits and beliefs, and a shift toward mindful living. Here's a deeper dive into the proposed keys:

Question Your Roles and Identities: Often, the roles we adopt come from external factors: societal expectations, familial roles, peer pressure, or personal experiences. While some of these roles might empower us, others can be restrictive. They may reduce our vast potential to mere labels. So, it's essential to take a step back and scrutinize these identities. Ask yourself, "Does this role or label empower me, or is it a box I've unknowingly confined myself to?" By challenging these preconceived notions, you pave the way for growth and the possibility to redefine or shed these roles.

Assess Your Self-Perception: Our relationship with ourselves significantly influences our thoughts, emotions, and actions. If you hold limiting beliefs about yourself, you're likely to make choices that reaffirm these beliefs. However, if you view yourself with love, understanding, and confidence, your actions will reflect this positive self-perception. Spend time understanding your inner dialogue. If it's mainly negative or self-deprecating, it's time to shift toward self-love and acceptance. Recognize your worth and remember that self-growth is a continuous journey; every step, no matter how small, counts.

Mind Your Daily Habits and Routines: The saying "You are what you repeatedly do" couldn't be more accurate. Our daily actions, habits, and routines shape our present and future. It's not about grand gestures but the small, consistent actions that lead to significant change over time. Assess your daily habits. Are they leading you toward growth and your desired future? Or are they just comfortable patterns keeping you in the same place? Remember, comfort doesn't always equate to growth. Sometimes, stepping out of your comfort zone, trying something new, or altering a habit can be the catalyst for profound transformation.

In essence, transformation is an ongoing journey of self-awareness, reflection, and active change. It requires you to continuously engage with yourself, to question, learn, unlearn, and relearn. As you embark on this journey, remember to be kind to yourself. Change isn't easy, but with commitment, awareness, and persistence, it's wholly within reach.

Unwavering Selfhood

Amid societal pressures and expectations, maintaining authenticity can be a battle. This chapter delves into the importance of staying true to oneself, the trials one might face in the process, and the rewards that come with unwavering self-belief.

Navigating the world as a people-pleaser felt like being a chameleon, constantly changing to fit the environment or the desires of others. This constant shifting was exhausting and, more importantly, led to a loss of self-awareness and self-worth.

In my self-awareness journey, I realized that this constant need to appease others, this perpetual apology for simply existing, was draining my spirit. It wasn't just about the apologies for inconveniences; it was an apology for my dreams, my passions, my quirks, and all the things that made me, me. My life became a constant series of adjustments, never sticking to my true form but shifting into whatever I thought would be the most acceptable or least disruptive.

And so, I came to understand that every time I shifted into a mold someone else preferred, I was quietly whispering to myself that the real me wasn't good enough. I was conditioning my own mind to believe that my authentic self wasn't worthy of love, respect, or acceptance.

The journey to breaking free from apology isn't about becoming indifferent to the feelings and needs of others. Instead, it's about realizing that you have just as much right to take up space, to have opinions, and to be your authentic self as anyone else does. The transformative moment comes when you decide that your self-worth isn't negotiable.

Embracing your authentic self doesn't mean rejecting self-improvement. It means understanding that while growth is a constant journey, the path should be carved by our own desires and needs, not by trying to fit someone else's mold. By seeking profound self-awareness, I began to delineate between the constructed personas and the real me. The more I understood and accepted, the less I felt the need to apologize.

The most freeing proclamation one can make is that they are unapologetically human, imperfect but earnest, flawed but growing. And in that acceptance, we find a strength that no amount of external validation can provide. When we step into the world as our authentic selves, we not only give ourselves the gift of freedom, but we also implicitly give permission to others around us to embrace their true selves as well.

So, ask yourself, in your quiet moments, stripped of expectations and societal pressures: Who am I? And as you discover and embrace the answer, you'll find the power to be unapologetically you.

Living unapologetically means to boldly claim our truths. How did we come to view ourselves in a certain light? Was it a comment from a parent that suggested we weren't enough? Was it a peer's teasing that left scars on our self-esteem? Or perhaps it was a societal narrative that consistently conveyed that we did not belong.

Releasing these false beliefs isn't merely about shedding a burden; it's about correcting a fundamental injustice to oneself. By holding onto beliefs that are untrue, we are, in essence, keeping stolen goods. And just as one would return an item wrongly taken, we must return these misconceptions to their sources. This doesn't mean confronting every individual who contributed to these beliefs. Instead, it's about mentally and emotionally releasing their hold, acknowledging the untruth, and metaphorically returning them.

The journey to self-discovery and self-acceptance isn't a simple one. There are moments of pain, vulnerability, and confronting harsh truths. But the destination—a life lived authentically and unapologetically—is worth the struggle. It is a life where one's value isn't borrowed or influenced by external voices but is intrinsic, genuine, and unwavering.

In this journey toward self-rediscovery, it's essential to release those borrowed beliefs that don't serve us anymore. Hand back the lies, the myths, and the misguided hopes to those from whom they originated. Embrace the liberating truth—your worth is innate. You've always been enough. And you always will be.

Worth & Lovability

You are worthy. This isn't a statement up for debate or a belief that requires evidence. It is an inherent truth, timeless and unwavering. Your worthiness is an intangible essence, much like the air you breathe or the love you give. It isn't conditioned by your actions, accomplishments, or lack thereof.

Consider a newborn. Gazing into their eyes, you don't see a scorecard of achievements or a litany of failures. You see innocence, potential, and a life bursting with possibilities. They haven't delivered groundbreaking speeches or scaled mountains. Their resumes are blank, their bank accounts nonexistent. They don't even know their own name. Yet, the very sight of them can bring grown adults to tears, compel them to make sacrifices, and fill them with an overwhelming sense of love and protection. Why is that?

Because the baby's worth is intrinsic. It isn't determined by their utility, their skills, or their knowledge. They are precious simply because they exist. This unadulterated worthiness isn't unique to infants; it is consistent across every stage of life. Just as it remains unchanged from infancy to old age, it remains constant from one individual to the next. No one is exempt.

Yet, as we grow older, we become ensnared in society's intricate web of expectations and validations. These societal constructs often masquerade as determinants of worth, leading us to measure our value by our success, appearance, wealth, popularity, or other fleeting metrics. Over time, this erodes the primal understanding of our innate worthiness. We begin to believe that we must earn our place and that our value is conditional.

But think about it. If a child's value isn't derived from their achievements, why should ours be? When did we learn to equate our self-worth with our accolades? Why do we believe that our value diminishes with each mistake and grows with every triumph?

Herein lies the challenge. Unlearning these misconceptions is a journey that demands introspection, courage, and conviction. Recognizing and embracing our inherent worth is paramount, not just for our personal well-being but for the collective good. When we stand firm in our worthiness, we encourage others to recognize their own. We foster environments of acceptance, empathy, and love.

Stepping into your greatness requires a foundation built on the bedrock of self-worth. You can't soar to new heights while tethered by chains of doubt and self-deprecation. Cut them loose. Your worth isn't something you've been granted—it's something you've always had.

Let's talk about lovability. The elusive search for love and acceptance often sends us on a spiral, leading us outside of ourselves on a never-ending quest for validation from others. We believe that love is a commodity to be received, an external acknowledgment of our worth. But in this pursuit, we often overlook the most profound source of love—the kind that resonates within our very core.

It's easy to be swayed into thinking that love is something we earn from others, that it's a response to our actions or our words. We often tie love to conditions and prerequisites. "If I act in this way, then I'll be loved." "If I achieve that milestone, then I'll be worthy of affection." Such beliefs, though commonplace, are deeply misguided. Love isn't transactional; it's transformational.

The perception of love as external makes us vulnerable to the whims and fancies of those around us. Every gesture and every word becomes a potential validation or rejection. This leaves us in a fragile state, constantly oscillating between the highs of perceived acceptance and the lows of assumed rejection. But this oscillation is a mirage, stemming from the incorrect belief that love is something granted to us from the outside.

To truly understand love, one must realize that it begins within. Love is an emotion, a state of being that we can choose to embody regardless of external circumstances. True love is self-generated, self-sustained, and isn't contingent upon someone else's validation. When we love ourselves wholly, recognizing our intrinsic worth and value, we become impervious to rejection. After all, how can someone reject us when we are firmly anchored in self-love?

Rejection, in its essence, is an external judgment. But just as a mirror reflects an image without passing judgment, any perception of rejection is merely a reflection of another's beliefs and insecurities. It's not a commentary on your worth or lovability. Yet, if inside you harbor doubts about your worth, you're more likely to internalize this reflection as truth. This is why the feeling of being rejected is often less about the act itself and more about the beliefs you hold about yourself.

The fear of rejection dissipates when you understand that your worth is non-negotiable and that love, true love, is an inside job. Embracing this empowers you to navigate life with grace and confidence, knowing that you are enough, always have been, and always will be. When you deeply internalize this, you'll find that rejection loses its sting, for it's impossible for someone to take away what was never theirs to give. Your value, your worth, your love—they've always been within you, waiting for you to recognize and embrace them.

Indeed, society often projects an ever-elusive scale of worthiness based on materialistic gains, accolades, or superficial benchmarks. The allure of these markers can be so intoxicating that we often lose sight of our inherent worth, replacing it instead with a relentless pursuit of external validations.

Imagine for a moment a scale that measures worthiness. Now, think of the countless variables we place on that scale: income brackets, educational degrees, societal roles, relationship statuses, and the list goes on. It's as if we've outsourced the definition of our worth to a constantly shifting set of standards. But by doing so, we're attempting to capture a deeply personal, intangible quality with arbitrary, external markers.

No matter how many degrees we accumulate, no matter the zeros in our bank accounts or the titles before our names, they can never truly represent our worth. Because worth isn't something you earn; it's something you recognize. It's not about accumulating more; it's about understanding the depth of your current value.

Asking the world to define your worth is like asking the waves to remain still. It's unpredictable and ever-changing. Instead, we must find grounding in the bedrock of our own self-belief, understanding that our value isn't a commodity to be traded or acquired. It is an intrinsic part of who we are.

The truth is, our worth isn't contingent on "ifs" or "whens." It doesn't arrive in neatly packaged Amazon boxes. It's not bestowed upon us once we've ticked off a checklist of societal achievements. Our worth is a steadfast constant, unaffected by external factors. It's the gentle, unwavering voice inside that assures us, "You are enough, just as you are." And once we truly internalize this, no external measure can sway our conviction in our intrinsic value.

Imperfectly Perfect

Claiming your inherent worth, diving deep into your innermost essence, and reconciling with both your strengths and weaknesses are essential to embracing your authentic self. To live imperfectly means to step out of the shadows of societal standards and the confines of self-imposed limitations. It means embracing every aspect of oneself, recognizing that every facet, every flaw, every strength, and every perceived weakness contributes to the tapestry of our unique human experience.

What if instead of running away from our flaws, we leaned into them? Instead of seeing them as something to hide or fix, we saw them as crucial elements of our story, even our identity? Our imperfections are not barriers to our growth but catalysts. They are not hindrances but gateways to introspection and personal evolution.

It's an empowering realization to know that our vulnerabilities are not necessarily detriments. They are avenues for connection, understanding, and depth. These so-called "weaknesses" could indeed be overextended strengths, manifesting at an intensity that might seem out of balance. For example, a person with an overabundance of empathy might become overly emotionally invested, or someone with unmatched focus might become too rigid in their ways. But with awareness, calibration, and intention, these traits can be harnessed constructively.

Our life is, in many ways, an endless course of self-study. Each experience, each flaw, each victory, and each setback are a chapter, guiding us toward a more profound understanding of ourselves. And as we navigate this journey, it's crucial to remember that it's not about seeking external validation but about forging an internal compass calibrated to our own truth.

Living imperfectly means understanding that we are the architects of our belief systems. It is about actively engaging with our thoughts and discerning which ones uplift us and which ones hold us back. When we stumble upon limiting beliefs, it becomes our prerogative to challenge them, dissect them, and rebuild them in a way that aligns with our authentic selves. It's not merely about passive introspection but active reconstruction of our thought patterns.

"The How To" of Living Imperfectly

1. Live free from the "S." As we have mentioned—the S is the first component in the Model. It stands for situation, and as we learned earlier, it is neutral and void of emotional interpretation. Living free from it requires us to detach from the situational intricacies that often become the narratives we bind ourselves to. When we fixate on our situations and circumstances, we unknowingly hand over the keys to our mental and emotional kingdom to external factors. Instead, realizing that situations are intrinsically neutral until we assign them value empowers us to reclaim our narrative. By understanding this, we choose the meaning, and in doing so, we craft OUR reality.

2. Listen to your intuition; it holds profound insights. This doesn't mean neglecting logic or reason, but it involves

recognizing the powerful instinctual understanding we often have about things. By marrying intuition with logical discernment, we can often arrive at decisions that are holistic, balanced, and aligned with our true selves.

3. Live in the middle. Find equilibrium. Release judgment. Embrace a perspective that sees beyond binary choices or extreme polarities. Every situation, every person, and every experience exists in shades of grey, and it's in this realm of nuance that true understanding lies (much more about this later).

4. Live in alignment with universal laws. Understanding the principles that govern existence is how we win in this life. Whether it›s the law of attraction, the principle of rhythm, or the principle of polarity, these laws offer a blueprint for understanding life›s ebbs and flows. Our suffering comes from not understanding and embracing these truths.

Our potential is vast and boundless. But it's fear and the avoidance of discomfort that often holds us back. Fear of the unknown, fear of rejection, fear of failure. But by committing to our capabilities, understanding our worth, and allowing ourselves to feel—truly feel, without judgment or avoidance—we open the door to a life of authenticity and fulfillment.

To truly flourish, we must release our attachment to the "known," to pre-defined paths, to the familiar patterns that have kept us stuck. We need to embrace the uncertainties, lean into our potential, and trust in both our journey and ourselves. The magic often happens not when everything is planned out but when we allow ourselves to explore, learn, grow, and truly live in each moment.

Living imperfectly is a bold embrace of one's identity and authenticity. It's a profound act of self-empowerment, signaling a transformation from a life lived on the peripheries of one's potential to step into the center stage of one's story. It's a commitment to the soul, a promise to oneself that the days of self-betrayal are over. It's a rallying cry to your inner spirit, urging it to break free from the chains of societal expectations and self-imposed limitations.

This is not a journey for the faint-hearted. Living imperfectly is a dance with vulnerability. It means confronting those shadows, those insecurities, and the age-old scripts that have long dictated how we should think, feel, and behave. It requires immense courage to unravel these threads and weave a new tapestry of self-belief and self-trust.

The act of living without apologies is an affirmation of your sovereignty. It's understanding that you're the author of your narrative and that every choice, every step, and every breath is an extension of your truth. It's a celebration of your imperfections, understanding that they're not signs of brokenness but markers of uniqueness.

Being unapologetic is about refusing to dim your light for the comfort of others. It's realizing that while seeking validation and approval is a natural human tendency, your worth isn't tied to external opinions. Remember, beautiful, your worth is inherent, unchanging, and infinite.

Moreover, living unapologetically is a realization of profound self-reliance. It's knowing deep within that while companionship, guidance, and mentorship can be enriching, you don't require external saviors. The hero of your story has always been and will always be you. ***No one is required for your saving.***

It's a transformation that doesn't happen overnight. It's a journey with its own set of challenges, but with each step, there's growth. With each decision made from a place of authenticity, there's liberation. And with each moment lived without apologies, there's the profound joy of living a life true to oneself.

Awakening to the truth of who we are is an intricate journey of introspection, reflection, and action. By delving deep into our thought models and habits, we embark on an expedition of self-discovery, constantly challenging our perceptions and reinventing our realities.

At the heart of personal transformation lies a potent Triad for Exploration: our thoughts, feelings, and actions regarding ourselves. This triad forms the cornerstone of our self-perception and dictates the quality of our lives.

Firstly, what we think about ourselves shapes the narrative of our identity. These thoughts are the script from which we operate, the blueprint of our self-concept. They can either construct a fortress of confidence or a prison of doubt.

Secondly, what we feel about ourselves is the emotional echo of our thoughts. Our feelings are the internal climate in which we live every day; they color our experiences and inform our sense of well-being. They can nourish us with warmth or chill us with neglect.

Lastly, what we do in relation to our thoughts and feelings is where the rubber meets the road. Our actions are the tangible expressions of our internal dialogues and emotional landscapes. They are the brushstrokes that paint our reality, the steps that carve our path forward.

Understanding this triad is akin to holding a compass that directs us toward our true north. It invites us to introspect deeply, align our emotions with our aspirations, and act in ways that reflect our most authentic selves. Let's explore together.

1. What We Think About Ourselves

Our self-concept, or what we think about ourselves, is a pivotal axis around which our life experiences revolve. Our internal narrative, often shaped by years of accumulated experiences, beliefs, and feedback, becomes our guiding compass, influencing every choice we make and interaction we have. Yet, it's essential to understand that this compass can sometimes be flawed due to external influences and past traumas.

Innate Habits and Personal Power

Each one of us possesses a set of habits, reactions, and tendencies that are deeply ingrained within us. Some of these habits serve us well, while others might hinder our progress. To unleash our full personal power:

Self-reflection: Regularly introspect on these habits. Are they serving your current goals and values, or are they remnants from a past self?

Mindfulness: Become an observer of your thoughts without judgment. By detaching and watching our thought processes, we can identify patterns and triggers.

Revisiting Our Thoughts, Understandings, and Beliefs

Our past experiences, the culture we're raised in, and the voices that surrounded us during our formative years play a massive role in shaping our beliefs.

Questioning the Status Quo: Challenge the stories you've always told yourself. Just because you've always believed something doesn't make it an absolute truth.

Embrace Flexibility: Allow your beliefs to evolve. As you grow and change, it's natural for your beliefs to shift in response to new experiences and insights.

Breaking Free From Misconceptions and Borrowed Beliefs

We often carry beliefs handed down to us by family, society, or experiences without ever questioning if they resonate with our true selves.

Identify the Origins: Trace back your beliefs. Is this genuinely what you feel, or is it something you were conditioned to believe?

Actively Choose: Decide which beliefs you want to retain and which you want to release. Remember, beliefs are choices; make sure they're your own.

Accepting Ourselves as We Are

At the heart of living unapologetically is a profound acceptance of oneself, warts and all.

Compassion Over Criticism: Treat yourself with the same kindness and understanding as you would a dear friend.

Celebrate Growth: Instead of focusing solely on the end goal, celebrate the journey and the growth that comes with it.

In essence, our thoughts about ourselves shape our reality. By actively choosing, refining, and nurturing these thoughts, we can step into our power and live life on our own terms, unapologetically.

Self-Esteem vs. Self-Confidence: A Deeper Dive

Both self-esteem and self-confidence play critical roles in how we perceive ourselves and how we interact with the world. However, they address different aspects of our self-perception. To understand them better, let's dissect their core differences and the ways they manifest in our daily lives.

Definition:

Self-Esteem:

Refers to the overall sense of self-worth or personal value. It is more about how you feel about yourself and your intrinsic worth, irrespective of external accomplishments or feedback.

Self-Confidence:

Is about believing in one's abilities to handle different situations or to perform specific tasks. It's task or situation-specific, focusing more on capability rather than overall worth.

Origin:

Self-Esteem:

Typically has deeper roots, often stemming from childhood experiences, consistent internal validation, or the kind of reinforcement one receives about one's inherent worth over a lifetime.

Self-Confidence:

Can be built over time through experiences, training, and repeated practice in particular areas. Achieving mastery or competency in certain skills can boost self-confidence.

Manifestation:

Self-Esteem:

Is more stable and consistent, reflecting a fundamental belief about oneself. For example, feeling that you deserve happiness and respect, irrespective of successes or failures.

Self-Confidence:

Can fluctuate depending on the situation. For instance, a person might feel self-confident in their job but not confident when trying a new sport or activity.

Impact on Behavior:

Self-Esteem:

Affects broader aspects of life. High self-esteem might make individuals resilient in the face of criticism, while low self-esteem might lead to chronic self-doubt and fear of judgment, affecting relationships, mental health, and overall satisfaction with life.

Self-Confidence:

Has more specific implications. A person with high self-confidence in public speaking might readily give speeches or presentations, while someone with low confidence might avoid or dread these situations.

Enhancement:

Self-Esteem:

Boosting self-esteem often requires deeper introspection and possibly therapy or coaching to address core beliefs and values about oneself. It's about nurturing a kinder, more accepting relationship with oneself.

Self-Confidence:

Can be enhanced through practice, training, and positive experiences in the specific area. For instance, practicing a musical instrument regularly can increase confidence in one's musical abilities.

When you have a *robust self-esteem:*

You believe in your intrinsic value.

External validation, while nice, isn't a necessity.

Failures don't diminish your perception of your worth.

Deciphering Confidence:

Confidence, on the other hand, is the belief in one's abilities to handle specific situations. It's context-dependent. You might have confidence in your professional skills but lack it in social settings.

When you have *robust self-confidence*:

You trust in your capabilities.

You are willing to take risks because you believe in your ability to navigate challenges.

Mistakes are seen as opportunities for growth, not personal deficiencies.

The Intertwining of Esteem and Confidence:

Imagine attempting to build a house (confidence) on unstable ground (low self-esteem). No matter how beautiful or sturdy the house is, if the land beneath is shifting, the structure's stability is compromised. Similarly, genuine confidence is built on the solid foundation of self-esteem.

Here's why:

Unwavering Foundation: When you inherently believe you are worthy, setbacks in your endeavors won't shatter your confidence. Instead, they become moments of learning.

Reduced Fear of Failure: With strong self-esteem, the fear of failure doesn't paralyze. You know that even if you falter, it doesn't make you any less valuable or worthy.

Authenticity in Confidence: Your confidence becomes genuine. You're not putting on a facade or emulating what you think confidence should look like. Instead, it's a true reflection of your belief in your abilities, grounded in the knowledge of your worth.

Flexibility in Growth: With solid self-esteem, you can more easily adjust and adapt. If one method or approach doesn't work, your foundational belief in your worth allows you to pivot without doubting your overall capabilities.

It's evident that confidence and self-esteem, while distinct, are deeply intertwined. To foster unwavering confidence, one must first cultivate and nurture an unwavering belief in one's intrinsic worth. Without the assurance that you are enough, just as you are, genuine confidence remains elusive. In the dance of self-belief, esteem leads, and confidence follows.

The Illusion of External Validation:
Unraveling Common Misbeliefs

Throughout our lives, societal norms and expectations shape our self-perception, often leading us to seek validation from external sources. This quest for external affirmation can sometimes divert us from understanding and recognizing our inherent worth. I touched on these already by way of false formulas, but I want to go a little deeper with these commonly held beliefs:

1. If people like you, then you are likable.

The craving for social acceptance is a fundamental human need stemming from our evolutionary drive to belong to a tribe. However, allowing the opinions of others to dictate our self-worth is limiting. People's opinions are shaped by a myriad of factors, many unrelated to you. Being likable should be about being authentic to oneself, not merely reflecting what others want to see.

2. If you got better grades, you are more successful.

While academic excellence is commendable, it's a narrow metric for gauging overall success. Some of the world's most influential thinkers and innovators did not necessarily excel academically. True success is holistic, encompassing personal growth, emotional intelligence, and a sense of purpose.

3. If you are thinner, you are happier.

Body image issues plague many, fueled by societal and media representations of "ideal" bodies. But equating thinness to happiness is a fallacy. Genuine happiness stems from self-acceptance, purpose, relationships, and mental well-being.

4. If you were prettier, you would be more popular.

Physical attractiveness might offer initial advantages in social settings, but lasting popularity and genuine connections are built on character, empathy, and authenticity.

5. If you made more money, you would be a high performer.

Financial success can be a byproduct of high performance, but it's not its sole indicator. Many high performers prioritize impact, innovation, or mentorship over monetary rewards.

6. If you looked more like that woman on the cover of that magazine, you would have more confidence.

Confidence does not spring from mirroring a societal ideal of beauty. Instead, it blossoms from recognizing your worth, embracing your strengths, and acknowledging that imperfections don't diminish value.

7. If people acknowledge and validate you, then you are good enough.

Seeking external validation can be a never-ending chase. It's essential to understand that you are intrinsically good enough, irrespective of external affirmations. Your worth isn't contingent upon others' acknowledgment.

Self-worth should be an intrinsic belief, unaffected by external validations or societal metrics of success. While it's natural to desire acknowledgment and admiration, it's vital to discern that these are not the sole determinants of our value. Unshackling ourselves from these external markers and looking inward for validation leads to a more fulfilling, self-affirmed life.

Driving Forward With Esteem

Our self-perception, the lens through which we view ourselves, acts as the driving force in our lives. If we see ourselves as valuable, capable, and deserving, we become protagonists in our life story, creating our destiny. In contrast, if we're constantly questioning our worth based on external markers, we become mere passengers, letting life happen to us rather than for us.

Self-esteem is the compass by which we navigate our life journey. By anchoring it in the unchanging truth of our worth, we not only ensure a steady course but also open up a world of infinite possibilities.

Esteem Over Confidence: Valuing the Essence of Being

In the lexicon of personal development and self-help, two terms frequently make their rounds: "confidence" and "esteem." While both are essential components of a healthy psyche and are often spoken about in tandem, there exists a pronounced disparity in the attention they receive.

Confidence is dazzling, overt, and palpable. It's the show-stopper—the shining armor we wear as we tackle challenges, display our talents, and navigate social spaces. It's about our "doing," our achievements, and the competence we display in our actions. Due to its outward-facing nature, confidence naturally garners admiration and attention. We live in a world that places enormous value on accomplishments and productivity, so it's no surprise that confidence, a reflection of our doings, often takes center stage.

On the other hand, there's esteem. Esteem is quieter, deeper, and intimately tied to our core. Unlike confidence, which is rooted in our capabilities and actions, esteem is about our intrinsic worth—our "being." It's the silent foundation upon which our entire sense of self is built, the internal compass that guides our feelings of worthiness and self-respect.

Yet, despite its profound importance, esteem often plays second fiddle. In our fast-paced, achievement-driven society, the emphasis on "doing" overshadows the essential nature of "being." However, it's vital to understand that while confidence might empower us to conquer the world outside, it is esteem that nurtures our inner world. Without a robust sense of esteem, even the most confident individuals can feel hollow, unanchored, and lost.

In the journey of self-awareness and growth, it's essential to recalibrate our focus. Confidence is undoubtedly crucial, but it must be built on the bedrock of strong esteem. For at the end of the day, beyond our accolades and achievements, it's our intrinsic worth and the respect we accord to ourselves that truly define our happiness and fulfillment.

In our quest for self-expression, let's remember that while the world may applaud our confidence, it's our esteem that truly shapes the essence of who we are.

2. What We Feel About Ourselves

The emotions and feelings we experience are like the vibrant threads that weave the fabric of our inner world. They are direct responses to the thoughts that flow through our minds like thermometers gauging the temperature of our mental processes. At the heart of this intricate interplay lies a profound truth: acceptance is a gift of love—both to ourselves and to the world.

Our feelings and emotions are the compasses of our inner land-scapes, guiding us through the terrain of our thoughts. When our thoughts are nurturing, kind, and filled with self-love, our emotions bloom with warmth, joy, and contentment. In contrast, when our thoughts are judgmental, critical, or self-deprecating, our emotions may darken with sadness, anxiety, or despair.

Love, in its purest form, begins within. It's the love we extend to ourselves that sets the tone for how we navigate the world around us. Self-love is not selfish; it's self-preservation. It's the acknowledgment that we, too, are deserving of compassion, care, and kindness—just as much as anyone else.

When we offer the gift of acceptance to ourselves, we open the door to a profound transformation. We recognize that we are human, with our quirks, imperfections, and complexities. We understand that it's okay to have moments of vulnerability, doubt, and struggle, for these are all part of the rich tapestry of life.

Love is a force that radiates outward, touching not only our own lives but also the lives of those we encounter. When we accept and love ourselves, we become beacons of love for others. Our relationships are infused with authenticity, empathy, and compassion.

Acceptance is, in essence, an act of love directed toward ourselves and the world. It's a recognition that we are all interconnected and that by nurturing the garden of self-love, we contribute to the growth of love in the world. When we love ourselves, we are better equipped to love and support those around us.

Acceptance isn't resignation or complacency; it's the first step on the path to growth and transformation. When we embrace ourselves as we are, we are building on the foundation of self-awareness and self-compassion. From this solid ground, we can embark on journeys of self-improvement, not out of self-criticism, but out of a desire to grow and evolve.

The interplay between love, feelings, emotions, and acceptance is a profound dance that shapes our inner and outer worlds. Love begins within as an acknowledgment of our own worthiness. It ripples outward, enriching our relationships and the world. Acceptance is the key that unlocks the door to self-love, and in offering this gift to ourselves, we find the power to transform our lives and contribute to a more loving and compassionate world. Love, after all, is the greatest gift we can give—to ourselves and to others.

The Inner Mechanics of Self-Love

For a sentiment that's universally sought, love is something most people find difficult to define or genuinely understand. Especially when it comes to loving oneself, the waters tend to get even murkier. This is because our perceptions of love are often wrapped in layers of societal conditioning, personal experiences, and inherited beliefs.

Decoding Personal Love Constructs

Throughout our lives, we're bombarded with messages about what love is supposed to look like or feel like. Movies, books, and songs romanticize love, making us believe it's an eternal high, always passionate and intense. Yet, true love, especially self-love, is quieter, deeper, and steadier.

How You Value Yourself:

This is the crux of self-love. It's not about narcissism or blind self-adulation. Instead, it's about understanding, forgiving, and embracing yourself. It's about recognizing your strengths, accepting your weaknesses, and striving for growth without harsh self-judgment.

Searching for External Love Tokens:

Often, in the pursuit of validation, we chase love externally. We might seek validation through relationships, achievements, or even physical appearance. Yet, these are fleeting, external markers and don't genuinely contribute to our core self-love.

Dismantling Love Myths

The beliefs we hold about love often hold us back. Here's a closer look:

Love is Hard/Difficult: Love should feel natural. If it's constantly hard or feels like a struggle, it might not be genuine love, or it might be entangled with other emotions or expectations. Real love is never hard, nor is it difficult.

Love is Conditional: Real love, especially self-love, isn't based on conditions. It doesn't fluctuate based on achievements, appearance, or status.

Love Comes at a Cost: Love isn't a transaction. You shouldn't have to "pay" for love, either through sacrifices, changing your true self, or compromising your values.

Love is Earned: This belief often stems from childhood or past relationships where love was withheld as a form of punishment or control. But love isn't something you earn; it's something you inherently deserve.

Understanding that love is an "inside job" is transformative. It shifts the locus of control back to you. When you internalize the idea that you are in charge of loving yourself and that this self-love isn't contingent upon external validations, you harness immense power. This doesn't mean external love isn't valuable or fulfilling, but it does mean that it isn't the sole or even primary source of your sense of love or worth.

Remember, others can only love you to the extent that they love themselves. Similarly, you can only genuinely love others when you truly love and embrace yourself. Your relationship with yourself sets the tone for every other relationship in your life.

While it's human nature to seek love and validation from others, the most potent and transformative love is the love you cultivate within. When you nurture self-love, you become less reliant on external validations, leading to a more authentic, fulfilled life.

Let's dig deeper ...

Deserving Love:
The Dual Act of Giving and Receiving

The human heart is an expansive entity. It holds within its chambers the capacity for immense love, but it's often shackled by the chains of our beliefs, past hurts, and misconceptions. Two of the most profound questions we grapple with are: Do I deserve to give love? And do I deserve to receive love?

Giving Love: When it comes to giving love, many people often feel hesitant. This hesitation may stem from past experiences where love was taken for granted or perhaps even rejected. There's a vulnerability in offering one's heart, and if you've been hurt before, the act of opening up again can be daunting. However, every individual is innately deserving of expressing love. Love isn't a finite resource; it multiplies with sharing. Denying yourself the act of giving love is like holding back a river—it goes against the natural flow of your being. And we mustn't forget: you are the feeler of your love, give it freely.

Receiving Love: This is where most people hit a wall. Feelings of unworthiness, past traumas, or societal conditioning can lead to a deep-seated belief that one isn't deserving of love. If someone has spent a significant part of their life feeling rejected or unloved, as in waiting for an absent father's acknowledgment or love, they "may" inadvertently set up barriers against receiving love, even when it's freely offered.

The Reciprocity of Love:
Giving and Receiving Within Ourselves

In the intricate dance of human relationships, love flows like a river, constantly moving, shifting, and replenishing the landscapes of our hearts. We often speak of giving and receiving love as separate acts, as if they exist on opposite ends of a transaction. But what we sometimes forget is that we are the ultimate benefactors of both. In the grand exchange of love, the more we give, the more we receive. And in this beautiful paradox, we discover a profound truth: the true rewards of love are felt within ourselves.

When we extend love to others, be it through acts of kindness, words of affection, or simple gestures of compassion, we create a ripple effect that touches not only their lives but also ours. Love is not a finite resource; it's boundless and boundlessly replenishing. The more we give, the more love flows through us, nourishing our souls and filling our hearts.

Yet, it's essential to recognize that the act of giving love isn't solely about making others happy or seeking external validation. It's about nurturing the wellspring of love within ourselves. When we express love, we feel its warmth, its power, and its transformative energy. We become intimately acquainted with the depth of our capacity to love, and in doing so, we unlock the doors to our own inner abundance.

Remember, love isn't a commodity to be bartered or traded. It's not a transaction with a ledger of credits and debits. Love is a sacred energy that flows freely and unconditionally. When we love, we don't keep score or expect something in return. We love because it's an authentic expression of our true selves, a reflection of the beauty and compassion that resides within us.

In the grand symphony of love, we are both the composer and the audience. We feel the music of love within our hearts, a harmonious melody that resonates with our deepest desires and values. The joy we derive from giving love is not dependent on how it's received; it's a celebration of our ability to be channels of love in the world.

While others may benefit from the love we share, the truest and most profound beneficiaries are ourselves. We become vessels of love, conduits of its boundless energy, and in doing so, we experience a richness of spirit that knows no bounds.

Love is not just an external force; it's an internal journey of self-discovery and self-fulfillment. The more we love, the more we win—not in worldly treasures or accolades but in the deep sense of purpose, connection, and joy that loving brings. We feel our love more than anyone else, and that, in itself, is a gift beyond measure.

Unshackling the Heart

The truth is, your worth isn't dependent on someone else's actions or decisions. No external validation, not even from a parent, can determine your capacity to be loved or to express love. Love isn't transactional; it's inherent. I understand that I've been emphasizing this point repeatedly, and I want to make it clear that it's a deliberate choice driven by care and love.

This goes beyond mere conceptual understanding; it's about genuinely sensing the accessible truth. When you accept that you are deserving of love just as you are, without conditions or alterations, you open yourself to the universe's abundance. You don't have to wait for anyone to come back or for circumstances to be perfect. Don't make the same mistakes I did. Every moment you spend waiting for someone else to validate your worth is a moment lost from embracing the love you inherently deserve.

Love is your birthright. It's not a reward for good behavior or an outcome of meeting specific criteria. So, give love generously and receive it openly. Embrace your inherent worthiness and let love flow unconditionally.

Love is often viewed as an emotion—something that swells up within us in the presence of someone or something. But what if love was more than just an emotion? What if love was a state of being, an intrinsic part of who we are? This might sound radical, especially in a world where love is often commodified, traded, and manipulated.

Yet, when we strip away external factors, we're left with an undeniable truth: our very essence is love.

The Chains of Conditional Love

Modern society places a myriad of conditions on love. We're taught, subtly and overtly, that love requires reasons. As a result, our love is chained by "buts" and "ifs." This conditional form of love binds us to fear. Why? Because there's always a lurking apprehension about those conditions being unmet. If our love is based on a person's behavior, status, or any external factor, it becomes fickle and vulnerable to the ebbs and flows of life.

Expressions like:

"I love my spouse, but ..."

"My child is wonderful, but ..."

... are indicative of love with conditions attached. They limit love's expansive nature and turn it into a confined emotion contingent on behavior or circumstances. This isn't genuine love; it's love with strings attached.

Love as Freedom

True love knows no bounds, no conditions. It simply is. When we embrace love as our natural state of being, we free ourselves from the chains of expectations and conditions. When we realize that no one outside of ourselves can truly "give" us love, we gain a profound sense of freedom. Sure, others can mirror or reflect love, but the feeling of love we experience comes from within. This is why expecting others to fill our love void is an exercise in futility. It's like expecting someone else to breathe for us.

Choosing Love Over Fear

When we choose to live in a state of love, we choose freedom over fear. Fear tells us love is scarce, conditional, and outside of ourselves. Love, on the other hand, reminds us of our inherent worth, our interconnectedness, and the abundant love that exists within and around us.

Choosing love is a daily act. It's a conscious decision to BE love, to show love, and to experience love in its purest form. It's recognizing that love isn't just something we feel but something we are.

In this state, love becomes as natural and ever-present as breathing. And just as we don't need to be reminded to breathe, when we embody love, we don't need external validation to feel it. We simply exist in it, continuously and unconditionally.

Being the Wellspring of Love

In our interconnected existence, it's easy to forget that our emotional experiences are deeply personal and internal. Often, we project our innermost feelings and beliefs onto the world around us, thinking they originate from external sources. However, when it comes to love, the truth is clear: you are its source, its wellspring.

Feeling Love From Within

Each individual uniquely perceives love. When you feel a rush of affection, it's a product of your emotions, your heart, and your soul. No one else is experiencing that precise moment of love in the same way. Similarly, when another person feels love, it is their unique experience that you can't fully feel or understand. Thus, our perceptions of love, though universally shared in essence, are deeply individual in experience.

Mirror of Self-love

The age-old adage, "You can't pour from an empty cup," rings true when we talk about love. One's capacity to love others is a direct reflection of their self-love. If you harbor resentment, self-doubt, or self-loathing, your ability to love others genuinely gets hindered. It's akin to trying to illuminate a room with a dim light. Only when the light shines bright can it radiate warmth and brightness everywhere.

Choosing to love without strings attached is the ultimate act of spiritual awakening. It lets you align with a congruent consciousness, creating a bridge between the physical and spiritual realms. Such a connection isn't just about personal fulfillment; it's about feeling the oneness, the unity of existence.

Embracing Love Freely

When you become an embodiment of love, barriers fade. The societal walls that often separate individuals crumble, revealing the interconnected tapestry of life. This is the power of free-flowing love. It doesn't bind; it liberates. It doesn't judge; it accepts. And in this vast expanse of boundless love, we find our true selves, our purpose, and our connection to the divine.

Emotional Literacy

Start by naming your emotions. This simple act can make them less daunting.

Acceptance: All feelings, whether pleasant or unpleasant, have a place. Denying or suppressing them only gives them more power.

Cultivation: Actively work toward cultivating feelings that align with the best version of yourself. If confidence is a goal, visualize situations where you felt most confident.

We've already examined our thoughts about ourselves, considering the roles of self-esteem and self-confidence. We've also explored our feelings and the gift of love. Now, we'll turn our attention to our actions and how they align with our thoughts and emotions.

3. What We Do in Relation to How We Think and How We Feel

Actions are tangible manifestations of our inner dialogues and feelings. They are the most visible indicators of who we believe we are.

Behavioral Analysis: Recognize patterns in your behavior. Do you often shy away from challenges? Do you self-sabotage when you're close to achieving something?

Intentional Action: Start taking small steps toward behaviors that resonate with your true self. If you seek courage, start with small acts that push you out of your comfort zone.

Consistency: Rome wasn't built in a day, and neither is personal transformation. Consistent effort, despite setbacks, is key.

In essence, to awaken to our true selves, we must become detectives of our own psyche. We need to explore every corner, understand every narrative, and challenge every belief that doesn't serve our higher self. Through this continuous exploration of thoughts, feelings, and actions, we don't just discover who we are—we actively create who we wish to become.

The Age-Old Question: Why DON'T People DO What They Know?

For countless coaches, mentors, and advisors, the perennial question that keeps them awake at night is this: "Why don't people do what they know?" It's a conundrum that spans various domains, from weight loss and fitness to personal development and career advancement. As someone deeply immersed in the world of coaching, this question has likely been the source of frustration, fascination, and, for me, sleepless nights.

The Common Scenario: Knowing the What and How

As a coach, I've encountered numerous individuals who sought my guidance and expertise. They come to me with specific goals in mind, whether it's shedding pounds, conquering a marathon, or excelling in their careers. I would meticulously lay out the blueprint for success, providing them with a crystal-clear roadmap of what to do and how to do it. The plan is foolproof, and the path to success seems well-lit.

However, here lies the perplexing reality: despite having the knowledge of what needs to be done and the precise steps to take, a significant portion of individuals still struggle to translate this knowledge into action. It's a common phenomenon that has left so many of us scratching our heads in bewilderment. Why does this gap persist between knowing and doing, even when the path forward appears so clear?

The Missing Pieces: The Power of "Who"

Enter the missing pieces of this intricate puzzle—the "Who." While Simon Sinek's concept of "Start with Why" has gained significant acclaim, it's essential to recognize that without the "Who," even the most compelling "Why" can fall short.[3] The "Who" represents who you are as a state of being—a thinking and feeling state that underpins all your actions.

In the grand scheme of motivation, it's not solely the "What" and "How" that drive us, nor is it merely the "Why." The linchpin of motivation is our identity, our "Who." It's our core beliefs, values, and self-concept that ultimately determine whether we take action or succumb to inertia. Regardless of how impeccable the plan or how grand the "Why" may be, it's our internal sense of self—the "Who"—that acts as the catalyst for action.

The "Who" as the True Driver of Action

Consider This: When individuals align their sense of self, their identity, with the desired actions, they become more inclined to take consistent steps toward their goals. It's not merely about knowing the "What" and "How"; it's about embodying the "Who" that is congruent with those actions. When someone sees themselves as a healthy, disciplined, and capable individual (the "Who"), they are far more likely to engage in behaviors that align with that self-concept.

The Transformational Journey: Bridging the Gap

Understanding the profound influence of the "Who" on motivation and action is a pivotal realization. It highlights the importance of helping individuals not only define their goals and understand the "Why" behind them but also cultivate an empowering self-concept that supports those goals. It's about guiding them on a transformational journey where they become the "Who" they need to be to achieve what they desire.

---

3   Simon Sinek, Start with Why: How Great Leaders Inspire Everyone to Take Action, Portfolio, 2011.

The perennial question of why people don't do what they know finds its answer in the synergy of the "Who." While the "What" and "How" provide the roadmap, it's the "Who" that fuels the journey. Recognizing and nurturing the "Who" within is the key to unlocking your true potential and bridging the gap between knowing and doing.

The Path to WHO

The Nexus of Thought, Feeling, and Action

When we consider human behavior, it's often oversimplified as mere reactions to external stimuli. However, a deeper exploration reveals a rich interplay between our thoughts, emotions, and the subsequent actions they inspire. These components aren't separate entities but rather a cohesive flowchart, each influencing and being influenced by the others.

Each day, our minds process tens of thousands of thoughts. While many of these thoughts are fleeting or benign, others significantly shape our emotional state. A positive thought can elicit feelings of joy, motivation, or gratitude. In contrast, a negative thought can spiral into anxiety, anger, or sadness. This intricate dance between thought and emotion directly influences our actions. For instance, feeling appreciated at work due to positive reinforcement can lead to increased motivation and productivity; it's opposite plays out as well.

Emotions as the Catalyst

Our emotions are powerful motivators. They can spur us into action or paralyze us into inaction. But these emotions, in essence, are byproducts of our thoughts. When faced with a challenging situation, if our immediate thought is, "I can't handle this," feelings of anxiety and overwhelm ensue. Conversely, thinking, "This is tough, but I'll find a way," can evoke determination and resilience.

Actions Speak Louder

It's said that actions speak louder than words, but perhaps, more fittingly, actions speak louder than thoughts or feelings. While our internal experiences shape our world, it's our actions that leave an indelible mark on it. The way we interact with others, the choices we make, and the paths we pursue are all extensions of our internal dialogue and emotional state.

Interconnectedness of Being

Every decision we make, every word we utter, and every relationship we nurture stems from the fusion of our thoughts and feelings. Our thoughts and feelings determine WHO we are, essentially our state of being. This is why self-awareness is paramount. Recognizing the patterns of our thoughts, understanding the emotions they elicit, and being conscious of the actions they precipitate is the foundation for personal growth.

Navigating Disempowering YOU States: Avoidance, Resistance, and Reaction

Emotions, in all their vivid intensity, can often act as a compass, guiding us through the mazes of our lives. However, not all emotions point us in the direction of empowerment and growth. Some, especially the more challenging ones, can lead us to strategies that hold us back—namely avoidance, resistance, and reaction. Let's delve deeper into how these strategies manifest when we encounter disempowering YOU states.

Avoidance: The Subtle Art of Dodging Discomfort

The tendency to avoid is a primal, instinctual reaction to perceived danger or discomfort. In the modern world, where threats are more emotional and psychological than physical, this mechanism often gets triggered in ways that are less about survival and more about evading emotional pain. However, what we often fail to realize is that in our attempts to escape discomfort, we may be inadvertently creating a cage of our own making.

1. Over-Indulgence: The Mask of Excess

When we speak of the "overs"—overeating, overspending, over-drinking—it's often a manifestation of our need to fill a void. These actions, while momentarily gratifying, are often attempts to numb or distract from an underlying emotional ache. They are the emotional equivalents of putting a plaster over a wound without cleaning it first.

2. The Busy Trap: Over-Doing as a Shield

In today's fast-paced society, being "busy" is often worn as a badge of honor. But for many, staying occupied is a convenient excuse to avoid confronting underlying issues. Overworking, for instance, might be celebrated as dedication or commitment, but can sometimes be a way to avoid personal problems, emotional confrontations, or even one's own feelings of inadequacy.

3. Digital Escapes: The Modern Maze

In the age of the internet and streaming, "overnetflixing" has become a notable means of avoidance. Series after series, movie after movie, we dive into fictional worlds, investing emotionally in characters' lives, often as a way to avoid facing the realities of our own.

4. Ignoring the Inner Self

The saddest form of avoidance is perhaps when we ignore or neglect our true selves. By failing to acknowledge and address our feelings, desires, dreams, or pains, we do a great disservice to our authenticity. Pushing away introspection or self-reflection can keep us stuck in patterns that don't serve our true interests or well-being.

The Cost of Avoidance

While avoidance might provide short-term relief, the long-term costs can be profound. Emotions, when ignored, don't just disappear—they often simmer beneath the surface, growing in intensity. Avoiding problems, especially in relationships, can lead to bigger confrontations down the road. Moreover, chronic avoidance can lead to feelings of emptiness, as if one is merely existing rather than truly living.

Embracing the Uncomfortable

The antidote to avoidance isn't confrontation but compassion. It involves turning inward with kindness, acknowledging our feelings without judgment, and giving ourselves permission to be human. When we allow ourselves to feel, to be present with our emotions, we often find that they lose their grip over us. By facing what we fear, we often realize that the shadows on our path are cast by us standing in our own light.

Resistance: The Emotional Fortress

Resistance is a powerful psychological force that often stems from a deeply rooted need to protect our self-image and the narratives we've constructed about ourselves and the world. Our brains are wired for coherence and consistency. When something threatens that equilibrium—be it an opposing viewpoint, an unexpected event, or even introspective insights that contradict our long-held beliefs—resistance often becomes our go-to response.

1. The Root of Defensiveness: The Right to Be Right

Humans have an innate desire to be seen as "right." We have covered this previously, but it is important to realize that this isn't just about ego; it's also about the brain's craving for certainty and the fear of the unknown. Recognizing that we might be wrong shakes the very foundation of our perceived reality. So, when challenged, the brain goes into a defensive mode. It's not merely about proving a point; it's about preserving our mental model of the world.

2. The Blame Game: Pointing Outward to Avoid Looking Inward

Blame is a manifestation of externalizing responsibility. When we blame others, we shift the onus of responsibility away from ourselves. It's a convenient way of saying, "It's not me; it's you." By doing this, we sidestep accountability, but we also miss out on opportunities for personal growth.

3. The Dance of Denial: Twisting Truths

Arguing, embellishing, and even lying are ways in which we twist reality to fit our narrative. When we alter the truth, we're not necessarily trying to deceive others; sometimes, we're trying to protect ourselves from facing a truth that might be too uncomfortable or confronting.

4. The Universality of Resistance

It's crucial to understand that resistance isn't exclusive to any individual. Everyone has experienced it, fueled by their brain's desire for consistency. It's not about "us vs. them;" it's about recognizing that the other person is also operating under the influence of their brain's imperatives.

5. Choosing Humanness Over Happiness

While happiness is a desirable state, it's transient. True fulfillment comes from acknowledging and embracing our shared humanness. It's about understanding that each of us is navigating this complex web of life, doing our best with the tools and knowledge we have. When we choose to see the humanity in others, even those we disagree with, we pave the way for genuine connection, compassion, and, eventually, peace.

Resistance, while a natural defense mechanism, often stands in the way of understanding, growth, and connection. By recognizing its patterns and origins, we can make conscious choices to respond with empathy and open-mindedness, fostering an environment of mutual respect and understanding.

React: The Impulse to Counter

In the symphony of human emotions and responses, reacting often takes center stage. A reaction is an impulse—a visceral, immediate response to stimuli without much thought or analysis. It's the brain's quick defense mechanism, propelling us into action, often bypassing the filters of reason or understanding.

1. Lashing Out: The Reflex Response

Just as the body jerks back from a hot flame, the psyche, too, has its reflexes. When confronted with something unsettling or adverse, the immediate reaction can be to lash out, to push away the threat, be it real or perceived. This reaction can manifest as angry words, abrupt actions, or even aggressive gestures.

2. Fighting Against: Battling the Perceived Threat

The fight-flight-freeze response is hardwired into our biology. When facing an apparent threat, our system chooses to fight against it. In emotional or psychological terms, this means challenging a different viewpoint, speaking against an opposing opinion, or even confronting someone we feel threatened by.

3. Retaliation: Getting Even

Reacting can sometimes mean retaliating—trying to get back at someone for what they did. It's the classic "eye for an eye" approach, where the focus shifts from understanding the cause to merely settling the score.

4. Defensiveness: Guarding One's Turf

At its core, defensiveness is a protective mechanism. When our beliefs, actions, or identities are challenged, the natural inclination is to defend them. This can involve justifying our actions, explaining ourselves, or even redirecting the blame.

5. Seeking Validation: The Need for Proof

In the realm of reactions, seeking validation or finding proof is a way to ground our beliefs and feelings. It's as if by finding external evidence, we can validate our reactions and feelings, lending them legitimacy in our eyes and, we hope, in the eyes of others.

6. Losing Our Center: Emotional Overwhelm

In intense reactive states, it's not uncommon to feel like we're "losing our mind." Emotions flood the system, rational thought can take a backseat, and we might say or do things that, in a calmer state, we'd never consider.

The Road Ahead

Understanding our reactive patterns is the first step toward greater emotional intelligence and self-awareness. Recognizing that reactions are instinctual and not always representative of our reasoned selves can pave the way for more mindful responses. It's not about suppressing reactions but about navigating them with greater understanding and choosing how we want to proceed.

The Quest for External Validation: The Disempowered Self

When we feel disempowered, it's akin to a light dimming within us. This dimness drives us to seek illumination outside of ourselves, believing that somewhere, somehow, someone else holds the key to our happiness, security, and well-being. This quest can lead us down paths that are often tumultuous and misguided.

1. Seeking External Comfort and Security

Disempowerment creates a void, a sort of emptiness within that we often scramble to fill. We might seek validation in the arms of another, in the accolades of our peers, or in the many distractions the world provides. Whether it's fleeting moments of comfort, the thrill of new experiences, or the allure of substances, we become seekers, hoping that somewhere out there lies the remedy to our internal unrest.

2. The Myth of Rescue

Deep within our psyche exists a narrative, one where a hero comes and rescues us from our woes. Cultivated by tales of knights in shining armor, we sometimes, in our moments of despair, wait for someone or something to come and save us. But the truth is more liberating—the hero we await is within us.

3. Restoring Faith in Ourselves

Restoration is an active process. It demands introspection, acknowledgment, and a desire to change. It's about understanding that while we might have lost our way, our inherent worth and capability remain untouched. By accepting our vulnerabilities and celebrating our strengths, we begin rebuilding that lost faith.

The Road to Empowerment

Recognizing these patterns is the first step toward reclaiming empowerment. Rather than allowing emotions to push us toward avoidance, resistance, or reaction, we can choose a different path: acceptance. This involves acknowledging our feelings without judgment, giving ourselves the space to feel, and then using rational thought to decide the best course of action.

In the end, it's essential to remember that while emotions are powerful, they are also transient. With understanding, patience, and self-awareness, we can navigate even the most disempowering YOU states and emerge stronger on the other side.

Empowerment: The Fuel for an Unapologetic Life

Empowerment is a dynamic force that propels us toward a life characterized by authenticity, confidence, and a resolute sense of self. It's the inner spark that ignites our journey toward living unapologetically. We have already scratched the surface with this invitation, but let's dive deeper. What does it truly mean to live unapologetically?

Living unapologetically doesn't imply a disregard for the feelings or perspectives of others. Instead, it's about embracing your true self, your values, and your aspirations without diminishing your worth or altering your path to seek validation from others. It's recognizing that your life is your own canvas, and you have the power to paint it with bold strokes that reflect your unique essence.

The Journey Toward Empowerment

The journey toward empowerment and living unapologetically is a deeply personal and transformative one. It's not always linear, and there will be moments of doubt, fear, and uncertainty. However, it's these very moments that offer opportunities for growth and empowerment.

1. Understanding Our Relationship with Self

Who we are is a culmination of our thoughts, feelings, and actions. How we perceive ourselves, how we feel about that perception, and how we act based on those feelings define our day-to-day experience.

2. Questioning, Reflecting, and Reinventing

In the journey of self-empowerment, questioning is the compass, reflection the map, and reinvention the destination. By challenging preconceived notions about ourselves, reflecting on our true desires, and reinventing our mindset, we create a life aligned with our authentic selves.

3. Ownership and Empowerment

The key to empowerment is ownership. Owning our thoughts, feelings, and actions and realizing that they're uniquely ours gives us a sense of agency. This realization that we're in the driver's seat of our lives is profoundly empowering.

Remember, it's not about achieving a state of perfection but embracing our imperfections. It's about understanding that our flaws don't diminish our worth but rather make us human. And in this acceptance, in this profound understanding, lies our true power.

The Path to Becoming Unapologetically You:
The STEAR Practice

Embracing oneself fully and living unapologetically isn't a mere switch that can be flicked on or off. It's an evolving journey that requires dedication, introspection, and, most importantly, practice.

Becoming unapologetically you is not a destination but a continuous process. It's about constantly applying the STEAR practice, reflecting on your journey, and making the necessary shifts. As you continue on this path, remember that every step, no matter how small, is a testament to your commitment to embracing your authentic self. Celebrate your progress, learn from setbacks, and always prioritize self-love and trust above all.

The STEAR practice, an acronym symbolizing the cognitive and emotional processes involved, forms the foundation of this transformative journey.

Shifting Paradigms with STEAR:

S – Situation: Recognize the external events or circumstances that trigger negative self-perceptions or reactions.

T – Thoughts: Identify the thoughts and internal narratives that arise in response to the situation.

E – Emotions: Understand the emotions that these thoughts evoke. Do they lead to feelings of shame, insecurity, or distrust?

A – Actions: Acknowledge the actions or reactions driven by these emotions. Are they in alignment with your authentic self, or are they merely defensive mechanisms?

R – Results: Observe the outcomes of your actions. Do they lead you closer to or further away from becoming unapologetically you?

The Initial Shift: Separating Situations From Thoughts

As we covered, our lives are inundated with a myriad of experiences and situations, but what truly defines our emotional response and, ultimately, our actions is the interpretation and meaning we assign to these experiences. This first step in transformation is fundamental as it lays the groundwork for every decision, action, and emotion that follows.

Understanding the Distinction:

Situation (S): This is an objective occurrence or state of affairs. It's fact-based and doesn't possess an inherent emotional charge.

For instance: "I weigh X pounds" is a situation. It's factual and verifiable.

Thought (T): Thoughts are subjective interpretations, beliefs, or narratives we construct about a particular situation. They are not universally accepted facts but are colored by our past experiences, cultural upbringing, biases, and more.

For instance: "If I were thinner, I would be more loveable" is a thought. It's an interpretation and not a universal truth.

Dissecting the Situational Thoughts:

When you place yourself as the central situation, as in "YOU" being the situation, it means understanding your core without the influence of external factors.

S: YOU

T: "If I were thinner, I would be more loveable." This thought stems from a place of shame, where self-worth is being equated with physical appearance

T: "I am not supported; therefore, I can't pursue this." Here, the feeling of insecurity is dictating one's belief in their abilities and the external resources one thinks one needs.

T: "I don't know how, so I will wait." This thought arises from a place of distrust in oneself to learn, adapt, or find a solution.

The pivotal step is to be able to observe these thoughts without getting emotionally entangled with them. By recognizing them as interpretations rather than absolute truths, we can give ourselves the freedom to question them. It's like looking at clouds; they may take various shapes, but ultimately, they're just clusters of water droplets. Likewise, our thoughts are just clusters of beliefs, biases, and previous experiences.

Without branding them as "right" or "wrong," we can ask, "Is this serving me? Is there another way to view this? Could there be another interpretation that's more empowering or positive?"

This observational awareness gives us the space to choose our reactions rather than being slaves to our initial interpretations. It becomes the foundation upon which we build our emotional resilience, self-belief, and unapologetic authenticity.

Key Shifts for Transformation

From Shame to Love: Instead of internalizing external judgments, embrace unconditional self-love. Understand that mistakes and imperfections don't define your worth. Start by forgiving yourself and embracing your journey with compassion and understanding.

From Insecurity to Capability: Recognize that you possess the innate capability to overcome challenges, learn, and grow. Instead of doubting your worth or abilities, focus on your strengths and potential. Empower yourself with knowledge, skills, and a growth mindset.

From Distrust to Trust: Instead of second-guessing every decision or seeking external validation, trust in your journey and your instincts. Understand that while external inputs can offer guidance, the final decision and trust must come from within.

Choosing Our Thoughts and Feelings Intentionally

By asking ourselves, "How do I want to show up?" we consciously determine the energy we bring into a situation. When faced with challenges, posing the question, "What would the best version of me do right now?" helps align our actions with our values and principles. This intentional thought process brings clarity and aids in making decisions that resonate with our authentic selves.

Living in Alignment

By practicing this alignment consistently, we actively distance ourselves from the trappings of the ego. Instead, we draw nearer to our true essence—our highest self. This self is unburdened by societal norms and uninfluenced by fleeting external judgments.

Embracing Freedom

In this space of alignment and acceptance:

We become *free from seeking permission*, understanding that our worth isn't defined by others.

We release the exhausting act of *pretending and people-pleasing*, embracing our authentic selves.

We let go of the need for *external validation and acknowledgment*, knowing our value is intrinsic.

We unshackle ourselves from the weight of *perfectionism*, celebrating our imperfections as facets of our unique journey.

We understand that our salvation doesn't lie outside but within, making us *free from the need to be saved*.

We give ourselves permission to *experience the full spectrum of emotions* without judgment.

We redefine love, trust, and worthiness, realizing that they're birthrights, not commodities to be earned.

Acceptance isn't about complacency or surrender but empowerment. It's about acknowledging where we are, embracing it, and understanding that we have the power to change, evolve, and grow. It's recognizing that our journey's worth isn't determined by the start or the challenges along the way but by how we choose to navigate them.

This acceptance brings profound freedom. It's the freedom to be authentically us, unapologetically. Living unapologetically doesn't mean living without responsibility or consideration. It means living without regrets, without seeking external validation, and, most importantly, without doubting one's intrinsic value.

It's the realization that our past doesn't define us, our mistakes don't bind us, and our potential is limitless. This freedom, stemming from acceptance, is the greatest gift we can give ourselves.

The Elusive Nature of Confidence

Confidence, that feeling of self-assuredness and belief in one's abilities, is a quality many aspire to possess. However, it often eludes us, leaving us feeling uncertain and insecure. The question then arises: Why does confidence remain just out of reach for so many?

The HOG—Hierarchy of Greatness

The concept of the "HOG," or the Hierarchy of Greatness, offers an insightful perspective on why confidence can be elusive. It suggests that our society has conditioned us to believe in a false hierarchy of greatness, where certain achievements, traits, or external validations are placed above others in terms of importance and worthiness.

In this hierarchy, some accomplishments or attributes are elevated to the status of greatness, while others are devalued or dismissed. For example:

Traditional Career Success: Society often places a high value on traditional markers of career success, such as a prestigious job title, a large salary, or recognition from peers and superiors. These achievements are often equated with confidence.

Physical Appearance: The emphasis on physical beauty and attractiveness can lead people to believe that their worthiness and confidence are tied to their appearance. This can create insecurity and self-doubt.

External Validation: Seeking constant approval and validation from others, whether through social media likes, compliments, or praise, can become a means of measuring one's self-worth and confidence.

Comparisons: Comparing oneself to others who seem to have achieved more in terms of societal standards can erode confidence, as it reinforces a sense of inadequacy.

Dissecting the Myth of Hierarchical Greatness

Society often presents greatness as a ladder with clearly defined rungs that individuals must ascend to reach the pinnacle. We're led to believe there's an established hierarchy of excellence, with the elite few at the top and the vast many at the bottom. However, such a perception, while deeply ingrained, is but a skewed representation of reality.

The Complexity of Defining Greatness

Greatness is a multifaceted and subjective concept that means different things to different people. It encompasses a wide range of qualities, achievements, and attributes, making it difficult to pin down with a single, universally agreed-upon metric. When we consider the diverse perspectives and values of individuals, it becomes clear why greatness is such a fluid and elusive idea.

For starters, the criteria that dictate this hierarchy are often arbitrary and heavily influenced by cultural, societal, and temporal biases.

What's deemed "great" in one era or culture may be disregarded in another. Mozart, for instance, died without the recognition he deserved, only to be revered centuries later. Would the hierarchy have placed him differently during his lifetime compared to now?

If you were to ask ten different people about their metrics for greatness, you'd likely receive ten different answers. Some might equate greatness with financial success, measuring it in terms of wealth and material possessions. Others might emphasize popularity, defining it by the number of followers or fans they have. For some, greatness may be associated with making a significant contribution to society or engaging in philanthropic endeavors.

Even if we were to agree on a specific metric of greatness, such as financial success, another challenge arises: determining the boundaries of greatness. At what point does one cross the line from being great to being excessive? How much wealth or fame is too much? This lack of clear demarcation further complicates the pursuit of greatness and the associated confidence.

Measuring greatness on a linear scale negates the diversity of human potential. How can we compare the greatness of an artist to a scientist, a teacher to an athlete, or a philanthropist to an entrepreneur? Each brings unique value to the world, and each achieves excellence in distinct domains. Insisting on a singular hierarchy diminishes the multifaceted brilliance of humanity.

Then, there's the personal journey to consider. Many who've reached what's considered the "top" have voiced feelings of emptiness, while those deemed "lower" often find profound fulfillment in their pursuits. Clearly, the internal experience doesn't always align with the external designation. Is someone truly greater if their achievements bring neither personal satisfaction nor genuine benefit to others?

Perhaps the most significant challenge is that greatness is a moving target. What society deems as great today may evolve over time. The qualities or achievements that are celebrated today might not hold the same significance in the future. This shifting landscape makes it difficult for individuals to set concrete goals and benchmarks for themselves.

Hence lies the problem with this external construct. It doesn't necessarily reflect one's true value or potential and often leads to a cycle of chasing external validation and trying to fit into predefined molds of success, which can ultimately undermine confidence, making it seem out of reach.

By dispelling the myth of hierarchical greatness, we free ourselves to pursue a more authentic, fulfilling, and uniquely brilliant journey of excellence.

Lateral Self-Belief

To reclaim confidence, it's essential to shift away from the HOG and toward a more holistic and self-affirming perspective.

The Horizontal Confidence Paradigm

The idea of horizontal confidence pivots from the conventional thinking that inadvertently places individuals on a vertical hierarchy of worth, achievement, or importance. As we have discussed, the notion of vertical hierarchy inherently suggests that there are individuals who are "above" or "below" others based on a variety of parameters—success, intelligence, appearance, wealth, or societal status. It's this conventional way of thinking that becomes the breeding ground for shame, pride, and a continuous comparison cycle.

Horizontal confidence, on the other hand, emphasizes the understanding that worth is not hierarchical. Instead, it offers a level playing field where everyone is of equal value. No one is any better than anyone else; we only differ by way of experiences.

Why are we stuck on this vertical access? One word … "SHOULD."

The Trap of "Should": The word "should" is a shaming word. It's insidious, suggesting that you ought to be something different than you currently are, always hinting at an unattained perfection. For instance, you "should" be more like someone else, or you "shouldn't" have certain emotions. Such thoughts serve only to reinforce feelings of inadequacy, hence lowering you on this self-imposed ladder.

Reality Check with "Should": What if we considered the fact that sometimes our behavior that leads to regret is a result of our humanness? Friendly reminder: acceptance does not equate to approval. Recognizing and accepting a certain behavior as a reality doesn't mean endorsing it; instead, it means acknowledging it to work toward improvement.

Breaking the Shame Cycle: Shame perpetuates a cycle of hiding, defensiveness, and finger-pointing. It's essential to realize that *no one can ever apologize enough to make your feelings of shame disappear.* Outsourcing the responsibility of your emotions to someone else, expecting them to resolve your internal struggles, is a futile endeavor. Most of the time, they aren't equipped to handle it.

Embracing Horizontal Confidence: Life is complex, and our responses to its many challenges can be equally intricate. Rather than confining ourselves to a vertical hierarchy where we constantly measure our worth against others, what if we operated from a horizontal line of confidence? Here, there's no need to constantly compare or compete, only to comprehend and be compassionate. It's a paradigm where acceptance leads the way. By focusing on growth, embracing our humanness, and understanding our strengths and weaknesses, we nurture competence. And with competence, *genuine* confidence follows.

In this new paradigm, every experience, emotion, and response becomes a part of our growth journey. The shift from a vertical to a horizontal perspective not only offers freedom from self-imposed pressures but also nurtures a more empathetic, understanding, and inclusive worldview.

Ultimately, the true essence of greatness lies in authenticity, purpose, and impact, not in climbing a hypothetical ladder. Instead of aspiring to ascend this illusory hierarchy, we should seek to carve our path, define our measure of success, and recognize the inherent value.

When we find ourselves ascending a steep slope, striving for peaks of perfection, we find ourselves in the valleys of self-judgment. Yet, when we level the playing field of this hierarchy, we grant ourselves the grace to step away from judgment and move into a space of self-discovery. Let me illuminate this with a personal story that encapsulates this transformative journey.

Navigating the Complex World of a Sports Mom

Being a sports mom is far from a walk in the park. It's a tumultuous roller coaster of emotions, investments, and high-stakes decisions. I remember a particular season when one of my kids was playing for a premiere organization. As the season neared its end, whispers and murmurs about positional biases and playtime grew louder.

I found myself at the center of these conversations, and soon, I became part of a small delegation that decided to approach the decision-makers: the coaches. My perspective was simple—addressing the concerns directly was a more transparent way to handle the situation rather than just gossiping at games and events.

In my earnestness to bring clarity, I was too forthright. I soon realized that my words, though honest, hurt two individuals I hadn't intended to—the coach and a fellow mom.

I never intended to inflict pain. But intent and impact don't always align. I had voiced my concerns, yes, but could I have been more tactful in my approach? Definitely.

If I had let the overwhelming "shoulds" take control, I'd be drowning in guilt. "You shouldn't have spoken out like that," my conscience would chide. "You're not being a team player or even a good mom," it'd continue.

But in sidestepping the pitfall of "should," I could look at the situation more objectively. Instead of berating myself, I embraced my flaws and my strengths. Compassion and curiosity replaced guilt and defensiveness.

Compassion allowed me to commend myself for having the courage to face the coaches and to also acknowledge that they deserved more nuanced feedback. On the other hand, curiosity made me reflect on why I reacted defensively. It also made me wonder about the coach's perspective and the reasons behind their reactions.

From this newfound understanding, I sent an email. It wasn't a template apology but a heartfelt note expressing regret not for my concerns but for the way I'd voiced them. I also recognized a need to improve my communication skills, leading me to delve deeper into understanding feedback mechanisms and effective communication.

The experience taught me the value of "progress over perfection." Life isn't about always getting things right; it's about learning from the times we don't. And as a sports mom, while the games might end, the lessons continue.

Living in the Middle

It's in the balance, the equilibrium, that true harmony is found. Let's celebrate the middle ground—neither in excess nor in lack. Together, we'll explore the magic of moderation and how finding one's center can lead to a life of enriched fulfillment.

Harmony is not found at the extremities but in the balance that exists between them. The middle ground, often overlooked in our world of extremes, is where real magic happens. It's the space where we're neither pulled in by overwhelming desires nor pushed away by intense aversions. As we delve deeper into this concept, we'll uncover the beauty of moderation and discover why finding your center can be the key to a life of profound contentment.

Living in the Middle—Self-Love

At the core of our being is the emotional spectrum that defines our human experience. How we feel acts as the catalyst for our actions, the driving force behind our decisions, and the essence of our very existence. But a crucial insight that often goes unnoticed is that the price for the results and achievements we yearn for is frequently paid in the currency of negative emotions.

The world might teach us to chase pleasure and avoid pain, but the truth is, to grow and evolve, we must embrace a gamut of feelings, including those that might be uncomfortable. The aspirations we set for ourselves, whether they pertain to personal development, relationships, or professional milestones, come packaged with emotions like disappointment, frustration, and moments of failure.

Attempting to think positively while being submerged in negative emotions is an exercise in futility. True transformation requires us to not only acknowledge these feelings but to also experience and process them fully. It's only by facing them head-on that we can hope to transcend them.

However, if we perpetually seek solace only in our minds and avoid confronting these challenging emotions, we'll find ourselves stuck in a loop of fleeting comfort and persistent dissatisfaction. True self-love, the kind that propels us forward, involves acknowledging these feelings, leaning into them, and using them as stepping stones to our next level of personal growth.

In the pursuit of living in the middle, we must remember that balance doesn't mean avoiding extremes altogether. Instead, it means knowing how to navigate them, using the emotions they bring up as tools for introspection and growth, and recognizing that our true power lies not in dodging discomfort but in embracing and learning from it.

Facing Fear: Unmasking the Paradoxes

At the heart of our hesitations, the undercurrent of our uncertainties lies a profound emotion: fear. But this isn't the primal fear that our ancestors faced, like the fear of a predatory animal. No, our modern-day fears are more insidious, more deeply rooted in our psyche, often manifesting in a web of conflicting emotions.

1. Fear of Success

It might seem counterintuitive at first. Why would anyone fear success? Yet, many do. The weight of success, the responsibility and effort it carries, can be overwhelming. What if, after reaching a certain pinnacle, you discover that scaling the next peak requires a different set of skills or even a different mindset? This daunting realization can deter many from pursuing further accomplishments, fearing that their present success might set them up for future failure.

2. Fear of Ruin

On the flip side of the success coin is the fear of utter downfall. It's the nagging voice inside that constantly wonders, "What if this is the mistake that costs me everything?" This fear is entrenched in the idea that our decisions carry irreversible consequences, permanently marking our legacy.

3. Fear of the Outcome

This is the uncertainty that even if we give it our all, the results might not live up to our expectations. The sleepless nights, the sacrifices, the energy expended—what if, after everything, the outcome isn't as rosy as we'd imagined?

4. Fear of Rejection

The need for social acceptance and validation is a powerful driver of human behavior. Many of our choices are, consciously or subconsciously, influenced by how we believe others will perceive us. The fear of judgment, of not fitting in, or of being ridiculed can be paralyzing. This fear is bolstered by the thought that detractors will feel validated if we don't succeed, echoing the sentiment, "I knew they couldn't do it."

5. Fear of Loss

This fear capitalizes on our tendency to overestimate losses and underestimate gains. It's the voice that whispers worst-case scenarios in our ears, making us second-guess every step. By always focusing on what could go wrong, we might miss out on what could go wonderfully right.

Confronting these fears is not about eradicating them; it's about understanding them. Recognizing the nuances of each fear helps us navigate them more effectively. It's essential to remember that fear, in itself, is not the enemy. In fact, it's a testament to our deeply human capacity to care, to hope, and to dream. The real challenge is not letting these fears dictate our path but using them as signposts, guiding us toward self-awareness and growth.

Embracing Fear: The Pathway to Boundless Possibilities

There's an adage that goes, "What you resist, persists." At its core, this wisdom applies aptly to fear. So many of us are hardwired to escape fear, to move in the opposite direction whenever it looms. Yet, ironically, every time we run from it, we deepen its hold on us.

234 | PILLAR 2

Choosing Fear Over Future

It's a weighty realization that the simple act of selecting our fears over our dreams circumscribes our potential. Each time we yield to trepidation, we're essentially forfeiting the expansive love and infinite possibilities that reside within us. It's as if we're surrendering to a self-imposed cage, depriving ourselves of the very essence that makes us limitless.

Science itself stands testament to the transformative power of confronting fear. For instance, when we lean into a challenging or intimidating scenario, our brain releases dopamine. This neurotransmitter isn't just associated with pleasure; it's also intricately linked with motivation, reward, and learning. So, in a way, every time we face our fears, we're biochemically programming ourselves to not only survive but thrive in similar future situations.

Running Into Fear

Recognition alone is insufficient; acceptance is key. In our shared human journey, fear isn't an outlier. It's an integral part of our narrative. Instead of perceiving fear as a monstrous adversary, what if we saw it as a guide, leading us toward growth? By willingly stepping into the embrace of fear, by truly experiencing and processing it, we forge a path that neither shuns nor gets dominated by it. This acceptance heralds progress.

There's a transformative power in voicing the unspoken, in shedding light on what's kept in the shadows. To manifest change in our lives, we must have the courage to utter what we've silenced and acknowledge what we've evaded.

But imagine a world where self-acceptance becomes a habitual practice. A realm where our inner dialogue shifts from blame, shame, and judgment to one of curiosity and compassion. The question then becomes, what facets of yourself, in this very moment, do you need to embrace to make that profound transition?

Embracing the H.U.G.S. Methodology: A Deep Dive Into Empathy

HUGS—they're more than just a comforting gesture or a warm greeting. They symbolize a sense of closeness, understanding, and the human yearning for connection. For many, a hug is an intimate expression of empathy, a silent way of saying, "I'm here with you." But what if we could give ourselves this same comfort, not just physically, but emotionally?

H: Honesty

At the core of any genuine connection, be it with others or oneself, lies honesty. Before we can truly embrace ourselves, we must confront our truths, both pleasant and painful. Honesty is not about brutal self-criticism but about acknowledging our feelings, actions, and thoughts without judgment. It's about seeing ourselves as we truly are and understanding that every facet of us is valid and meaningful.

U: Unity

Unity is the essence of wholeness, reminding us that we are complete as we are. Every emotion, every flaw, every strength is a part of our unique tapestry. To be united within oneself is to harmoniously accept all parts of oneself. It's about celebrating the symphony of feelings, experiences, and perspectives that make us who we are.

G: *Grace*

Grace is kindness toward oneself. It's the gentle whisper that says, "It's okay" during times of distress. By extending grace to ourselves, we offer a safe space for our vulnerabilities and imperfections. In this nurturing environment, self-love thrives, and we begin to understand that mistakes and setbacks don't define us; our resilience and spirit do.

S: *Surrender*

Surrender is not about giving up but about letting go. It's about releasing the burdens of expectations, fears, and past regrets. By surrendering, we unshackle ourselves from the constraints of self-doubt and judgment. We allow ourselves to live in the present, to breathe, and to simply be.

Being a fervent hugger myself, I've always seen hugs as an essential part of my identity. The global pandemic and its mandate for social distancing tested this intrinsic part of me. The absence of these warm embraces during interactions, both new and familiar, felt alien, making even the most straightforward greeting an awkward dance. But as much as I value hugging others, I've come to recognize the importance of "hugging" oneself.

This metaphorical H.U.G.S approach isn't just about self-soothing during tough times but about consistently nurturing our inner selves. It's an invitation to journey inward. When we envelop ourselves in this embrace of empathy, we're not just healing past wounds; we're fortifying our spirit for the challenges and joys that life has in store.

Let's dig a little deeper, starting with honesty.

HONESTY: *The Beacon of True Self*

Honesty is often regarded as a virtue in relation to others. However, its most profound impact can be seen when applied internally to oneself. Honesty with oneself is akin to holding up a mirror, free of distortions or filters, reflecting our truest selves back to us.

So, what does this self-reflection reveal?

Showing Up: When you take a close look at yourself, you may realize that the persona you've been portraying isn't the full picture of who you truly are. Have you been wearing a mask, adopting what you believe are socially acceptable attitudes and behaviors, or perhaps holding back your true feelings and beliefs to fit in or avoid conflict? Now's the time to ask yourself if you're genuinely being you.

Thinking Patterns: Our thoughts lay the foundation for our reality. Recognizing our habitual thought patterns can shed light on why we react or behave in certain ways. Do you find yourself regularly veering toward negativity, or perhaps you're overly optimistic to the point of being invisible?

Feelings: "I'm fine." How many times have we uttered these words without truly meaning them? There's no shame in admitting when we're not okay. Whether it's joy, sadness, frustration, or contentment, recognizing and validating our emotions is crucial. This emotional honesty paves the way for healing and growth.

Actions and Inactions: Both what we do and what we refrain from doing shape our realities. By acknowledging our choices and understanding the reasons behind them, we reclaim our power. We begin to see that every choice, no matter how insignificant it seems, steers the course of our lives.

Recognizing the scarcity mindset, characterized by self-doubt, shame, or feelings of inadequacy, is pivotal. When we're mired in this way of thinking, it's challenging to embrace abundance in all forms—love, success, and happiness. But by shining the light of honesty on these limiting beliefs, we can begin to break free.

Acknowledging our thoughts and feelings doesn't mean we're conceding to them. On the contrary, this awareness empowers us to challenge and change them. It's about understanding that while our reasons for feeling or behaving a certain way may be valid, they aren't always beneficial or constructive.

Honesty of self is an invitation to grow from a place of love and understanding. It's about realizing that we hold the power to reshape our narratives. With honesty as our guide, we can navigate the winding paths of life with clarity, purpose, and a genuine sense of self.

UNITY: Coming Home to Yourself

Unity isn't just about collective togetherness; it's also a deeply personal journey of alignment. At its core, unity is about becoming whole, integrating all parts of ourselves, even those we often hide or run away from.

Inner Divisions: Often, the biggest rifts we experience aren't with the world around us but within ourselves. These divides manifest when our actions aren't aligned with our core values or when our words don't echo our true feelings. Every time we silence our inner voice for external validation, we widen the chasm between who we are and who we present to the world.

The Dilemma of People Pleasing: As we have previously discussed, people pleasing can often seem like a noble endeavor. We might believe that by putting others' needs and feelings before our own, we're being kind and considerate. But the truth is, when we continually neglect our own feelings and desires to accommodate others, we aren't just doing a disservice to ourselves but also to those around us. Authentic relationships are built on genuine interactions, not on pretenses. By presenting a facade, we deny others the chance to know and love our true selves.

The Lie of Incompleteness: Society often reinforces the belief that we're perpetually lacking. We're taught that there's always something more to be had, someone else to become. But the reality is, we're already whole. Everything we need, every piece of ourselves we think we're missing, is already within us, waiting to be acknowledged.

Embracing Unity: Unity demands honesty. It requires us to embrace both our strengths and weaknesses, our successes and our failures. It's about accepting that we are multifaceted beings, each facet as essential as the other. This acceptance isn't a passive act but a dynamic process of self-discovery and self-love.

In this pursuit of unity, we're not seeking to erase or negate any part of ourselves but to understand and integrate them. This holistic view doesn't just allow for self-acceptance but celebrates it. It's a return to our most primal state of being, an invitation to come home to ourselves.

By achieving unity within, we set the stage for genuine connections outside. We open ourselves up to authentic relationships, experiences, and, most importantly, an honest life, free from the constraints of pretense.

GRACE: *Embracing Yourself With Kindness*

When we talk about grace, we often imagine it as a divine virtue or a favor bestowed upon someone. But what about self-grace? This form of grace is essential yet often overlooked. It's about treating ourselves with the same level of kindness and understanding that we often extend to others.

Self-Judgment: One of the most significant obstacles we face in our journey toward self-acceptance is our own self-judgment. We scrutinize ourselves, holding ourselves to sometimes impossible standards, often stemming from societal expectations or past experiences. While we may readily forgive others, we are stringent and harsh when it comes to our own mistakes or perceived inadequacies.

The Imposter Syndrome: Many of us, irrespective of our achievements and capabilities, suffer from the impostor syndrome. As touched on before, it's that gnawing feeling that we're not as competent as others perceive us to be, that we've only gotten where we are by luck or by deceiving others. This self-doubt, if unchecked, can cripple our potential and rob us of opportunities.

The Gift of Grace: To bestow grace upon oneself is to acknowledge our humanity. It's about understanding that, like everyone else, we're on a journey with its highs and lows, triumphs and setbacks. Granting ourselves grace is an act of self-love. It's giving ourselves permission to be imperfect, to learn, and to grow at our own pace.

You Matter: It's a simple truth, yet one we often forget. Every individual's journey, experiences, and emotions are valid. Just because someone else's challenges might seem "bigger" or "more important" doesn't diminish our own. There isn't a finite reservoir of significance or relevance. Every person's story, including yours, holds intrinsic value.

The Infinite Pie of Worth: Imagine if our worth were like a pie. Just because someone takes a slice doesn't mean there's less for everyone else. In reality, our worth and significance aren't limited resources. There's plenty to go around, and acknowledging someone else's worth doesn't diminish ours. There's no cap on success, love, or mattering.

Embracing grace is more than just an act; it's a mindset. It's about moving forward with compassion, not just for the world but for ourselves. As we navigate life, let's remember to grant ourselves the same grace we so readily offer to others. Because at the end of the day, we're all works in progress, deserving of love, understanding, and, yes, grace.

SURRENDER: *Embracing the Power of Letting Go*

The word "surrender" often brings with it a negative connotation—that of defeat or giving up. But in the context of personal growth and emotional healing, surrender is about yielding to the power of the present moment, accepting what is, and releasing the need to control every aspect of our lives. It's about acknowledging our vulnerability and, in doing so, finding our strength.

Facing Our Emotions: To truly heal, we need to face our emotions head-on. Often, we're told to "stay strong" or "move on" when we're going through challenging times. While the intention behind these words might be well-meaning, they can inadvertently lead to emotional suppression. By not acknowledging and processing our feelings, we're merely postponing the inevitable confrontation with them.

Going in to Let Go: Surrender requires a deep, inward journey. It's about diving into our psyche, confronting the shadows, and then bringing them to light. It's not about brushing our feelings under the carpet but rather sitting with them, understanding them, and then releasing them. This process might be uncomfortable and even painful, but it's a necessary step toward genuine healing.

The Illusion of Control: We often hold onto things because we believe we can control or change them. This includes our emotions, especially the painful ones. But emotions aren't meant to be controlled; they're meant to be felt. When we try to regulate how we feel, we're not only denying our authentic experience but also expending energy on a futile endeavor. True power comes from accepting our lack of control over certain aspects of life.

The Mind-Heart Connection: While the mind is a powerful tool that can help us understand and process our experiences, healing isn't just a cognitive endeavor. True healing involves both the mind and the heart. Emotional wounds can't be mended by thought alone; they require the salve of felt experience. Cognitive coping is a start, but to experience profound transformation, we need to immerse ourselves in the full spectrum of our emotions.

Solving the Right Problem: Sometimes, we get so fixated on a particular issue or emotion that we fail to see the underlying cause. By constantly addressing surface problems, we might feel temporary relief, but the root issue remains unresolved. True surrender is about recognizing and addressing the core of our emotional distress.

Surrender, in its essence, is an act of bravery. It's about opening ourselves up, being vulnerable, and trusting in the process of life. When we surrender, we're not giving up; we're giving in to the flow of life, understanding that sometimes, healing requires us to let go of our preconceived notions and embrace the journey, with all its twists and turns.

The Mind:
An Ally or Adversary in Personal Growth?

Our minds, often considered the pinnacles of human evolution, hold an immense capacity for reasoning, learning, and problem-solving. But within the vast cognitive machinery lies a counterintuitive tendency—our minds may sometimes act as barriers to our own growth and transformation. The intricacies of the brain's mechanisms, which were largely designed to protect us, can sometimes keep us from absorbing new insights that could propel our personal evolution.

The Mind's Defensive Mechanisms

To better navigate the journey of self-growth, we need to be acutely aware of the mind's three typical defensive reactions:

Conceptualization: Conceptualization is our mind's way of placating us into believing that we "get" something without truly internalizing its depth. It's the superficial nodding in agreement, the "been there, done that" attitude. It's as if the mind says, "Oh, this idea? We know it."

Ever found yourself in a seminar or reading a transformative book, nodding along in agreement but then failing to enact the insights you agreed with in your daily life? That's the first sign of your brain's passive acceptance. This means recognizing the truth but failing to put it into action. It's almost like appreciating the beauty of a tool but never actually using it to build anything.

But true understanding involves deeply integrating knowledge into our lives. It's not enough to just "know" conceptually; we need to embody it and live it. Recognizing this difference is vital. Every time we find ourselves nodding in acknowledgment, it's beneficial to ask, "Am I living this truth, or do I just recognize it?"

Manipulation: Here, the mind's cunning comes into play. When presented with a new idea or perspective, our brains can twist it, molding it to fit within our pre-existing frameworks. It's a way of pacifying the discomfort that comes with confronting an idea that might challenge our deeply held beliefs. We reshape the idea until it aligns with what we already "know," thus neutralizing any threat to our mental status quo. It's comfortable to hear what we want to hear and to interpret information in a way that reinforces our existing beliefs. But real growth demands we recognize this habit and challenge it. Only then can we truly understand others and, in doing so, broaden our own horizons.

However, in doing this, we often miss out on the transformative power of the original insight.

Rejection: When all else fails, when the mind can neither fit a new idea into its existing schemas through conceptualization or manipulation, it employs the most direct defense: outright rejection. Our brain, in its quest for cognitive ease, often outright rejects ideas that don't immediately fit into its understanding. It's the brain's last-resort firewall, dismissing the new insight as irrelevant, wrong, or nonsensical. This might manifest as skepticism, mockery, or plain indifference. But each time we dismiss an unfamiliar perspective, we lose an opportunity to learn and grow.

Beyond the Mind's Limitations

To truly evolve, we need to go beyond these automatic mechanisms. It involves a degree of mental humility, accepting that, sometimes, our minds might be our own biggest hurdles. A commitment to self-growth means being vigilant of these tendencies and challenging them. It's about making the mind an ally, not letting it become an unconscious adversary.

Embracing transformation often requires us to relinquish some of the strongholds our minds have over our perceptions. It's about questioning, reevaluating, and, sometimes, unlearning. Because transformation doesn't just involve adding new layers of knowledge on top of old ones; it often requires tearing down outdated structures to make room for the new.

The Heart-Mind Connection: Embracing Emotions as Teachers

Often, the discourse on personal growth revolves around the concept of an "open mind." Seminars, self-help books, and motivational speakers emphasize the importance of freeing our minds from prejudices and preconceived notions to truly learn. And while this is undoubtedly a critical step, it's only half the equation. An open mind without an open heart is like a ship with sails but no wind.

The Open Mind Fallacy

An open mind is often misconstrued as a mere intellectual acceptance of new ideas. But in reality, true openness is more profound. It's about accepting not just new ideas but new emotions, feelings, and experiences. However, the very proclamation, "I have an open mind," is often a defense mechanism, an intellectual shield against vulnerability.

Emotions as Gateways

Every emotion we feel—be it joy, sadness, anger, or excitement—offers a unique lens through which to view the world. They are raw, unfiltered, and free from the biases of our intellectual minds. By embracing these emotions, by truly feeling them, we gain insights that an open mind alone cannot provide.

For instance, it's one thing to understand the concept of loss intellectually. It's another thing entirely to truly feel the pang of grief in your heart. That emotion, though painful, offers a depth of understanding that the mind alone cannot fathom.

The Power of the Open Heart

An open heart is receptive to the myriad of feelings that life offers. It doesn't shy away from discomfort or pain, recognizing them as teachers in their own right. This acceptance allows us to grow not just in knowledge but in wisdom. It transforms learning from a mere accumulation of facts to a holistic experience.

For true learning and growth to occur, we must be prepared not just to change our minds but to change our hearts. It's about embracing the uncertainties and vulnerabilities that come with feelings. When we do this, we transcend the limitations of the intellect and tap into a deeper, more profound understanding of life.

Navigating Success With Heart

Success is not just about achieving milestones or acquiring knowledge. It's about integrating that knowledge into our lives, letting it shape our character, and using it to enrich our experiences. This requires not just an open mind but an open heart, ready to feel, learn, and grow.

In essence, detaching from the confines of certainty that our minds cling to and diving deep into the ocean of emotions with an open heart is the path to true enlightenment and personal growth. Only by merging the openness of both mind and heart can we truly embrace the full spectrum of life's teachings.

Unlearning: Dismantling Past Paradigms

Every person is a compilation of beliefs, values, and experiences, all deeply rooted in their psyche. As we journey through life, we often don't realize that the paradigms we function within might be outdated, unhelpful, or even detrimental. This chapter is dedicated to understanding the concept of unlearning—the process of shedding those outdated beliefs to make room for new, empowering truths.

Old Paradigms vs. New Perspectives: As I have mentioned throughout our journey together, many of our core beliefs are imprinted in us from a young age, stemming from our upbringing, societal influences, and personal experiences. However, as we evolve, so should our beliefs. Holding onto old paradigms might be comfortable, but it can hinder our growth. The first step in the unlearning process is recognizing these outdated patterns and being willing to view the world through a fresh lens.

Active vs. Passive Consumption: In our pursuit of knowledge, we often oscillate between two types of consumption: active and passive. Passive consumption is akin to absorbing information without critical thought—like binge-watching a series or mindlessly scrolling through a feed. Active consumption, on the other hand, involves engaging with the material, questioning it, and integrating it into our belief system. For effective unlearning, we need to lean more into active consumption. This involves challenging what we read or hear and determining its applicability to our current life.

Assumptions of Unlearning

Incomplete Knowledge: Accepting that our understanding of a subject might be incomplete is humbling. This doesn't mean that what we know is wrong but that there could be more to it, different perspectives we haven't considered, or new advancements that have added layers to the topic.

Unlearning as a Continuous Journey: Unlearning is not a one-time event but a continuous journey. As we grow and evolve, so will our perspectives. We should be prepared to shed beliefs that no longer serve us and embrace new truths that resonate with our current selves.

Unlearning is as essential as learning. It's about not being anchored to our past but being open to the infinite possibilities of the present and future. By consciously choosing to challenge our beliefs and being open to new insights, we pave the way for personal evolution and growth.

Crafting a Life of Authenticity

Imagine a life where you're not constantly swayed by external validation, where your worth isn't determined by societal metrics, and where you love freely and unconditionally. This is the life waiting for you, a life molded not by resistance but by acceptance.

Creating such a life requires courage. The courage to face our resistances, to embrace the lessons they offer, and to let go of what no longer serves us. It's about understanding that we are not flawed beings in need of fixing but whole individuals capable of profound love, growth, and transformation.

The journey from resistance to love is not just about breaking barriers but also about understanding and embracing the lessons hidden within them. As we navigate this journey, we not only discover the depths of our capacity to love but also the boundless potential that resides within us. Through learning and unlearning, we pave the path toward a life of genuine fulfillment and authentic love.

The Unlearnings Required for Authentic Living

To live an authentic life, it's not just about acquiring new knowledge and insights but also about letting go of outdated, limiting beliefs and behaviors. Here are some of the crucial unlearnings that we have covered in our time together so far. These unlearnings are required to pave the way to a life of authenticity, fulfillment, and happiness.

1. The Myth of Perfection

Unlearn: The belief that perfection is attainable and necessary.

Why: Chasing perfection can lead to chronic dissatisfaction. Our imperfections make us unique, relatable, and human. Embracing imperfection can lead to richer experiences, greater resilience, and deeper connections.

2. External Validation

Unlearn: Seeking validation from outside sources to affirm our worth.

Why: External validation is fleeting and unreliable. Our self-worth should be rooted in self-awareness, self-acceptance, and our intrinsic values rather than external accolades or approval.

3. Fear of Failure

Unlearn: Viewing failure as the end rather than a step in the journey.

Why: Failures are valuable learning experiences. They provide insights, build resilience, and often lead us to better paths.

4. Fixed Mindset

Unlearn: The belief that our abilities are static and unchangeable.

Why: A growth mindset, where we view challenges as opportunities to grow and evolve, enables us to adapt, learn, and thrive in changing circumstances.

5. Unhealthy Comparisons

Unlearn: Measuring our worth based on others' achievements or lifestyles.

Why: Everyone's journey is unique. Comparing ourselves to others can diminish our own accomplishments and hinder our personal growth.

6. Immediate Gratification

Unlearn: The need for instant rewards and outcomes.

Why: Good things often take time. Patience, persistence, and long-term vision are keys to sustainable success and happiness.

7. Limiting Beliefs

Unlearn: Any beliefs that restrict our potential or dictate what we "should" or "shouldn't" be.

Why: These beliefs can keep us trapped in cycles of doubt and stagnation. Recognizing and challenging them frees us to pursue our true passions and potential.

8. Reliance on Comfort Zones

Unlearn: Avoiding discomfort or unfamiliar situations.

Why: Growth often requires stepping outside of what's familiar. Embracing discomfort can lead to new opportunities and personal evolution.

9. Conditional Happiness

Unlearn: The idea that happiness will come when certain conditions are met (e.g., "I'll be happy when I get that job/promotion/partner").

Why: True happiness is an inside job. It comes from gratitude, present-moment awareness, and finding joy in the journey itself.

10. Sacrificing Self-Care

Unlearn: Placing others' needs consistently before our own.

Why: Self-care is not selfish. It's essential for our well-being and ensures we can be there for others in a more meaningful way.

In essence, the best life living requires a delicate balance of learning and unlearning. By shedding the beliefs and behaviors that no longer serve us, we create space for new growth, deeper connections, and a life that aligns with our truest selves.

A Few Of My Personal Unlearnings

Perfection Is Overrated: One of the most profound realizations I had was understanding that aiming for perfection doesn't necessarily lead to happiness. In fact, it often left me feeling unfulfilled and frustrated as I constantly compared myself to an unrealistic standard. I had to unlearn the idea that perfection equated to success and replace it with the understanding that it's okay to be a work in progress.

Busyness Is Not a Badge of Honor: I used to pack my calendar to the brim, thinking that being busy was a sign of importance. It took a moment of exhaustion and overwhelm to understand that being constantly busy wasn't making me productive; it was making me miserable. I had to unlearn the need to always be "on" and instead "in."

Saying "No" Is Okay: I used to say "yes" to everything, mistaking this habit for kindness. The reality was that I was often overcommitting, leading to burnout and resentment. I had to unlearn the idea that saying "no" was a sign of rudeness and reframe it as a necessary act of self-care.

Seeking External Validation Ruined My Life: The desire for approval had me chasing accolades, likes on social media, and compliments from others. I had to unlearn the need for external validation and cultivate a sense of self-worth from within. I've come to understand that my value is inherent and not tied to the fleeting opinions of others.

Avoiding Vulnerability Disconnected Me From Not Only Others but Myself: I used to equate vulnerability with weakness. Keeping my guard up was a protective mechanism to avoid getting hurt. But in doing so, I missed out on genuine connections and intimacy. I unlearned the belief that vulnerability is a liability and embraced it as a strength, paving the way for deeper relationships and self-understanding.

Control Is an Illusion: I once believed that I could micromanage every aspect of my life to avoid uncertainty and unpredictability. This unlearning was a humbling experience. Embracing the unknown and releasing the need to control every outcome has allowed me to experience life with more freedom and spontaneity.

Unlearning these deeply ingrained beliefs and habits hasn't been easy. It's a continuous journey of self-reflection and growth. However, with each unlearning, I've discovered a deeper sense of self-awareness, authenticity, and a more profound appreciation for the ebb and flow of life.

Throughout my life, the process of unlearning has been as crucial as learning, often revealing itself in unexpected ways through my experiences. Allow me to share some personal anecdotes, hoping they might resonate with you or spark insight into the unlearnings that can pave your path to growth and liberation.

Boundaries, Lies, and the Cupcake Incident

Back in the day, I used to be the ultimate people pleaser, constantly dancing to the tunes of others, hoping that they'd reciprocate with approval. It's almost amusing how far I would go to avoid confrontations or disappointments. For many years, I operated under the guise of thinking that saying "yes" to everything would cement my place in the good books of others. But eventually, I came to a startling realization: I was compromising my own well-being in the process.

It took some time, but I learned to prioritize myself. The first step was recognizing and setting up boundaries. I devised a set of rules—first, no more lying or pretending. If something didn't resonate with me, I would be upfront about it. The second rule was to ensure that whatever I committed to, I did with a good attitude. And lastly, if something didn't align with my personal values or it was an outright no.

The implementation of these rules was a challenge, especially when I had conditioned myself to be agreeable all the time. But here's where the "cupcake story" becomes significant.

One day, a friend asked me to bake cupcakes for her daughter's school event. Now, anyone who knows me is aware of how much I dislike baking. It stresses me out! But in my old "people-pleasing" days, I would have begrudgingly agreed, spending hours cursing the oven and then resenting my friend for even asking. But not this time. I paused, took a breath, and said, "I love you, and I want to help, but baking isn't my strong suit. Maybe I can assist in another way?"

To my surprise, she laughed and replied, "I don't like baking either!" It was a revelation. First, I thought all good moms baked. Second, she wasn't mad. Third, I wasn't mad that I took on yet another obligation that I didn't want to do and then, to make it worse, lie about being "happy" to do it. That day, the "cupcake incident" became my gold standard for how I approached requests. It taught me that it was okay to say no, that honesty was appreciated, and more often than not, it wouldn't spell the end of relationships.

But there's a deeper lesson in all of this … when we constantly agree to things out of obligation, not only are we lying to ourselves and others, but we are also robbing them of opportunities to handle disappointment or to find alternative solutions. Every time we step in, eager to be the savior, we deny them the chance to face life's challenges, to grow, and to find their own way.

In a world where authenticity is often masked by pretense, it's revolutionary to be genuine, to have boundaries, and to let others have their own experiences. And through it all, I've learned that people don't need a version of you shaped by their expectations; they need the real you.

I'm Fine

Growing up, our household dynamics were as unique as they come. My mother, a single beacon of strength, carried the weight of the world on her shoulders. Raising three children by herself wasn't just a test of resilience; it was a daily challenge that she faced with an admirable combination of grit and grace.

My younger brother's battle with spinal meningitis, diagnosed when he was just a toddler, added another layer of complexity to our already complicated lives. His condition necessitated constant attention, a series of medical procedures, and countless sleepless nights. My mother, in her indomitable spirit, always rose to the challenge, ensuring that he received the best care possible.

Amidst the chaos, my elder sister matured rapidly, assuming responsibilities far beyond her years. From helping with household chores to assisting in looking after our brother, she inadvertently slipped into the role of a co-guardian. Her youthful years were consumed by responsibilities, and the joys of childhood became fleeting moments, overshadowed by our family's overarching challenges.

Then there was me. Observing the intricacies of our family's struggles, I learned early on to be self-sufficient. Perhaps it was my coping mechanism, or perhaps it was a bid to alleviate my mother's burdens, but I became adept at suppressing my feelings and emotions. No matter what challenges I faced personally, I chose to put on a "brave" front, convincing myself and those around me that everything was "fine." I became the invisible pillar, providing silent support but never making my presence loudly known. Over time, this guise of perpetually being "fine" became my identity.

In my mind, everyone else's needs and concerns seemed to surpass my own. Rather than seek support or express my feelings, I decided it was better to be the uncomplicated one, the "easy child." But in doing so, I unintentionally erased a part of my identity. Amidst the whirlwind of my family's challenges, I faded into the background, effectively becoming a spectator in my own life. This self-imposed invisibility had consequences, shaping my perceptions and interactions as I grew older. The belief that I needed to be self-reliant, to never be a burden, became deeply ingrained in my psyche. It was both a strength and a silent sorrow.

Growing up with the habitual response of being "FINE" was not just a mere reflex; it was a protective shell I had constructed around myself. Every time I asserted that I was fine, it was a way of self-preservation, of minimizing my space in the universe so as not to be a bother or burden. However, as the years wore on, this seemingly innocuous word became a heavy anchor, pulling me deeper into a realm where my emotions, desires, and very essence were suppressed.

The unlearning was an arduous journey. The revelation that my proclamation of being "FINE" was, in essence, a denial of my own existence was a profound one. It wasn't merely about suppressing emotions or trivializing my experiences. Instead, it was a fundamental rejection of my own being, my worth, and my place in the world.

It took time and introspection to understand that my brother's mattering and my own were not mutually exclusive. His challenges, his journey, and his significance in our family did not diminish my own worth or the space I held in our shared universe. One person's significance does not overshadow another's. It was a revelation that mattering isn't a zero-sum game; there's ample space for everyone to coexist, each with their unique worth and essence.

My life had been haunted by an unmet need—the need to feel seen, to be acknowledged, to matter. The true transformation came when I decided to validate myself. The choice to believe that I mattered, irrespective of external circumstances or comparisons, was liberating. It was a conscious decision to reclaim my space, to affirm my existence, and to embrace every facet of my being.

Choosing to matter was not about seeking validation from others but about recognizing and honoring my intrinsic worth. It was about understanding that my existence, emotions, and experiences were valid and valuable. And in this newfound realization, I found not just acceptance but a profound sense of belonging—to myself, my family, and the world.

The Void

Growing up, the echoes of an absent father shaped my world. The hollow sound of silence where there should have been laughter, lessons, and love became a constant reminder of a void in my life. Like a jigsaw puzzle missing its final piece, I grew up feeling incomplete, always searching for validation in external accomplishments and external voices.

As a child, my heart nurtured the naive hope that if I just did more or was more—smarter, faster, funnier, prettier—maybe, just maybe, my father would notice and come back. Maybe my achievements would light up the dark path he had taken, guiding him back to me. Every award, every accolade, every praise became a beacon, a silent call out to him. But the silence from his end remained deafening.

What was even more taxing was the inner dialogue I constantly engaged in. "Maybe if I had been better, he would've stayed," was a recurring thought. It was a vicious cycle; the more I achieved, the more insatiable my hunger for approval became. I believed, deep down, that my value was inextricably tied to my achievements and to others' perceptions of me. The weight of this belief was crushing.

As I grew older, I began to recognize the toll this mindset took on my mental and emotional health. I was running a never-ending marathon, chasing after a sense of self-worth that always seemed just out of reach. And then came the epiphany … the key to my freedom wasn't outside—it was within.

One evening, while reflecting on a journal entry from my teenage years, I had a profound realization. I had been my own jailer, imprisoning myself in a cage of external validation. The power to free myself, to truly see my inherent worth, had always been in my hands.

It was transformative. The clarity that I did not need to prove my worth to anyone, not even my absent father, was liberating. I recognized that worthiness wasn't a distant shore I had to swim toward but solid ground I already stood upon. I didn't need the world to tell me I was enough; I just needed to believe it myself.

I won't say that the journey to self-acceptance was easy or instant. It took time, introspection, and conscious effort. But it was the most worthwhile journey I've ever embarked upon. Today, I am free. Not because the world says so, but because I know, deep in my bones, that I am worthy. I no longer seek permission to live my life; I embrace it wholeheartedly, cherishing every moment, every emotion, every experience—because I choose to. For myself. On purpose.

Overdoing to Underfeel

In a world that often praises the "hustle" and idolizes the "go-getters," it's no surprise that many of us have adopted an "over" mindset— overworking, over-committing, over-planning, and even overthinking. Each "over" serving as a shield, a barrier against confronting the real issues lurking beneath the surface. For me, this "over" lifestyle was my tried-and-true method of escaping feelings. But in reality, it was an emotional band-aid, a temporary fix for a more profound wound.

It started innocuously enough. If I felt anxious, I'd just work a little more. A pang of sadness? A shopping spree would surely dull the ache. Moments of doubt? Maybe if I accomplish just one more thing today, I'd feel valuable. Over time, it became a pattern. A pattern so deeply ingrained that I barely recognized it for what it was—a defense mechanism.

I over-spent and over-ran not because they made me genuinely happy or fulfilled but because they gave me a momentary escape. An escape from confronting what I was truly feeling. An escape from the vulnerable act of diving deep into my emotions, understanding their origins, and addressing them head-on.

The realization was like waking up from a long slumber. It hit me one day as I was lacing up my running shoes, not out of the joy of running, but to avoid feeling overwhelmed. Why was I running away from my feelings instead of toward understanding them?

Feelings, I've come to understand, are like messengers. They carry with them information and insight into our inner worlds. By constantly avoiding them, I was missing out on an opportunity. An opportunity to grow, to heal, and to truly understand myself.

Embarking on the journey of facing my feelings head-on wasn't easy. It meant confronting painful memories, acknowledging mistakes, and often, just sitting with the discomfort of an emotion until it passed. But with each confrontation came clarity. With each acknowledgment, a lesson learned.

Over time, the need to "overdo" started diminishing. The shopping sprees reduced, the mindless running decreased, and in their place came moments of introspection, journaling, meditation, and genuine self-care.

Life is too short to spend it in perpetual motion, trying to outrun what we feel. Emotions are an integral part of our human experience. By confronting them, by genuinely feeling them, we not only understand ourselves better but also pave the way for genuine healing and growth.

In retrospect, unlearning the habit of emotional escapism was one of the best things I've ever done. It has brought depth and richness to my life, an authenticity that no amount of overdoing could ever match. It has taught me that true strength isn't in avoiding feelings but in facing them with courage and grace.

Unbecoming to Become: The Power of Unlearning

In the ever-evolving landscape of human understanding, where the fields of personal development, neuroscience, and quantum science intermingle, a peculiar irony stands out. Sometimes, unlearning holds more transformational power than learning. As we navigate the intricacies of our lives, there's a continuous interplay between what we've absorbed over the years and what we need to let go of.

The process of unlearning is akin to shedding. It's a recognition that the cocoon that once protected us, the very same patterns and beliefs, can also restrict our wings from spreading. Our thoughts, beliefs, and perceptions, instilled over decades, often operate in the background, driving our decisions, actions, and, ultimately, our outcomes. But here's the catch: we can't overhaul what we're oblivious to.

If personal growth is a journey, then unlearning is the compass recalibration. It's not merely about forgetting but rather about conscious disassociation from habits, thoughts, and beliefs that no longer serve our higher purpose. It's recognizing that while our past experiences and learnings have sculpted us, they don't have to define our trajectory.

We've all heard the saying, "If you keep doing what you've always done, you'll keep getting what you've always got." But how often do we pause and reflect on this? To evolve, to shift our life's narrative, requires a holistic approach of introspection, reflection, and, yes, unlearning.

For instance, the belief that one's value is tied to productivity, or the idea that vulnerability signifies weakness, or even the concept that asking for help equates to incompetence—these are just a few examples of ingrained beliefs that many of us might hold. To break free and carve a new path requires us to confront these beliefs head-on, scrutinize their origin, and then decide whether they have a place in our future narrative.

In a world saturated with information, the real challenge often isn't acquiring more knowledge. Instead, it's discerning which parts of our internal programming need an update or a rewire. And while the journey of unlearning, this "unbecoming," might be fraught with challenges, the rewards—a life lived more authentically, consciously, and in alignment with our true selves—are immeasurable.

In the end, the journey toward personal mastery is less about accumulating and more about refining. As we peel back the layers of conditioning, as we challenge the status quo of our internal world, we get closer to our essence. And in that essence, in that core of authenticity, lies our true power. The power of unbecoming to become our best selves.

Unbecoming to Reveal the Authentic Self

Life often feels like an endless game of roles. From the moment we are born, society bestows upon us a multitude of labels, expectations, and responsibilities. Be a dutiful child, a model student, a devoted parent, a dedicated employee—the list is endless. We assume countless roles, fitting snugly into the boxes that society prescribes, sometimes without questioning if they align with our true essence. And in that perpetual act of conforming, there's a chance we lose sight of who we truly are, buried under layers of societal expectations and our own conditioned beliefs.

Becoming more of who we want to be invariably demands a deep dive into unbecoming everything we thought we should be. It's a journey of introspection, questioning, and eventually shedding. It's like untying knots in a tightly coiled rope, making space for it to breathe, to stretch, and to be used for its true purpose.

Unbecoming isn't about discarding or belittling past experiences or our previous selves. It's an acknowledgment that while certain traits, behaviors, or beliefs may have served us at some point, they might not align with our present aspirations or desired future. It's a conscious act of releasing weights that hold us back, be it outdated beliefs, stifling routines, or toxic relationships.

However, this process of unlearning and unbecoming is not just about elimination. It's also about revelation. Every layer we peel back, every redundant belief we challenge, brings us closer to our core, revealing our authentic selves.

The challenge? Admitting that we don't have all the answers. Recognizing that growth isn't about accumulation but often about subtraction. It requires humility to accept that maybe, just maybe, there's a different, better way. It demands courage to challenge long-held beliefs and comfort zones.

Moreover, being awake doesn't mean we have it all figured out. Being awake means recognizing our blind spots, the areas in our lives that operate on autopilot, unexamined and unquestioned. It means challenging those areas, stirring them from their slumber, and shining a light on them with the unyielding power of our consciousness.

In this intricate dance of becoming and unbecoming, there is a rhythm, a flow. As we unshackle from old paradigms, there's a liberation, a lightness. We find that as we make space by letting go of the old, the universe rushes in with new experiences, insights, and blessings that align more harmoniously with our true selves.

In the end, to evolve, to soar, and to truly live our potential, we must be willing to let go of who we thought we were to reveal and embrace the magnificent being that lies within. This is the beauty and power of unbecoming.

Forgiveness: Inspired by the Source

The Pinnacle of Acceptance: The Therapeutic Power of Forgiveness

In the vast landscape of human emotions and experiences, acceptance stands as a beacon of healing. It offers a pathway out of the maze of hurt, resentment, and anger, leading us toward a life of serenity and self-awareness. But to fully immerse oneself in acceptance, there's a final summit to conquer … forgiveness.

Unveiling Forgiveness

Many misconstrue forgiveness as a sign of weakness or as a simple act of moving on. But forgiveness, in its purest form, is a deliberate choice to release oneself from the shackles of bitterness. It's an acknowledgment of the hurt, not a denial of it, coupled with a conscious decision not to let that hurt define one's life.

The Dual Paths to Forgiveness

Forgiveness often bifurcates into two paths: forgiving oneself and forgiving others. While both are interconnected, each presents its own set of challenges.

Forgiving Oneself: This often proves to be the more challenging journey. Accepting our own imperfections and mistakes requires confronting our vulnerabilities. By extending compassion to ourselves, we pave the way for personal growth and self-understanding.

Forgiving Others: This requires us to transcend our ego, moving past the instinct to hold onto resentment. It's about seeing beyond the act of hurt and recognizing the shared human frailty.

The Journey Toward Release

The road to forgiveness is rarely linear. It's punctuated by moments of doubt, relapse into old patterns, and periods of deep introspection. However, with patience and persistence, one can navigate through the stormy waters of resentment and reach the shores of understanding. The essence lies in the realization that holding onto pain serves no purpose other than deepening our own wounds.

The Aftermath of Forgiveness

When the weight of past hurts lifts, a profound peace settles in. It's as if a heavy cloud has been lifted, revealing a clear blue sky. This serenity isn't just the absence of anger or hurt; it's a positive state of being where love, understanding, and gratitude flourish. It fosters deeper connections with others and a more harmonious relationship with oneself.

Forgiveness, as the pinnacle of acceptance, is the key to unlocking a life of true contentment. It's not merely an act but a state of being, a continuous journey of love and understanding. As we venture into the depths of our hearts and souls, let's remember that in forgiveness, we find our truest liberation and our most profound peace.

Forgiveness: The Emotional and Mental Catalyst for Growth

Forgiveness, often seen as an act of benevolence or even a moral obligation, runs far deeper than mere action. It is a catalyst, a transformative force that alters the course of our emotional and mental well-being. It serves as a bridge between the shadows of our pasts and the light of our futures, allowing us to tread with a heart unburdened by resentment.

At its core, forgiveness is about liberation. The act of forgiving doesn't merely erase memories; it changes our relationship with them. We no longer view past transgressions through a lens of bitterness or pain but through understanding and compassion. This shift doesn't mean we deny the pain or excuse the act; it means we've chosen to release its power over us.

Often, we tether our identities to our experiences, especially the painful ones. They become stories we recount, reinforcing our victimhood with every retelling. But when we truly forgive, we make a profound internal shift from a space of remembering to a space of evolving. The narrative changes. We are no longer defined by the hurt we've felt but by the strength we've gained from letting go.

Forgiveness is less about the other person and more about our own inner journey. It's a declaration that says, "I value my peace over my past." This act of grace, self-love, and acceptance creates an environment where joy, trust, and serenity flourish.

Forgiveness is perhaps the most potent form of acceptance. When we forgive, we acknowledge the imperfections of human nature, including our own. We recognize the fragility and brevity of life and the futility of clinging to past grievances. This acceptance is not a sign of weakness but a testament to our emotional depth and maturity.

Forgiveness is transformative, a beacon that illuminates our path forward. It's not just about absolving someone or seeking closure; it's about redefining our relationship with our past, present, and future. As we journey through life, let us remember that the true power of forgiveness lies not in forgetting but in transcending, not in erasing memories but in creating a space where love, growth, and healing prevail.

Forgiveness: The Key to Inner Liberation

Forgiveness is often misconceived as a gesture solely for the person being forgiven, yet in truth, its most profound gift is the liberation it offers to the one bestowing it. Before we delve into the act of forgiveness, let's first understand the broader landscape that underscores our experiences.

Cause and Effect—The Dance of Experience

The cosmos runs on the principle of cause and effect, a rhythmic balance that ensures everything happens for a reason. Recognizing this, we realize that every experience, no matter how seemingly random, plays a part in our evolution.

Self-Acceptance—The Pillar of Healing

To heal and forgive, one must commence by accepting oneself, both the brilliance and the shadows. This acceptance involves:

Creatorship: Understanding that we are the architects of our experiences and, in doing so, acknowledging our power to mold our destiny.

Inherent Worth: Embracing our intrinsic value, regardless of external validations or achievements.

Embracing Imperfection: Recognizing that our journey isn't about reaching a state of perfection but rather a continual process of growth, where even missteps hold value.

Life's Dualities: Life, with its blend of highs and lows, offers lessons that we can harness for our advancement.

Intuitive Connection: Trusting that innate inner wisdom that connects us to a broader universe, enabling us to navigate life's myriad challenges.

Active Engagement: Understanding that while we don't always need to know every step of the journey ahead, our proactive involvement can shape its course.

Wholeness in Acceptance: To fully integrate into our being, we must embrace all facets of our existence. This means even those parts we may not be proud of, for they, too, have lessons to impart.

Judgment—The Energy Drainer

When we judge, we divert our energy toward a negative frequency. This not only drains our vibrancy but keeps us entangled in the very thing we disdain. Every judgment we cast outward often reflects an internal insecurity or unaddressed wound.

The Path to Forgiveness

Understanding these nuances lays the foundation for genuine forgiveness. To forgive is to release oneself from the shackles of past traumas, judgments, and regrets. It's to acknowledge, without bitterness, the lessons each experience has offered and to move forward with a heart unburdened by resentment.

In essence, forgiveness isn't just an act; it's a state of being. A state that promotes healing, growth, and profound inner peace. As we tread this path, we don't just forgive others; we set our souls free.

The Cage of Judgment: Negative Projections and Their Consequences

Judgment, a seemingly innocuous act that we all indulge in, often hides a deeper and more damaging layer when it becomes a tool for negative projection. To project negativity through judgment is more than just an assessment of another; it becomes a reflection of our internal state and our relationship with the world.

The Illusion of Control

Often, our judgments are an unconscious effort to exert control over the uncontrollable. By placing people, situations, and life events into neatly labeled boxes, we create an illusion of order in a universe that's inherently unpredictable. Yet, this false sense of control doesn't empower us; it entraps us. We become puppeteers trying desperately to control the strings, unaware that we're the ones being controlled by our own need for dominance.

Resisting Reality

Judgment stems from a resistance to accept things as they are. In criticizing and condemning, we reject the present, hoping our judgments will morph reality into our desired shape. But life doesn't bend to our will through negativity. Instead, it mirrors back the discord we radiate, making us feel even more out of sync.

The Loss of Power

Each time we judge negatively, we relinquish a bit of our inner power. Instead of focusing on our potential and our journey, we externalize our energy, giving away our vitality to situations and people who should have no control over our emotional well-being.

Deferring Accountability

Blame is a byproduct of judgment. When things go awry, it's easy to point fingers, critiquing the world around us. But in doing so, we forsake our responsibility. We become passive observers, victims of circumstance, rather than active participants in our own narrative.

Self-Condemnation

The harshest critic often resides within. When we routinely judge others, we also set a stringent standard for ourselves. Every minor slip becomes a reason for self-derision. This perpetual state of self-condemnation stifles growth and prevents self-compassion.

Stifling Growth

A judgmental mindset is static. It doesn't foster growth, evolution, or change. It solidifies our beliefs, making us resistant to new perspectives and fresh insights. By pre-judging, we close the doors to learning and enlightenment.

Suppressing Our Genius

Each one of us has a unique gift, a genius that's waiting to be explored. But, ensnared in the web of negative judgments, we become too focused on the external world and its perceived flaws. This distraction prevents us from delving deep within and recognizing our true potential.

While judgment might appear as a shield, protecting us from the uncertainties of the world, it's often a cage. Breaking free from this cage requires self-awareness, understanding, a willingness to embrace life with all its imperfections, acceptance, and forgiveness. Only then can we truly experience the boundless possibilities of our existence.

Freedom From Judgment: The Path to Forgiveness

Judgment acts as a filter through which we perceive our reality, often distorting the truth in favor of our biases and insecurities. At its root, judgment stems from an inability to accept and forgive. By understanding the origins and the repercussions of our judgments, we can start our journey toward inner peace.

The Heart of Judgment: Lack of Forgiveness

At the center of our judgments lies an unwillingness or inability to forgive. Whether it's a slight from a stranger or a deep hurt from a loved one, holding onto these grievances keeps us in chains. But consider this: If our inner landscape was free of resentments and past hurts, would we be so quick to judge?

Questions to Ponder:

Reluctance to Forgive: Which past incidents or individuals still haunt your thoughts? Recognizing these instances is the first step toward healing.

Withholding Love: Whom have you closed your heart to? Sometimes, this may even be oneself.

Wanting Vengeance: Are there situations where you feel a desire for someone to "pay" for their actions?

Beliefs About Forgiveness: What narratives have you built around forgiveness? Some might see it as a sign of weakness, while others may believe it leaves them vulnerable.

The Illusions Surrounding Forgiveness

Many misconceptions surround the act of forgiving:

Getting off the Hook: Forgiveness doesn't equate to exoneration. It doesn't mean that the wrongs are forgotten or that they become acceptable. Instead, it means that we choose to free ourselves from the weight of resentment.

Submissiveness: Forgiveness is a sign of strength, not weakness. It takes immense courage to let go of past hurts and look forward with hope.

Opening Up to Mistreatment: By forgiving, you're not permitting repeated offenses. Boundaries can be set and self-respect maintained, even in a state of forgiveness.

Embracing Forgiveness

True forgiveness is a journey inward. It's about healing the wounds within us more than mending external relationships. It's a conscious choice to let go of the burdens of the past and to move forward unburdened. When we forgive, we're not doing it for the other person; we're doing it for ourselves to experience the peace and freedom that follows.

To step out of judgment is to embrace forgiveness wholeheartedly. It's to recognize the humanity in others and in ourselves. It's to understand that we're all products of our experiences, doing the best we can with the knowledge and tools we have. When we approach life with this compassion, judgment loses its grip, and we find ourselves in a state of grace.

The Ripple Effect of Forgiveness

True forgiveness does not exist in isolation. When we free ourselves from the shackles of resentment and hurt, we radiate a powerful, healing energy. This energy affects everyone around us, creating a ripple effect. The person you forgive, sensing this shift, may feel a subconscious nudge toward self-reflection and healing. It's a profound cycle where healing begets more healing, creating a world rooted in understanding and compassion.

Life will always be filled with challenges, misunderstandings, and hurts. But in every painful experience lies an opportunity—an opportunity to choose forgiveness and, in doing so, choose freedom, healing, and growth. By turning our gaze inward and embarking on this transformative journey of self-forgiveness, we open doors to unparalleled peace and empowerment.

True forgiveness is indeed a profound expression of love. It is not merely an action or a decision; it is a reflection of the deep love we hold within our hearts. The act of forgiveness itself is not the real miracle. The real miracle lies in the source that inspires us to forgive.

Love is the most powerful force in the universe, and it has the capacity to heal wounds, mend relationships, and transform lives. When we love deeply, we open ourselves to the possibility of forgiveness. It is love that softens our hearts, allowing us to let go of anger, resentment, and judgment.

True Forgiveness: The Love-Inspired Miracle

Forgiveness is often seen as an act of graciousness, a virtue, and a sign of emotional maturity. When someone forgives, it's hailed as a gesture of goodwill. But diving deeper into the essence of forgiveness, we find that it is not the act itself but the inspiration behind it that stands out. That very inspiration is rooted in love.

The Underlying Force of Love

At the core of every genuine act of forgiveness lies the profound force of love. It's love that softens our hearts, making space for understanding. It's love that prompts us to look beyond the hurt and see the human behind the act. It's love that allows us to shed the weight of resentment and embrace the lightness of understanding.

The Distinction Between the Act and the Inspiration

Forgiving someone can sometimes be an act of self-preservation, a way to find personal peace, or even a societal expectation. But true forgiveness, the one that heals both the forgiver and the forgiven, emerges genuinely from a place of love. This distinction is vital.

While the act serves as a mechanism to move forward, the love-inspired inspiration serves as the soul's deep yearning for harmony.

Love's Inherent Nature

Love, by its very nature, is all-encompassing. It sees the flaws and the mistakes and yet chooses to embrace the individual. This characteristic of love makes it the perfect foundation for true forgiveness. When forgiveness is motivated by love, it transcends the superficial layers of the act and reaches the depths of true understanding and compassion.

The Real Miracle

While forgiveness is a powerful act, the real miracle lies in the capacity of love to inspire it. It's in those silent moments where love whispers to the heart, urging it to let go of the pain, to understand, to heal, and to move forward. The miracle is in the transformation love ignites within, turning wounds into wisdom.

In the dance of life, where mistakes and misunderstandings are inevitable, love acts as the guiding light. It reminds us that every hurt is an opportunity to understand deeper, to love fiercer, and to forgive genuinely. For in the grand tapestry of human experiences, while forgiveness is a significant thread, it's the love that weaves it all together. It's love that stands as the true miracle, inspiring acts of forgiveness that heal and transform.

Acceptance—The Gift of Love

Acceptance is a powerful yet subtle force. It's a foundational block for personal growth, self-awareness, and inner peace. Importantly, accepting something doesn't necessarily mean you condone or approve of it. Acceptance simply means acknowledging what is without trying to change, resist, or judge it.

Guilt, on the other hand, is a powerful emotion that often arises from non-acceptance. It's a result of comparing our actions, thoughts, or feelings against an internal moral compass and finding them wanting. However, guilt does nothing but deny truth and impede the flow of love. Holding onto guilt is essentially denying oneself the opportunity for growth and healing. Instead, by understanding and acknowledging our inherent worth, both past and present, we pave the way for genuine self-love.

Every decision we've made, every step we've taken, has been informed by our level of self-love and self-understanding at that particular moment. It's essential to remember that every action was based on the best information and emotional resources we had at that time.

As we grow and evolve, our perspectives change. With this growth comes a deeper understanding of our past actions, and this newfound awareness offers an unparalleled opportunity for healing. It's a chance to revisit old wounds and to reassess and heal them with the wisdom we've garnered. This process is essential not just for personal evolution but for heart-centered living.

Stepping into self-compassion is transformative. It's about transcending the urge to judge oneself based on societal standards or past actions. It's about understanding that every individual's journey is unique, filled with its highs and lows, its mistakes and learnings. The more we embrace self-compassion, the closer we move to our true selves—awakened, authentic, and unburdened.

Acceptance is a profound act of love—for oneself and for others. By fully accepting ourselves, flaws and all, we gift ourselves the freedom to grow, to heal, and to live authentically. It's a journey away from the shadows of guilt and judgment and into the warm, nurturing embrace of love and compassion.

In the ebb and flow of life's relationships, the one with my father was marked by profound silence. Our interactions were limited to occasions draped in somber black—funerals. Our exchanges were brief, non-existent conversations, echoing the void between us. I often wondered if, like me, he, too, was imprisoned by shame. A shame that distanced a father from his daughter, building walls thicker than words.

2007 brought with it a permanent silence. My father passed away just a day shy of my 35th birthday. But rather than wallowing in the profound weight of grief and years of unresolved emotions, I gave myself a gift—the gift of letting go. Letting go of the narrative that had dictated my life's worth. The story that whispered that I was only worthy if my father actively chose to be part of my life.

I released the self-imposed shackles of who I thought I should be, choosing instead to embrace my true self. Without seeking validation. Without striving for perfection. Just unapologetically, authentically me.

As I navigated this new chapter, love became my compass. It guided me toward forgiveness. A deep, compassionate forgiveness for myself, for binding my self-worth to my father's actions. Realizing that it wasn't him who abandoned me, but I who abandoned myself in the labyrinth of misconstrued perceptions. And forgiveness for him, not out of obligation but from a place of genuine love for the person I've grown into.

Which narrative have you allowed to define your life? What story, steeped in past pains and misconceptions, holds you back? Remember, you have the power to choose. To let go. To redefine your story and step into your most authentic self. The essence of who you truly are is waiting to be discovered if you can unchain your truths from misconceived stories. Embrace acceptance, let go of those narratives, and pave the way for a future you design. Your freedom, your truest self, lies on the other side of that choice.

PILLAR 3

The Gift of Freedom—Self- Awakening

When we embark on a journey of introspection, often it is our darkest moments, our most painful memories, that provide the most profound opportunities for growth and awakening. I've often believed that our vulnerabilities, when acknowledged and addressed, can pave the way to our strongest transformations. With your indulgence, I'd like to share a personal one from my past, a shaming story that had once cast a long shadow over my sense of self. But rather than letting it tether me to pain, I chose to see it as a beacon, guiding me toward a deeper understanding of myself and the world around me.

As we delve into this final segment of the book, I hope that my story will serve as an illustration of the awakening potential that resides within each of our struggles. It's not always easy to face our pasts, to scrutinize the moments that brought us low. But there's an intrinsic power in doing so, a power that can propel us forward with newfound wisdom and resilience.

In sharing this tale, my hope is to shed light on the transformative potential of introspection and self-compassion. By recognizing the lessons inherent in our experiences, no matter how painful, we open ourselves up to growth, healing, and a deeper connection to our authentic selves.

So, as we transition into this last section, I invite you to join me on this exploration to witness the metamorphosis that can occur when we allow ourselves to truly see, feel, and learn from our past. Through my story, I hope to illuminate the path for others, showcasing the profound impact of understanding, forgiveness, and the pursuit of enlightenment.

Growing up in Hudson, IA, was like living inside a snow globe—small, encapsulated, and seemingly untouched by the rapid pace of the world outside. The town, with its close-knit community and warm-hearted locals, always held a special charm for me. Our humble abode in the mini-mall apartments, which might seem modest to many, was a sanctuary filled with love, laughter, and countless memories.

Our proximity to the kindergarten building was one of the apartment's many perks. I recall it being a clustering of old, red circular buildings, each apartment in the shape of a pie. The kindergarten building was just a stone's throw away from the long, all-inclusive 1–12 grade building.

One of my most vivid memories from those kindergarten days was a sunny morning laden with the promise of joy. I was dressed in one of my favorite outfits—a dress that I believed made me look like a princess. In my hands was a box of cupcakes. I don't quite recall the occasion—perhaps it was someone's birthday—but I remember the flutter in my heart, the excitement bubbling up as I thought of my classmates' reactions.

As I walked, I imagined their faces lighting up, the oohs and aahs, and the shared laughter.

Setting the cupcakes aside, I joined the morning ritual— the "circle." But as I sat cross-legged, a chilling realization washed over me. I had forgotten to wear underwear beneath my dress. The weight of shame pinned me to the ground. Why couldn't I get something as simple as dressing right? Why was I weird? Who could possibly like me now? In the midst of my young euphoria, had I become irresponsible?

When filtered through the lens of adulthood, it's simple. The cupcakes, their promise of joy, had eclipsed everything else. But the shame, instead of being a fleeting embarrassment, imprinted a false mantra in my mind—excitement is a distraction; it leads to irresponsibility.

This false doctrine dominated my life, convincing me that life wasn't a journey of joy but a serious pursuit. College life echoed this sentiment. I was the sober student, the epitome of diligence until a single wine cooler led me to confess love to strangers. The subsequent embarrassment only fortified my self-imposed boundaries. Every foray into spontaneity seemed to be met with dire consequences, be it being thrown in a dryer or left on the highway.

The journey of self-acceptance is not just personal; it's generational. As I embrace my true essence, I want to liberate my children from these shackles, too. I want to teach them that they don't need consequences to feel or external validation to be.

In a world that often dictates conformity, the bravest act is to just BE.

The shackles of resentment are self-imposed, but so is the power of release. Embark on a journey where forgiveness is the key and the doors opened lead to a realm of boundless freedom and love.

The soul's journey through life is one of exploration, discovery, and transformation. It starts with self-awareness, where we unravel the layers of our being, understanding our patterns, desires, and the myriad facets that make us unique. Then, we navigate through self-acceptance, learning to embrace every part of ourselves with love and compassion and recognizing our inherent worth. As we traverse these realms, we are being set up for the most profound chapter of our journey—self-awakening.

Awakening the self is not a linear journey that follows a clear set of steps or a predetermined map. Instead, it's a deeply personal odyssey, one that unfolds uniquely for every individual, drawing from the well-springs of inner consciousness. This voyage spans three vast terrains of the mind: subconsciousness, mindfulness, and super-consciousness.

Subconsciousness: Often referred to as the undercurrent of our minds, the subconscious stores past experiences, beliefs, and memories. It's the backdrop against which our life unfolds, silently influencing our behaviors, reactions, and patterns. Many of our deep-rooted beliefs and automatic reactions stem from this realm. While it operates below our active awareness, its impact is profound, often guiding our actions and decisions in ways we don't consciously recognize.

Mindfulness: As we begin to awaken, we step into the realm of mindfulness. Here, we become keen observers of our own thoughts, emotions, and actions. No longer are we merely reacting to life's events; instead, we're actively engaging with them, assessing our responses, and choosing our next steps with deliberation. Mindfulness is the bridge between the subconscious and the super-conscious. It's where we begin to question, reflect, and seek deeper understanding, breaking free from the automatic patterns set by our subconscious.

Super-consciousness: Venturing beyond mindfulness, we arrive at the realm of super-consciousness. This is the pinnacle of self-awareness, where we tap into a higher wisdom, transcending the limitations of our individual experiences and egos. It's a state of heightened intuition, profound insight, and universal connection. Here, the self aligns with something much larger, understanding life from a vantage point that sees the interconnectedness of all things.

These realms are not distinct territories we cross one after the other. They overlap and intertwine, and sometimes, we might find ourselves oscillating between them. But the path to awakening is not about reaching a destination; it's about expanding the horizons of our understanding.

In the quest for self-awakening, it's vital to remember that *our mind can only grasp what aligns with its current capacity.* Each phase of awakening prepares the mind, broadening its capacity to embrace the next. But no book, guru, or external guide can lead us to awakening. They might point the way, but the journey is ours to undertake. The path to awakening is a personal odyssey, and the mind must find its own way, drawing from its innate wisdom and the experiences that have shaped it.

The journey of personal growth often navigates through a labyrinth of emotions, experiences, and revelations. But at its core, the quest is always one of transcendence—moving beyond our limitations, whether they be physical, emotional, or mental. This journey culminates in the pillar of awakening, where transcending our confines is the essence.

Every individual, knowingly or unknowingly, is bound by invisible chains. These chains may be past traumas, deeply ingrained beliefs, societal norms, or even self-imposed limitations. The process of awakening challenges us to recognize these confines and actively work to break free from them. But this isn't a mere act of rebellion or defiance; it's an evolution.

Transcendence in the context of awakening is not about rejecting or discarding parts of ourselves. Instead, it's about rising above, seeing the bigger picture, and realizing that our true essence is not bound by any chains, no matter how strong they seem. This realization brings an unparalleled sense of freedom. It's the kind of freedom that doesn't just mean the absence of constraints but signifies a profound understanding of one's infinite potential and boundlessness.

In this awakened state, freedom becomes our natural way of being. It's not just a concept or a momentary feeling but a lived experience. We begin to operate from a place of abundance, unburdened by past regrets or anxieties about the future. Decisions come from a place of love and wisdom, and our interactions with the world around us become more intentional and meaningful.

In essence, the pillar of awakening serves as a beacon, guiding us toward our most liberated self. While the journey to reach this state might be challenging, filled with introspection and moments of doubt, the destination offers a reward like no other: the gift of true freedom.

Freedom is the embodiment of our highest potential, the actualization of our true selves. It's about breaking free from the shackles of societal expectations, internal limitations, and self-doubt to create a life that's authentically ours.

In self-awakening, we transcend the ordinary, embracing the extraordinary potential within us. It's a realm where we realize that there is so much more to life than just going through the motions, merely existing without truly living. It's where we come alive, bursting forth with creativity, passion, and purpose. It's where we realize that settling is no longer an option because our souls yearn for more, for greatness, for meaning.

Sadly, too many of us are caught in a loop of complacency, thinking that a "good" ordinary life is all that's available to us. There might be occasional sparks of longing for something more, but they're quickly snuffed out by the overwhelming weight of daily routines and societal expectations. This chapter seeks to reignite those sparks, to fan them into roaring flames of desire and determination.

The truth is every one of us has the potential to lead an extraordinary life. Yet, it remains untapped in many, buried under layers of fear, doubt, and conditioning. My hope is that this section will serve as an awakening, a clarion call to your soul, urging you to reach out and claim the incredible life that's waiting for you.

Remember, the world isn't just waiting for the extraordinary. It's waiting for you. Your unique blend of talents, passions, and experiences has the power to make a difference, to bring about change, and to inspire others. All you need to do is awaken to your potential and set yourself free.

The path to freedom and self-awakening is yours to walk. With each step, you'll find yourself drawing closer to your true essence, to a life filled with purpose and passion. The journey may be challenging, but the rewards are beyond imagination. Embrace the gift of freedom and awaken to the extraordinary life that awaits.

Awakening and superconscious living represent an evolution of the human spirit and mind, transcending the limitations of ordinary consciousness and leading to a deeper understanding of oneself and the universe. Here are the key components to this profound journey:

Self-awareness: The foundation of any awakening process, self-awareness involves recognizing our patterns, beliefs, emotions, and behaviors. It's the ability to introspect and see ourselves without judgment.

Mindfulness: This is the practice of being fully present in each moment, observing thoughts, feelings, and sensations without getting attached or reacting to them. It's about cultivating a state of pure awareness.

Intuition: Superconscious living often involves heightened intuition. It's the ability to understand or know something without any direct evidence or reasoning process.

Interconnectedness: Recognizing that everything is connected, that we are part of a vast, intricate web of life, and that our actions reverberate in the larger scheme of things.

Compassion: As we awaken, our hearts expand. We begin to feel more empathy and compassion not just for ourselves but for others and the world at large.

Transcendence: This involves moving beyond the ego and personal desires to a state where universal love and the greater good are the guiding principles.

Alignment With Universal Truths: Recognizing and aligning life with cosmic or universal principles, understanding that there are truths that go beyond our individual experiences.

Holistic Wellness: An understanding that the body, mind, and spirit are interconnected. This leads to a lifestyle that prioritizes holistic health and wellness, integrating practices like meditation, yoga, and clean eating.

Detachment: Not in the sense of becoming aloof or indifferent, but the ability to remain centered amidst the chaos, understanding the impermanent nature of life.

Continuous Learning: Superconscious living involves being a perpetual student, always open to new knowledge, experiences, and growth.

Living With Purpose: It's about aligning with one's higher purpose or calling, making decisions and actions that resonate with this inner truth.

Embracing Uncertainty: Accepting that life is uncertain and unpredictable and finding peace and contentment in that fact.

Incorporating these components into one's life does not necessarily mean living in a constant state of bliss or detachment from the world. Instead, it's about navigating life with heightened awareness, wisdom, and a deeper sense of purpose, ensuring that each action and thought stems from a place of love and understanding.

Sovereign Selfhood: The Elevation of Mastery

Deep within every individual is a well of untapped potential. This is the foundation of one's sovereign selfhood, a place where self-mastery melds seamlessly with the genuine essence of who we are. It's not about conquering the self but about harmonizing and embracing every facet of our being.

Self-mastery is a culmination of personal responsibility and consistent practice. It involves understanding and acknowledging the intricacies of our minds and emotions, recognizing the deep-rooted patterns, and consciously pivoting toward intentional choices. Every experience, every emotion that we go through, is a direct reflection of how we perceive and react to it. This realization is powerful, for it embodies the essence of sovereign selfhood. It's knowing that the ball is always in our court and that our reactions, actions, and eventual outcomes stem from our choices.

Embracing this sense of accountability for our higher good is an exhilarating freedom. When one acknowledges this personal responsibility, there is a seismic shift. No longer does one see the world as an oppressive force but as an open field full of opportunities.

It's imperative to discern between genuine accountability and the shadows of blame and shame. While both are reactions to situations, they come from vastly different places. We covered this previously, but it is worth repeating. Blame points fingers outwardly, attributing responsibility to external sources. Shame, on the other hand, internalizes these feelings, casting doubt upon one's worth and capabilities. Both are detrimental and stem from the ego's need to protect itself.

Sovereign selfhood requires one to rise above these ego-driven reactions. To recognize them, understand them, and then let them go. Because true power doesn't lie in accusations or self-depreciation; it lies in acceptance and growth. Every time we succumb to blaming circumstances or people for our emotional states, we give away a part of our power.

In psychological terms, the situations or comments that provoke strong, often negative reactions are termed "triggers." However, seeing them as "unforgiven opportunities" shifts our perspective. It's an invitation to look inward, to explore the roots of our reactions, and to heal those fragments of our psyche that remain wounded.

In this state of elevated mastery, every challenge is an opportunity, every reaction a lesson, and every choice a step closer to our genuine self. The journey toward sovereign selfhood isn't a linear one. It's filled with introspection, challenges, growth, and, most importantly, immense rewards. It's about reclaiming our power, acknowledging our worth, and standing tall in our own unique essence.

The Reflection of Inner Conflict

On the surface, it often appears as if our conflicts and disagreements are external, seemingly originating from others. We point fingers, attributing blame, thinking, "It's their fault" or "They just don't understand." This projection is a convenient deflection from the reality that most disagreements, in fact, stem from the internal conflicts we grapple with.

Every time someone passes a judgment or offers an opinion about us, it's essential to understand that it's rooted in their personal experiences, limitations, and biases. In essence, they're viewing the world through their unique lens, which is shaped by their life experiences, fears, and desires. Their judgments, then, are less about us and more about their own internal struggles and limitations. However, the way we react or respond to these judgments speaks volumes about our own inner conflicts and limitations.

Ego plays a tricky game here. It seeks validation, craving external affirmation to fortify its existence. The ego tells us that these judgments matter and that we need to defend our honor, and in doing so, it keeps us trapped in a cycle of seeking external validation. It convinces us that the external world determines our worth, leading us down a path where we constantly seek approval and fear disapproval.

When we operate from this space, freedom becomes elusive. We become slaves to others' opinions, contorting ourselves to fit into molds that others deem acceptable. This need to prove ourselves, to constantly seek validation, keeps us shackled, preventing us from experiencing genuine freedom and self-expression.

Growing up, the phrase "Don't take it personally" was like a soothing balm my mom would apply to my emotional wounds. It was her way of reminding me that the world didn't revolve around my feelings and that others' opinions of me were just that—opinions. She instilled in me the belief that the only opinion about me that truly mattered was my own. And while this belief fortified me to some extent, it wasn't entirely foolproof.

As I journeyed through life, even with my mother's words echoing in the back of my mind, I still felt the sting of criticisms, the weight of judgments, and the pain of rejection. Why did things still feel so personal, even when I tried to remind myself that they weren't? The answer was simple yet profound: While other people's opinions may not define me, the feelings they triggered within me were very real and very personal.

This realization was a turning point. Instead of dismissing my reactions to others' opinions and judgments, I started to lean into those feelings. I began to ask myself, "Why does this particular comment or action trigger such a strong emotion in me?" Rather than seeing these triggers as something negative, I viewed them as signposts pointing toward areas within myself that needed healing or understanding.

Every time I felt hurt, offended, or angered by someone's words or actions, I took a moment to introspect. What past wounds were these current situations poking at? What insecurities were they highlighting? And, most importantly, how could I heal these wounds and insecurities so that I no longer felt triggered by external circumstances?

This inner work wasn't always easy. There were times when I wished I could just dismiss things and move on, but I knew that would only be a temporary solution. The real work was in diving deep, facing my wounds, and healing them from the inside out.

Now, when I say I don't take things personally, it comes from a place of genuine healing and understanding. It's not about ignoring or dismissing others' opinions; it's about recognizing that my reactions to them are a mirror reflecting parts of myself that need attention. Every trigger, every emotional response, is an opportunity for growth, healing, and awakening. It's a call to look inward, to understand myself better, and to evolve into a more conscious and whole version of myself. It's an invitation to get better practiced at LOVE for myself.

The Empowerment of Sovereignty

True mastery of self isn't just about learning new strategies or acquiring new knowledge. At its core, it's about setting higher standards for our own lives. This doesn't mean cultivating unrealistic expectations or becoming overly self-critical. Instead, it means actively choosing not to settle for patterns of thinking, feeling, and behaving that no longer serve our growth.

Consider the power and the freedom of these choices:

Taking Ownership: The moment we stop seeing ourselves as victims of circumstances and begin to recognize that we are, in fact, the architects of our reality, profound change begins. By owning our stories and experiences, we empower ourselves to rewrite them.

Internal Accountability: By taking responsibility for our feelings, we reclaim our power. Feelings become our internal compass, directing us toward areas within ourselves that need attention, healing, and love.

Emotional Fluidity: Resistance to negative emotions is like trying to hold back the ocean with our hands. By allowing these emotions, understanding their origin, and processing them, we can navigate through life with a heightened sense of emotional intelligence.

Freedom From External Validation: Understanding that others' judgments and opinions of us are often a reflection of their inner world liberates us. When we know our worth, external voices lose their power.

Embracing New Possibilities: Our past is a treasure trove of lessons, but it shouldn't be a prison. Using it as the only gauge for future possibilities stifles our potential. The desires and dreams we harbor are indicators of what's possible for us.

Authenticity Over Borrowed Beliefs: In a world that constantly tells us who to be, finding our genuine selves can be a challenge. But it's crucial to sift through externally imposed beliefs and identities, returning them to their origins and carving out our unique path.

Recognizing Inherent Worth: Our value isn't determined by a tally of our achievements. True worth is intrinsic. It's not earned or bestowed; it simply is.

Life as a Creation: When we shift our perspective to see life as something we actively create rather than something that merely happens to us, we tap into a wellspring of potential. We can then view adversity not as a cruel twist of fate but as an opportunity for growth.

Making these shifts in perception and behavior isn't merely about personal growth. It's a revolutionary act of rebellion against societal norms that would have us remain small, controllable, and predictable. It's about choosing to live on our terms with authenticity, purpose, and passion. And when we make that choice, the chains of the past fall away, and the horizon ahead is limitless. These are the choices required for both your awakening and the freedom you deserve.

Embracing Freedom Through Surrender and Self-Mastery

Christmas Wishes and Cabbage Patches

Christmas was a season of joy and wonder, a time when love and tradition converged in a beautifully orchestrated ballet. Our Christmas Eve service was nothing short of ethereal, with the candle lighting ceremony and the echoes of "O' Holy Night" resonating deeply within me, sometimes drawing tears. Post-service, we'd eagerly unravel the mysteries that the gifts under the tree held. Yet, the main event, the pinnacle of anticipation, was reserved for Christmas morning. That's when Santa wove his magic.

Year after year, Santa brought along the coveted item from my wish-list, always tucked in my special spot. The ritual was one of hardly any sleep and surging excitement for the morning when I'd rush downstairs to find that cherished gift awaiting me. This particular year, at age ten, my heart yearned for a Cabbage Patch doll. It was the era before the convenience of online wish lists and instant gratifications. Growing up, we had two key occasions for presents: birthdays and Christmas. With my birthday nestled in the heart of summer, Christmas was my winter solace. And this year, my entire being pined for that doll.

A Cabbage Patch doll wasn't just a toy; it represented a companion, a confidante, and endless moments of imagination and love. My mind overflowed with scenarios of us being inseparable, of whispered secrets and comforting hugs. In my heart, I was certain Santa would fulfill this longing. My older sister, always the insider to my little world, confirmed my hopes. She knew, somehow, that Santa had answered my call. Elation bubbled within me like never before.

Christmas morning, barely touched by dawn's first light, I sprinted downstairs. My spot on the couch should've been adorned with my wish. Yet, it lay bare. The confusion and panic were immediate. Why wasn't it there? In a desperate bid for answers, I woke my mom. Her face, usually a haven of warmth and assurance, mirrored my own confusion. My sister, however, had a different suggestion. "Look in the fridge," she said, her voice oddly evasive.

Dashing through our kitchen, I yanked the refrigerator door open. And there it was. Or, rather, there it wasn't. A head of cabbage, anthropomorphized with eyes, nose, mouth, and limp spaghetti strands for hair, stared back at me. Confusion melted into disbelief. Was this a cruel joke? How could Santa, the epitome of love and joy, do this to me?

The truth unraveled soon. That year, the Cabbage Patch doll was the "it" toy. Parents were duking it out in stores, with some even ending up behind bars, all to bring a smile to their child's face. My mother, despite her diligent search, couldn't nab one. In a twist of misguided affection, my sister decided to craft her own version of the toy, hoping it might fill the void.

While the incident might seem comical in hindsight, for the younger me, it was a traumatic episode. Santa's omission felt like a testament to my unworthiness. If fathers could abandon and forget, why not a mythical gift-bringer? That Christmas, instead of joy, I was cloaked in feelings of inadequacy. It felt like yet another proof of being less than, of not being enough.

Life's moments shape our beliefs, sometimes in ways more profound than we realize. And while that Christmas might have temporarily marred the magic for me, it was also a reminder that the essence of the festive season wasn't just in receiving but also in understanding, the freedom in forgiveness, and, above all, love.

Freedom, a word often misunderstood, is not about breaking chains in the outside world but about releasing the chains we have self-imposed. True freedom stems from a place of surrender, acceptance, and profound forgiveness of oneself and the surrounding world. Such freedom paves the way for self-mastery, which in turn enhances one's sense of liberty.

I remember my own journey, which was replete with internal battles and external misrepresentations. I'd become a master of disguises, presenting a version of myself crafted to appease and please others. The irony? In attempting to avoid conflicts, I had created a much larger one within myself.

Hiding behind a façade, I sought validation. Each nod of approval, each word of appreciation, though heartwarming, was for a persona I had crafted, not for the real me. It was like receiving applause for a role in a play while the real actor stood backstage, unseen and unappreciated. And when you're busy pretending, even when surrounded by people, loneliness has a way of creeping in. It's the isolation of knowing that people only see your mask, not your true self.

I remember the constant weight of expecting someone to finally "see" me, to recognize my efforts, to validate my existence. The endless wait for apologies that might never come, thinking that those words of remorse were the keys to my inner peace.

And amidst all these external validations, I also battled inner turmoil. The ever-persistent doubt, the fear of being found out, and the crippling belief that maybe I was never going to be "enough." Each piece of feedback, instead of being constructive criticism, felt like a personal attack, cementing my belief in my insufficiency. The flexibility of thought was lost in the quagmire of needing to be "right." And in the event I took the moral high ground, I yearned for recognition for my sacrifices.

At the root of all this was a profound mistrust—a skepticism not just toward others but toward life itself. This skepticism was nurtured and amplified by my own past experiences and deeply ingrained beliefs.

The journey to freedom began when I recognized these patterns, realized that I had the power to change my narrative, and accepted myself, both the awesome and the messy. It was a shift from seeking control to embracing surrender, from external validation to profound self-acceptance, from a carefully crafted persona to genuine selfhood. In that surrender, in that acceptance, I found freedom. And with that freedom came the self-mastery that allowed me to navigate life with grace, compassion, and authenticity.

Embracing Resilience Through Conscious Living

Embarking on this journey of self-discovery and introspection has fundamentally shifted my approach to life. It has equipped me with an armor of resilience, not against external adversities but against my internal storms. Each situation, no matter how seemingly adverse, is perceived through a lens of opportunity rather than victimhood. I've come to realize that life doesn't just happen to me; it unfolds for me.

This profound understanding that I am the architect of my experiences has been transformative. Every situation is like clay in my hands. I mold it, shape it, and give it form and meaning. No longer do I passively accept the narrative presented to me. Instead, I actively engage in crafting my own story. The power to transition from the unconscious to the conscious, from passive acceptance to active engagement, has been a revelation.

By allowing people the space to be themselves and by releasing them from the shackles of my expectations, I've found a newfound freedom. It's a liberation from the need for external validation, a release from the desire to fit into molds crafted by societal norms. I no longer seek validation or hinge my worth on others' perceptions. My worth is intrinsic, unapologetic, and untethered to external opinions.

Engaging in open conversations, not as confrontations but as dialogues of growth, has become a norm. Feedback, instead of being a dagger aimed at my self-esteem, is now a tool for growth, a mirror reflecting areas of potential evolution.

My understanding of greatness has also undergone a sea change. The societal hierarchy, which once seemed so rigid and deterministic, has flattened in my perception. Every individual, including me, stands on an even platform, each with their unique strengths and vulnerabilities.

Negative emotions, which once were catalysts for reactionary behavior, are now signals, alerting me to delve deeper, to understand their root, and to harness them for growth. They've become instruments of introspection rather than triggers for irrational reactions.

In essence, this journey has been about harnessing the full potential of what's possible, about recognizing the infinite power within and channeling it to live a life of conscious choice and boundless growth.

The Eternal Journey of Self-Mastery

Self-mastery, a term that evokes images of ultimate accomplishment, is not a pinnacle to be reached but an ever-evolving journey. It isn't about reaching a definitive endpoint or acquiring a finite amount of wisdom. Instead, it's about a continuous process of self-exploration, reflection, and growth.

Life, in its endless tapestry of experiences, challenges, and opportunities, serves as our greatest teacher. Each moment presents a new lesson, a chance to delve deeper into the very essence of our being. Every hardship, every joy, every challenge, and every triumph offers a window into understanding ourselves better.

To believe we can ever fully master the vastness of human existence is to simplify the intricate, multi-dimensional nature of our lives. The beauty of our journey lies in its unpredictability, its endless potential for growth, and its ceaseless opportunities for self-improvement.

As we navigate through life, we should cherish the realization that the path to self-mastery is not about arriving but about embracing the journey itself. It's about appreciating each twist and turn, knowing that they serve a purpose, teaching us more about who we are and who we can become.

So, while we may never attain complete mastery over the vast complexities of human existence, we can commit ourselves to the quest. We can continually strive for deeper understanding, greater awareness, and boundless love for ourselves and the world around us. The quest for self-mastery is, after all, a testament to the beauty of the human spirit and its insatiable thirst for growth.

Neural Navigator: Commanding the Brain's Course

Our brain, a magnificent orchestrator of thoughts and emotions, is not always our best ally. But what if you could navigate its intricate pathways, turning every neural nook and cranny to your advantage?

Charting the Neural Seas

Picture your brain as a vast ocean, its waves representing thoughts, emotions, and memories. Just as a seasoned sailor learns to navigate choppy waters and unpredictable storms, we, too, can learn to steer through the tempests of our neural seas. The secret? Taking deliberate command.

The neurons and their countless connections are like the wind, currents, and tides. They shape our experiences, but they are not unchangeable. With awareness and intention, we can influence these neural patterns, ensuring they serve our greater good rather than hinder our progress.

Mindful Mastery

The cornerstone of awakening, becoming the boss of your brain, is mindfulness. By paying deliberate attention to our thoughts and emotions without judgment, we can recognize patterns that don't serve us. When an old narrative or negative self-talk emerges, mindfulness gives us the space to pause and choose a different response.

Consider neural pathways like well-trodden paths in a forest. The more frequently a path is traveled, the more defined it becomes. Similarly, the more we entertain certain thoughts or emotions, the stronger their neural pathways become. But just as a less-used forest trail eventually becomes overgrown and fades, we have the power to weaken and change unhelpful neural pathways by consciously choosing different thoughts and behaviors.

Understanding the Brain's Overprotective Instinct

From an evolutionary standpoint, the brain's primary goal has always been survival. The amygdala, often referred to as the "lizard brain," is wired to detect threats and respond with the fight, flight, or freeze reflex. While this served us well in prehistoric times when threats were largely physical, in today's modern society, these "threats" often manifest as challenges to our beliefs, social pressures, or unfamiliar situations. Consequently, the brain can overreact, perceiving these as life-threatening scenarios when, in reality, they might just be opportunities for growth and learning.

Interpreting Brain's Signals

It's like an alarm system that's set too sensitive and goes off at the slightest hint of disturbance. A flutter of self-doubt can escalate into full-blown anxiety, a minor disagreement can feel like a major confrontation, and stepping out of our comfort zone can seem as perilous as facing a predator.

However, just as we wouldn't want to rid our homes of an alarm system entirely, we don't want to mute our brain's warning signals. Instead, we should aim to recalibrate them. To do this, we must first understand that most of the "threats" our brain detects are not truly dangerous. By developing this understanding, we can filter genuine concerns from unfounded ones.

Regaining Control: The Power of Conscious Thought

Becoming the boss of your brain starts with creating a conscious awareness of its habits. When a negative thought or fear arises, instead of letting it control you, pause and ask, "Is this thought based on fact or fiction? Is it helping me or hindering me?" This process of introspection and analysis allows us to discern between valid concerns and irrational fears.

Moreover, understanding that emotions, however intense, are temporary states can be empowering. By observing them without judgment and without identifying with them, we can let them flow through us without becoming consumed by them.

Practicing Brain Boss Techniques

Mindful Observation: When faced with a strong emotion or reaction, instead of instantly acting on it, practice observing it without judgment. Ask yourself what triggered it and whether the intensity of your reaction is warranted.

Cognitive Reframing: Challenge negative or irrational beliefs by looking at situations from different perspectives. Try to find a more positive or constructive way to interpret events or feelings.

Affirmative Self-talk: Instead of indulging in self-criticism or doubt, cultivate a habit of positive self-talk. Reassure yourself, celebrate your strengths, and acknowledge your efforts.

Seek External Perspectives: Discussing your thoughts and feelings with trusted friends, mentors, coaches, or therapists can provide fresh insights and help you discern the brain's overprotective narratives from objective reality.

By consistently practicing these techniques, not only do we get better at recognizing when our brain is being an overzealous gatekeeper, but we also become adept at guiding it toward patterns that serve our growth, well-being, and ultimate happiness.

Decoding Sensations: Fear vs. Excitement

The brain, a marvel of evolution, processes an array of stimuli every moment. It interprets these stimuli based on past experiences, genetic predispositions, and cultural programming, among other factors. Fascinatingly, the sensations of fear and excitement, two seemingly distinct emotions, manifest in strikingly similar physiological ways. Both can lead to a pounding heart, sweaty palms, an adrenaline rush, and heightened senses. Yet, our perception of these two emotions and the narratives we build around them can be polar opposites. Why?

Interpretation Is Key

At the core, our interpretation of these sensations is influenced by our personal experiences, the context, and our existing beliefs. When boarding a roller coaster, the sensation of our heart racing might be interpreted as excitement due to the context of being at an amusement park, surrounded by joyous screams and laughter. However, the same sensation felt while walking through a dimly lit alleyway at night might be interpreted as fear.

The challenge lies in moments of ambiguity, where the context doesn't strictly dictate one emotion over the other. It's in these gray areas that our power of choice comes into play.

The Power of Perspective

Imagine being asked to speak publicly. The mere thought might send one person into a state of anxiety, their mind filled with fears of judgment or failure. In contrast, another might feel invigorated by the opportunity to share their ideas and connect with an audience. The situation remains the same, but the interpretations differ vastly.

Being the boss of your brain means recognizing these pivotal moments and actively deciding which narrative to adopt. Do we approach unfamiliar scenarios with apprehension, anticipating all that could go wrong? Or do we choose to see them as thrilling opportunities to learn, grow, and experience something new?

Harnessing the Dual Emotions

Here are some steps to shift perspectives and use the physiological similarities between fear and excitement to our advantage:

Reframe the Narrative: When faced with a challenging situation, consciously shift your internal dialogue. Instead of thinking, "I'm terrified of this new project," consider, "I'm excited about what I can learn from this new project."

Body Language Matters: Adopting a confident stance or engaging in deep breathing can send signals back to the brain to reinforce the narrative of excitement.

Visualize Positive Outcomes: Instead of dwelling on potential pitfalls, visualize the best possible outcome. This can sway your mind from fear to excitement.

Seek External Input: Sometimes, discussing your feelings with someone can help in reframing them. This person might offer a perspective you hadn't considered.

Practice: The more frequently you consciously choose excitement over fear, the more natural this choice becomes. With time, it becomes a conditioned response.

Life is filled with unknowns, challenges, and opportunities. Our interpretation of these events largely dictates our experiences. By recognizing the thin line between fear and excitement and choosing which side to lean on, we become the true bosses of our emotional landscape, wielding the power to transform potential threats into enriching opportunities.

Designing Destiny

Your life is the most significant project you'll ever work on. With every choice, you lay a brick; with every dream, you draft a blueprint. Let's explore what it means to be the chief architect of your destiny.

Every interaction and every experience in our lives revolves around the relationships we cultivate, not just with people but with our circumstances, our beliefs, and even our own selves. What if we redefined these relationships? What if instead of viewing time as a limiting factor, we perceived it as a vast landscape, abundant and ripe with potential? Instead of viewing money as a scarce commodity, what if we saw it as a reflection of the value we bring into the world?

In the past, you might have held onto rigid beliefs about life and its various facets. But with conscious effort and a shift in perception, you can rewrite these narratives. Turn food into an experience rather than a battle of "good" vs. "bad." Reimagine workouts not as grueling obligations but as invigorating challenges. See age, past experiences, and personal history not as limitations but as unique qualifications, making you the expert of your own story.

By transforming these thought patterns, we not only change our relationship with individual aspects of life but reconstruct the very foundation of our destiny. Every thought becomes a brick, every intention a cornerstone, and every action a pillar, together forming the magnificent mansion of our lives.

The design of our lives is woven with thoughts, memories, and experiences. Yet, one often overlooked truth is the monumental influence our internal dialogues have on the tapestry of our existence. The cars we drive, the homes we live in, the wealth we accumulate, and even the relationships we build, while significant, are not the sole determinants of our life's quality. What truly shapes our experiences and, by extension, the quality of our lives is the narrative we spin within our minds.

Every thought we entertain, every internal dialogue we engage in, acts as a filter through which we perceive the world around us. When we nourish our minds with positive, empowering thoughts and speak to ourselves with kindness and encouragement, we invariably enhance the vibrancy and richness of our life's tapestry.

Conversely, if our internal conversations are rife with criticism, negativity, and self-doubt, the world can seem bleak, no matter how ostensibly successful or prosperous we may be. Our mental landscape, colored by these thoughts, casts shadows on our experiences, relationships, and accomplishments.

The mastery of one's thoughts is, therefore, not just an intellectual exercise. It is a vital life skill, one that requires consistent practice and mindfulness. Taking charge of our thoughts and deliberately choosing positive, constructive, and empowering narratives can uplift our spirits and transform our lives. Being mentally conscious, being aware of our thought patterns, and actively directing our thoughts toward what serves our well-being and growth is what true empowerment is all about. It's about recognizing that we hold the reins to our life's narrative. It's about understanding that by elevating the quality of our thoughts, we can significantly enhance the quality of our lives.

So, every time you find yourself at a crossroads, every time you feel overwhelmed, or every time you feel elated, remember—it's not just about the external circumstances. It's about the stories you tell yourself, the thoughts you nurture, and the internal dialogues you engage in. Your life's quality, its vibrancy, its richness, is in your hands, or rather, in your thoughts. Choose them wisely.

Custodianship: Owning Your Actions

In a world where blame is often passed along like a hot potato, the act of taking responsibility can be revolutionary. Venture into the realm of true ownership, where accountability is not a burden but a beacon.

The Dance of Responsibility and Freedom

When we think of accountability, our minds might automatically conjure images of blame or shame. Society has conditioned us to see accountability as an admission of wrongdoing. However, at its core, accountability is about honesty, clarity, and growth.

Imagine you're standing at the center of a spider's web. Each strand leading outwards represents a choice you've made. Some choices bring joy, while others bring challenges. But every strand, every outcome, can be traced back to you. This doesn't mean you're to blame for every external circumstance. It simply means you have the power to decide how you respond.

Accountability shifts the narrative from "Why is this happening to me?" to "What can I learn from this?" It moves us from a passive stance, where life simply happens, to an active one, where we recognize our agency and power. It teaches us to see challenges not as setbacks but as opportunities for growth.

Furthermore, accountability is the bedrock of trust. In relationships, whether personal or professional, owning up to our actions fosters an environment of mutual respect and understanding. It communicates integrity, humility, and authenticity.

But how does one truly embrace accountability?

Self-reflection: Regularly take time to evaluate your actions and decisions. Ask yourself, "What role did I play in this situation? Could I have acted differently? What can I do better next time?"

Acknowledge Mistakes: We're all human, and mistakes are part of our growth journey. Instead of shying away from them, own them. Apologize if needed, and learn from them.

Seek Feedback: Don't be afraid to ask others for their perspective. They might provide insights into your blind spots.

Commit to Growth: Make a conscious commitment to grow from every experience. This proactive mindset can turn any situation, however challenging, into a stepping stone.

Shift Perspective: See accountability as a form of empowerment. It's not about weighing yourself down with blame but about lifting yourself with newfound wisdom.

Accountability threads its way through every choice, challenge, and celebration. By embracing it, we not only pave the path for personal growth but also create ripples that can positively impact those around us. It's not about carrying the world's weight on our shoulders; it's about understanding that our actions have weight, and we are the custodians of their consequences.

The Power of Self-Responsibility

As I have mentioned, taking responsibility for our lives doesn't mean we blame ourselves for every mishap or unfortunate event. Rather, it means understanding that within each circumstance, there's a realm of control we possess. This perspective allows us to move from a reactive stance to a proactive one. Instead of being at the mercy of external events, we become architects of our reality.

Purposeful Pursuits: More Than Just Goals

Goals are the destinations we aim for, but purpose is the compass that guides us. Delve into the deeper layers of setting aspirations that resonate with your soul's true calling.

The Allure of the Impossible: Rising Beyond SMART Goals

For decades, the concept of SMART (Specific, Measurable, Achievable, Relevant, and Time-bound) goals has dominated the world of personal and professional development. While these goals have their place, offering clarity and structure, they sometimes hinder our evolution by tying us to the realm of the "known" and the "done before." In the journey of self-awakening, aiming for what seems impossible can be a more transformative and empowering pursuit.

The Limitation of the Realistic

When we tether ourselves exclusively to realistic goals, we operate within a predefined boundary. These boundaries, while providing a safe and predictable structure, can also curb our aspirations, limiting us to the familiar. If a goal is labeled realistic, it often means it's been achieved by someone else before. This means we're merely following a well-trodden path rather than carving our own.

Impossible Goals: Catalysts for Evolution

Impossible goals, by their very nature, demand that we stretch, grow, and evolve. They challenge our perceptions, push our boundaries, and ignite a fire within that refuses to settle for the status quo. When we aim for the seemingly unreachable:

We Foster Innovation: To reach what seems unreachable, we must think differently, approach problems uniquely, and be willing to challenge established norms.

We Discover Hidden Reservoirs of Potential: Impossible goals force us out of our comfort zones, making us tap into skills, talents, and strengths we might not know we possessed.

We Transcend Limits: When we continuously push our boundaries, we soon realize that many of the limits we believe in are self-imposed. As we break past them, we rewrite our narrative of what's possible for us. We become a new "who."

Capacity vs. Ability

While ability speaks to our current skill set, our known competencies, and our present understanding, capacity addresses our potential—the heights we could reach, the talents lying dormant, and the horizons yet to be explored. Living in our ability keeps us anchored in the present. Living in our capacity propels us into a future of endless possibilities.

Championing the Impossible

As we journey through the landscapes of self-awakening, let's champion the idea of the impossible. Let's understand that while SMART goals provide clarity and direction, impossible goals offer challenge and transformation. They remind us that we're not just a product of our past but architects of our future, capable of building worlds beyond current comprehension.

In the dance of life, while SMART goals give us the rhythm, it's the impossible goals that provide the magic. As we chase the unreachable, we don't just discover new destinations; we discover ourselves.

The Power of Failure Resilience

Society whispers in our ears that failure is a dead end. But what if I told you it's a detour, one that often leads to richer, more scenic routes?

For many, the word "failure" conjures up feelings of inadequacy, embarrassment, and defeat. We've been conditioned to avoid it, fear it, and often deny it. But what if our perception of failure is, in itself, flawed? What if embracing failure is actually a pathway to our grandest self-awakening?

The Misconception of Failure

As we have discussed, we often equate failing with having failed, intertwining an action (or lack thereof) with our self-worth. This false conflation is where our fear finds its roots. But when we peel back the layers, failure is simply a result, a data point. It's feedback, not condemnation.

The Bigger Life Awaiting Beyond Failure

When we allow ourselves to detach from the sting of failure and see it as a guide rather than an end, we create a life of limitless potential. Here's how:

Innovation Through Iteration: Every significant innovation in history has come after countless trials, errors, and failures. Embracing failure fosters innovation because it promotes a mindset of iteration, tweaking, and eventual refinement.

Growth Through Challenge: Without the risk of failure, there's no challenge, and without challenge, there's limited growth. Welcoming failure ensures we're continually pushing our boundaries and evolving in the process.

Building Resilience: Each time we face failure and rise, we build resilience. This resilience becomes the bedrock on which we construct a life of bold endeavors and meaningful pursuits.

The Freedom in Failure Tolerance

When we become tolerant of failure, we grant ourselves the freedom to experiment, to be curious, and to venture into the unknown. The cage of perfectionism breaks open, and we soar on the wings of exploration. This freedom is liberating, offering us:

Choices: Without the paralyzing fear of failure, we can make choices based on passion, curiosity, and intuition rather than mere safety.

Adventures: With the willingness to fail, every endeavor, no matter its outcome, becomes an adventure, a story worth telling.

Depth: Embracing failure adds depth to our experiences. It teaches us empathy, humility, and the value of persistence.

A Life Unshackled by "What Ifs"

As we continue our journey into self-awakening, let's remember that the most vibrant lives aren't those free of failures but those enriched by them. Every stumble, every misstep, every closed door is a stepping stone to a life larger than we dared to dream.

In our lives, failures are but threads, weaving intricate patterns of lessons, growth, and triumphs. When we cherish these threads, we truly set ourselves free, awakening to the most profound freedom of all.

Challenges Transformed: Finding Strength in Adversity

Adversity. Merely the word can stir emotions of unease and discomfort. It paints images of setbacks, challenges, and difficulties that seemingly hold us back. But what if, instead of perceiving adversity as a barrier, we saw it as a stepping stone? What if every challenge was an opportunity cloaked in a test of our resolve? Let's journey through its transformative power.

Reframing Adversity: From Enemy to Ally

Our reactions to adversity define the trajectory of its impact. We have the choice to view it as a stumbling block or a stepping stone, and that choice is pivotal in determining whether adversity breaks or builds us. Let's delve into the transformative powers of adversity:

The Catalyst for Growth: Like the fire that forges the iron, adversity shapes and strengthens us. It forces us out of our comfort zones, pushing us to new limits, expanding our capacities, and making us smarter and stronger.

A Conduit for Curiosity: Challenges incite questions. Why did this happen? How can we overcome it? What can we learn? In seeking answers, we become more curious, paving the way for innovative solutions and ideas.

Courage in the Face of Challenges: With each adversity we encounter and overcome, we collect evidence of our resilience. This reservoir of past triumphs builds courage, empowering us to face even bigger challenges head-on.

The Asset of Adversity

By reframing adversity as an asset, we tap into its latent potential:

Resilience: Every challenge faced and overcome reinforces our mental and emotional resilience, making us more adept at bouncing back from future setbacks.

Wisdom: The lessons adversity imparts are unparalleled. They instill wisdom, a blend of knowledge with experience, guiding our future actions and decisions.

Connection: Shared adversities foster deep connections. They build empathy, understanding, and a shared sense of purpose among communities and individuals alike.

Adversity's Invitation to a Bigger Self

Adversity invites us, albeit forcefully at times, to step into a grander version of ourselves. It nudges us toward paths we might never have trodden, toward lessons we might never have learned, and toward strengths we might never have discovered.

Embracing adversity is a conscious choice, a decision to see beyond the immediate pain and recognize the potential growth lying beneath. It's a commitment to transform each setback into a setup for a grander comeback.

In our journey of self-awakening, let's honor adversity for what it truly is—not a cruel jest of fate but a gift, urging us to unveil our most authentic, resilient, and radiant selves.

Connection Chronicles:
The Art of Relating & Appreciating

Relationships are complex tapestries interwoven with emotions, expectations, experiences, and the myriad nuances of individual personalities. Within this intricate dance, we often find ourselves grappling with the weight of unmet expectations, blurred boundaries, and, all too often, the suppression of our true selves. Let's unravel these complexities, seeking the freedom that self-awakening offers.

The Weight of Expectations

Expectations, both spoken and unspoken, are inherent in relationships. They reflect our desires, hopes, and what we anticipate from our partners. Yet, when these expectations go unmet, they transform into breeding grounds for disappointment and resentment.

Self-Awakening Insight: Instead of laying our happiness in the hands of others, we must recognize that our inner peace is our responsibility. Expectations must be communicated, not assumed, rooted in understanding and compassion.

Blurred Boundaries: The Line Between "Us" and "I"

While relationships involve unity, they shouldn't engulf individual identities. Blurred boundaries can lead to loss of self, where personal desires and dreams are overshadowed by the collective "we."

Self-Awakening Insight: Boundaries aren't barriers. They're reflections of self-respect. Defining and communicating our boundaries helps protect our mental and emotional well-being and ensures that the relationship thrives on mutual respect.

Denial of Self: The Subtle Erosion of Authenticity

In our quest to be the perfect partner, friend, or family member, we often suppress or modify parts of ourselves. Over time, this leads to a chasm between our external persona and our true self, leading to feelings of emptiness and inauthenticity.

Self-Awakening Insight: Embracing our authentic selves with all our imperfections, vulnerabilities, and strengths paves the way for genuine connections. When we're true to ourselves, our relationships resonate with authenticity, depth, and understanding.

Charting a Course to Freedom

The journey of self-awakening in relationships demands introspection, communication, and, most importantly, self-love. By recognizing and addressing the weight of expectations, the blur of boundaries, and the denial of our true selves, we can steer our relationships toward healthier horizons.

Relationships, when navigated with awareness, become not just sources of comfort but also catalysts for personal growth. They mirror back to us our deepest fears, hopes, strengths, and areas of growth, propelling us further on our journey of self-awakening. Let's cherish them not just as bonds with others but as sacred paths to discovering and celebrating our true selves.

Choice & Love: The Dual Superpowers

In the vast universe of human emotions and actions, two elements stand out with their transformative prowess: choice and love. These twin pillars, when understood and wielded correctly, have the potential to revolutionize our lives, gifting us unparalleled freedom and self-awakening.

The Power of Choice: A Beacon of Autonomy

Choice is our internal compass, granting us the autonomy to navigate life's myriad paths. Every day, every moment, we're presented with a series of decisions, from the mundane to the momentous. These choices carve out our futures, stitch together our destinies, and shape our identities.

Self-Awakening Insight: Embracing the power of choice means recognizing that while we may not control every circumstance we encounter, we always control our reactions to them. This agency allows us to move from a space of reaction to one of intentional action, opening doors to realms of freedom we might never have imagined.

Love: The Universal Constant

More than just a fleeting emotion, love is a profound force of connection and transformation. It binds us, drives us, and uplifts us, connecting souls and bridging divides. In its truest form, love isn't just about romance; it's an unconditional acceptance of the self and others.

Self-Awakening Insight: To truly harness the power of love, one must begin with self-love. Embracing our flaws, celebrating our strengths, and nurturing our spirits pave the way for genuine love for others. It's a love unshackled from conditions, expectations, or judgments.

Marrying Choice With Love

When choice and love come together, they create a symphony of self-awakening. Choosing to love and loving our choices are acts of profound empowerment. They're declarations of our worth and testaments to our potential.

Self-Awakening Insight: To intertwine choice with love is to say, "I choose to accept and love myself unconditionally, and in doing so, I choose pathways that reflect this love and respect toward myself and others." It's a dance of freedom, where every step is both deliberate and joyous.

Unleashing the Superpowers

Choice and love, when truly understood and embraced, become not just aspects of our lives but the very essence of our being. They empower us to rise above challenges, to connect deeply with ourselves and the world, and to carve out a journey of self-awareness, growth, and freedom.

By tapping into these superpowers, we awaken to a world where every challenge is an opportunity, every connection is profound, and every moment is steeped in intentional love and conscious choices.

Decisions: The Bedrock of Self-Awakening

Previously, we touched upon the significance of decision-making, but let's delve deeper to understand how, through the very act of deciding, we enhance our own value and solidify our self-worth, our own self-awakening. Underneath this seemingly simple action lies the very essence of our autonomy, and it is within these choices that our paths to self-awakening and freedom unfurl.

Every decision, from the mundane to the momentous, acts as a pivot, changing the course of our stories. A single decision can shift our trajectory, elevating us to heights previously unimagined or, sometimes, pushing us into abysses of learning. And it is through these chosen paths that we awaken to the immense reservoir of power we hold within.

The Ripple Effect of Decisions: Picture life as an endless sea where each decision is a stone cast upon the water. Each choice creates ripples, spreading outwards and intersecting with the waves from other stones, symbolizing the outcomes and consequences of our actions. The smallest decision can send waves that travel far and wide, influencing the vast expanse of our life's journey. Our current position is the sum of all the ripples we've created, and the horizons we will explore are shaped by the stones we have yet to throw.

The Power Within: Many external factors influence our lives: upbringing, environment, and even chance. Yet, it's important to recognize that while these factors may set the stage, we, through our decisions, control the narrative. By consciously making choices that align with our true selves, we reclaim our power and pave the way for self-awakening. Every choice offers an opportunity to further our understanding of ourselves, enhancing our connection to our inner essence.

Unlocking Freedom: True freedom is not merely the absence of physical constraints but the liberation from limiting beliefs and self-imposed barriers. Decisions are the keys that unlock this freedom.

When we choose to break free from patterns that no longer serve us, to voice our truth, or simply act in alignment with our core beliefs, we experience the exhilaration of genuine freedom. This sensation is the hallmark of self-awakening.

Embracing the Unknown: Decisions often come with a shadow—the unknown. While this can be daunting, embracing uncertainty is pivotal for growth. The act of deciding amidst ambiguity strengthens our intuitive muscles, teaching us to trust our inner compass. With each decision made under such circumstances, our connection to our true self deepens, accelerating our journey toward self-awakening.

Our power is not merely in the circumstances we find ourselves in but in how we choose to navigate them. Decisions, in all their complexity, are our compass, our rudder, and our sail. As we harness this power, making choices that resonate with our core, we embark on the most profound journey of all—the journey of self-awakening and boundless freedom.

Let's take a minute to reflect on where we have been and where we are going as our journey together is nearing the end.

Reflection on the Journey of Consciousness

1. Life Happens to You: From Victimhood to Empowerment

In our lives, it's not uncommon to feel like a mere speck, tossed about by the whims of fate. Just when you think you've got a handle on things, life throws a curveball that takes you off your feet. It's unpredictable, chaotic, and often overwhelming.

For many, life feels like an uncontrollable force, a tidal wave that crashes without warning. Days start to blend into each other, punctuated by moments of joy, sorrow, triumph, and defeat. When events don't align with our expectations, it's easy to feel trapped, as though life is a storm we're caught in, with no shelter in sight.

At times, it might seem like life is a vast, unpredictable ocean, and we're just driftwood floating without purpose or direction. The challenges come one after the other: an unexpected bill, a falling out with a loved one, health concerns, or even global events that shake our very foundations. It's as if life is an endless series of obstacles, and all we can do is brace ourselves for the next blow.

Amidst the chaos, there's a voice inside each one of us, constantly narrating our experiences. This voice, the "storyteller," adds layers of interpretation to everything we encounter. It tells tales of injustice, of bad luck, of missed opportunities. The stories often have a central theme: "Why is this happening to me?"

The more we listen to this storyteller, the more our world shrinks. We become the protagonists in our tragedies, always on the defensive, perpetually seeking safety. Every setback reinforces the notion that we're at the mercy of an unpredictable universe.

But what if there's another way to view life? What if, instead of seeing life as something that "happens to us," we begin to see ourselves as active participants in a grand, unfolding narrative? This doesn't mean that challenges will cease, but our perspective on them can drastically change.

Imagine viewing life not as a series of threats but as a journey of lessons. Every challenge, every unexpected twist becomes an opportunity for growth, for deeper understanding. Instead of resisting life, we can embrace it, with all its uncertainties.

When we stop trying to "figure it all out" and instead open ourselves to the experience of the present moment, we move from a place of fear to a place of acceptance. This acceptance is not passive; it's an active acknowledgment that we are not mere victims of fate. We are co-creators of our reality.

Life, in all its unpredictability, is a dance. Sometimes, it's fast and frenzied, and at other times slow and graceful. The key is not to control the dance but to lose ourselves in it, to embrace each twist and turn, each rise and fall, with openness and curiosity.

By shifting from a mindset of victimhood to one of empowerment, we not only change our relationship with life, but we also reclaim our innate power. We recognize that while we can't control the waves, we can learn to surf. And in doing so, we find joy, purpose, and connection right here and now.

2. Life Happens by You: From Control to Collaboration

Emerging from a sense of victimhood, the realization that we have some semblance of control over life is a profound revelation. It's like finding an oar after being adrift at sea for so long. The second stage of higher consciousness, wherein one believes that "Life happens by you," is imbued with a sense of empowerment and agency. Suddenly, the world seems moldable, subject to our will and desires.

In this stage, the narrative shifts dramatically. We're no longer the passive recipients of life's whims; we become the directors, the orchestrators. There's a newfound confidence in our stride, a belief that we can dictate terms to life. While this sense of control is a marked improvement from feeling perpetually victimized, it carries its own set of pitfalls. The need to control can become obsessive. Everything starts to revolve around molding life to fit a particular mold, to meet specific expectations. It's as if we're trying to sculpt life, forgetting that it's a force in itself.

In this relentless pursuit of control, we often end up clashing with others who are on the same quest. Conflicts arise when two dominant narratives collide. Be it in personal relationships, workplaces, or larger societal structures, the need to exert control can lead to friction, misunderstandings, and even hostility.

In this phase, the mind believes in its paramountcy. Setting goals, crafting resolutions, and charting out life blueprints become central activities. There's a rush in setting a target and working toward it. It's about conquering, achieving, and, often, proving oneself. But with goals come the inevitable challenges of not meeting them, leading to self-criticism and disappointment. Intentions serve as a bridge between raw ambition and harmonious aspiration. They carry the warmth of feelings, hoping to manifest desires not just through sheer will but through genuine emotional longing.

However, as we continue to evolve in our understanding of life and consciousness, there comes a realization. True power doesn't lie in dominating life but in collaborating with it. Instead of trying to force life into a preconceived mold, what if we danced with it? What if, instead of rigid goals, we set flexible intentions, allowing life to shape them as it flows?

The path to awakening is not about overpowering life but understanding its rhythms, patterns, and flows. When we move from a space of trying to control everything to one where we work in tandem with life's natural course, we discover a harmony that was missing earlier. It's about recognizing that while we play a role in shaping our destinies, life itself is a partner in this dance, guiding, supporting, and sometimes leading the way.

The true magic happens when we transition from "life happens by you" to "life happens in you." It's a collaborative journey, one where the universe and the individual engage in a harmonious ballet, co-creating a melody that resonates with love, understanding, and mutual respect.

3. *Life Happens in You: Life Is a Mirror of the Soul*

Life's intricacies weave a complex tapestry, taking us through a spiraling journey of highs and lows, joys and sorrows. As we grow and evolve, our perspectives shift. While initially, we may perceive life as something that merely happens to us or by us, a deeper realization awaits as we ascend to the third level of higher consciousness: Life Happens in You.

Gradually, the blaring noises of victimhood and control begin to subside. It becomes evident that there's more to life than just trying to dominate it or being buffeted by its unpredictable waves. This is the dawn of introspection, where life isn't about the external events but the internal response. It's not the scenery outside but the observer within that takes precedence.

A profound revelation at this level is recognizing the distinction between living life and merely thinking about it. When we are constantly lost in our thoughts, we aren't truly experiencing the vibrancy and immediacy of the present moment. Instead, we're trapped in the confines of our minds, viewing life through the distorted lens of past memories and future anxieties.

In this cocoon of thought, our perceptions are colored not by the reality of what is but by our internal narratives. It's like staring at a beautiful sunset but only seeing the smudges on the window pane. We superimpose our biases, judgments, and stories onto the world, clouding its raw, unfiltered beauty.

An essential insight at this stage is recognizing the root of our suffering. It's not the events of life that cause pain but our interpretations of them. The same situation can elicit joy in one moment and misery in the next, depending solely on our internal narrative. The gray day isn't inherently depressing; it's our story about the gray day that casts a shadow on our mood. The realization that suffering is an internal creation stemming from our stories rather than objective reality is both humbling and empowering.

As we journey through this level of consciousness, we begin to embrace life from the inside out. We become more attuned to our inner landscape, understanding that our external experiences are reflections of our internal state. The world outside becomes a mirror, reflecting the world within.

The third level of consciousness, then, is a call to turn inward, to engage with life not as passive spectators but as active participants, shaping our reality from the inside out. It's about reclaiming our power, not over life but over our responses to it, recognizing that every external event is an opportunity for inner growth and self-awareness.

Life is an ever-evolving dance between external events and our internal responses. As we progress through our journey of consciousness, a profound shift begins to take root. We realize that the power to transform our experiences doesn't lie outside of us but deep within our innermost realms. This inner pivot, where we direct our gaze inward instead of outward, is termed the "You-Turn."

In our earlier stages of consciousness, our focus is predominantly on external circumstances. We either view ourselves as victims of life's whims or believe we must wrestle control from it. But as awareness deepens, an understanding emerges—that our true power lies not in altering the outside world but in understanding and transforming our inner one.

Embracing the You-Turn

The "You-Turn" is more than just introspection; it's a profound redirection of attention. Instead of getting entangled in the external drama, you dive deep into the inner theater of your mind and emotions. Here, in this sacred space, you come face to face with your limiting beliefs, fears, hopes, and dreams—the "spells" that dictate your reactions to the world.

By making this You-Turn, you're no longer just reacting to life; you're actively engaging with the root causes of those reactions. It's like tracing a river to its source or a tree to its roots. By understanding the origin, you gain the power to transform the entire flow.

At the heart of the You-Turn is a simple yet potent question: "What is asking to be seen?" This isn't about seeking problems or issues to fix. It's an invitation to be genuinely curious about your present-moment experience. It's a gentle probe into your current state without judgment or agenda.

Are there emotions bubbling up, thoughts darting by, or sensations tingling within? By asking this question, you bring a loving awareness to whatever arises, allowing it to unfold and express itself. This process of witnessing, without attachment or aversion, is where healing and transformation truly begin.

Embracing the Present With the You-Turn

In making the You-Turn, you're not running away from the world but rather running toward a deeper, truer version of it. It's about anchoring yourself in the present, fully embracing whatever sits here and now. The challenges, the joys, the sorrows, and the mundane—all are welcomed with open arms and a curious heart.

In essence, the You-Turn is a pathway to profound self-awareness and transformation. It's a journey from the surface turbulence of life to its deep, tranquil depths, from where you can truly see, understand, and transform your world. It's the shift from being at the mercy of life to dancing harmoniously with it.

4. Life Happens for You: Embracing Its Flow

In the fourth level of higher consciousness, we witness a significant paradigm shift. It's not just about acknowledging life but also about wholeheartedly embracing it. As we evolve in our understanding, we begin to perceive that every twist and turn of our existence, every challenge and celebration, isn't a mere accident or a hurdle. It's a purposeful orchestration meant to guide us, grow us, and, most importantly, gift us the lessons we need at that very moment.

In this heightened state of awareness, life is no longer an adversary or an entity we need to control. Instead, it emerges as a benevolent teacher, a guiding force, constantly maneuvering us toward our highest self. There's a deeply comforting and empowering realization here—every situation, no matter how seemingly trivial or overwhelmingly daunting, is part of a grand design tailored for our spiritual and personal evolution.

Every joy, sorrow, success, and failure isn't just an isolated event; it's a note in the grand symphony of our existence. And when we begin to perceive this symphony in its entirety, rather than getting caught up in individual notes, a beautiful harmony emerges. We realize that even the most challenging experiences are opportunities in disguise, pushing us to dive deeper, unlearn limiting beliefs, and break free from self-imposed boundaries.

Yes, the ocean of life will have its storms and calm spells. And while we can't control the weather, we can certainly learn how to sail better. Instead of resisting the waves, we learn to ride them. Instead of fearing the storm, we learn to find peace amid it. This doesn't mean we become passive or resign ourselves to fate. It means we operate from a place of trust and understanding. We recognize that **pain is inevitable, but suffering is a choice**. And this choice stems from how we perceive, process, and respond to our experiences.

Being in this state of consciousness means truly showing up for every moment of life. It's about being present, not as a mere spectator but as an active participant. It's about engaging with life, with all its imperfections and unpredictabilities, and understanding that every event is a stepping stone leading us closer to our true selves.

Our essence is vibrant, pulsating aliveness. But, over time, societal norms, limiting beliefs, past traumas, and the myriad "spells" we unknowingly cast upon ourselves can dim this innate vibrancy. They trap our energy, constraining our potential and dimming our light. But the beauty of life's intelligent design is that it constantly offers us opportunities to break free. Every challenge, every emotion, every inner conflict is an invitation to shed these layers and return to our natural state of free-flowing aliveness.

By shining the light of awareness on these bound energies, by being curious and attentive, we start the process of liberation. As these "spells" dissolve, we experience a surge of energy, a flood of joy, and the bliss of being truly open. This openness isn't just a state of mind; it's a state of being. It's a deep-seated realization that we are intricately connected to the intelligent unfolding of life.

Life, in all its wisdom, constantly extends a proposition to us: *to engage, to experience, to evolve.* It reminds us that it's all set up for our growth. Whatever arises is an opportunity to delve deeper, to unbind the trapped energy, and to revel in the beauty of existence. As we navigate this journey, it's essential to remember this profound insight: Life is *set up* to *bring up* what has been *bound up* so it can *open up*, to be *freed up*, so we can *show up* for life!

Embracing this proposition, we don't just exist. We thrive, dance, and become co-creators in the grand, intelligent design of life.

The fourth level of higher consciousness is about profound trust and surrender. It's about believing that the universe, in all its vast wisdom, is always conspiring in our favor. And our job? To dance with life, to learn from it, to grow with it, and to cherish every single moment of this wondrous journey.

5. *Life Happens Through You: Life as a Divine Conduit*

Every stage of higher consciousness is like peeling off layers of an onion, and with each layer removed, the core essence becomes clearer, purer, and more connected to the ultimate source of life itself. The fifth level of consciousness propels us into a realm where we no longer feel merely a part of life; we are its conduit. Life doesn't just happen to us, by us, in us, or for us—it expresses itself through us.

When we fully embrace the idea that life flows through us, we become instruments of a grand cosmic orchestra. The melodies we produce aren't just our own; they're the harmonies of the universe being channeled through our very existence. In this space, the distinction between the self and the universe starts to blur. We become the expression of life's will, and this realization brings with it a profound sense of purpose and connection.

The notion of trusting life isn't about blind faith or neglecting our agency. It's about recognizing the divine intelligence that underlies all existence. Even when life brings challenges or pain, in this state of consciousness, we understand these as lessons or experiences meant to refine our souls and deepen our connection to everything. Trusting life means we believe in its inherent wisdom, even when our limited human perspective can't fathom the bigger picture.

In this heightened state of awareness, every second becomes a sacred encounter with the divine. There's no room for taking things for granted. The mundane becomes miraculous, the ordinary becomes extraordinary, and every experience—be it joy, sorrow, pleasure, or pain—is an invitation to dive deeper into the heart of existence. The veil of illusion lifts, and we see the world for what it truly is—*a playground of consciousness,* a dance of energy, and a testament to life's infinite creativity.

With the realization that life is expressing its myriad forms through us, we begin to see our lives as threads in an intricate tapestry of existence. Every event, emotion, thought, and action is interconnected, contributing to a divine design that's far greater than ourselves. This interconnectedness brings a deep sense of gratitude. We recognize that our very existence is a culmination of countless factors, events, and interactions stretching back to the dawn of time.

The fifth level of higher consciousness is a beautiful paradox. On one hand, we experience a sense of expansion, feeling connected to the vastness of the universe. On the other, there's a homecoming, a return to our truest nature, which is pure, unbounded consciousness. Every step taken on this journey, even the painful and challenging ones, is a step closer to this ultimate realization. Life, in its boundless wisdom, is always guiding us back to our true essence, urging us to remember, realize, and rejoice in the miracle that is existence.

6. *Life Is You: Life's Grand Unification*

The journey through the various levels of consciousness brings us closer to an ultimate truth, one that is deeply profound and yet so simple. At the sixth level of consciousness, we touch the essence of existence, and here, we come to realize that life is not just within us or around us—life is us.

As we evolve in our understanding and awareness, the boundaries that once defined our identity begin to dissolve. The duality of self and other, inner and outer, you and the universe, all fade away. What emerges is a profound sense of unity. You don't just feel connected to everything—you recognize that you are everything.

The roles we play, the labels we attach to ourselves, the narratives we've built around our personal histories—all of these become mere stories. They are chapters in a much larger book where every story and every chapter is interlinked. In this expansive state, personal identity transcends to universal identity. You aren't just a drop in the ocean, but the entire ocean in a drop.

Life, in this state, is seen as a dynamic dance of consciousness. Everything is in a state of flux, continuously changing and evolving, and yet, paradoxically, everything remains eternal and unchanging in its essence. In this dance, you are not just a dancer. You are the dance, the song, the rhythm, and the audience.

Every moment becomes a miracle. The very act of breathing, of perceiving the world, of feeling emotions—all these are experienced with a sense of wonder. For in every experience, you are not just witnessing life; you are realizing your own nature as life itself.

This realization brings forth a love that's all-encompassing. With the understanding that all is one, compassion flows naturally. There is no "other" to judge, to fear, or to be in conflict with. All beings, all elements of nature, are seen as a reflection of oneself.

Reaching this level of consciousness is an awakening in the truest sense. It's waking up from the dream of separateness to the reality of oneness. It's recognizing that, at the core, all distinctions melt away. Life isn't just happening to you, by you, for you, or through you. Life is you. You are not a fragment of the universe. In your essence, you encompass it. As the ancient sages have always whispered, "Tat Tvam Asi"—You Are That.

The Evolving Landscape of Human Consciousness

In our human existence, most individuals find themselves ensconced in the initial phases of consciousness where life seems to act upon them ("to you") and where they exert control, believing life transpires because of them ("by you"). In the tumultuous interplay of these early stages, many remain unaware of the transformative gateway nestled between them, leading to expansive realms of consciousness.

The transition from the first two stages to the succeeding ones is not just a personal journey of enlightenment. It's an evolutionary trek, beckoning not just for individual betterment but for collective healing. As individuals awaken and progress through the phases of consciousness, they don't merely benefit personally. They radiate a healing energy, becoming beacons of hope, understanding, and compassion in a world often overshadowed by despair and confusion.

However, this journey of higher consciousness isn't linear, nor is it fixed. It's a dynamic and intricate dance. The paradox of our existence is that, on a grand scale, humanity is inching from the rudimentary phases of consciousness toward more advanced ones. Yet, on an individual level, one might oscillate between these phases multiple times in just a single day. Mornings might be spent in the throes of feeling acted upon by life, afternoons might witness moments of assertion and control, while evenings might offer profound insights, revealing the interconnectedness of all things.

Embracing this dynamic nature is pivotal. It's not about sidelining or negating any phase, nor about deeming one superior to another. All phases, from the earliest to the most advanced, are intrinsic facets of the human experience. Each holds its lessons, challenges, and opportunities. They all represent different melodies in the symphony of life.

As individuals and as a collective, it's essential to acknowledge this evolving journey without judgment. By recognizing, understanding, and embracing each phase, we cultivate an environment where growth isn't just encouraged but celebrated. And in this celebration, we find our paths to not just higher consciousness but to a more compassionate, interconnected, and enlightened world.

While our individual experiences can often seem tumultuous and even adversarial, there lies a deeper, profound wisdom in the fabric of existence. The journey to higher consciousness requires us to confront, challenge, and ultimately reform our understanding of trust, particularly our trust in life itself.

For many, the trials and tribulations of life—the unexpected setbacks, the heartbreaks, the seemingly insurmountable challenges—become evidence that life isn't trustworthy. We begin to believe that in order to navigate this unpredictable terrain, we must exert control, shape our destiny, and insulate ourselves from potential hurts and disappointments.

Yet, in this endeavor to control and predict, we inadvertently blind ourselves to the vast intelligence and wisdom of life. We forget that our personal narratives, as poignant as they are, form but a minuscule part of an immense, intricate tapestry. By focusing solely on our individual clouds of doubt, fear, and mistrust, we miss out on the vast meadow of possibility, learning, and growth.

What if, instead of viewing life through the lens of skepticism and distrust, we were to recognize its inherent wisdom? This isn't to say that life is always kind, fair, or predictable. But perhaps it's smarter than we give it credit for. Maybe, just maybe, the adversities we face are not arbitrary punishments but meaningful, albeit challenging, paths to growth, understanding, and higher consciousness.

To trust life is to surrender to its flow, to accept that we might not have all the answers or the ability to foresee every twist and turn. But in that surrender, there's freedom—the freedom to experience, to learn, to grow, and to evolve. It's the freedom to move beyond our confined narratives and step into the expansive meadow of possibility.

So, as we journey through the phases of consciousness, let us remember that the key to progression isn't just awareness or understanding. It's trust. By trusting the wisdom of life, by believing that it is, in fact, smarter than our limited perspectives, we open ourselves to truly profound transformations. It is in this deepened trust that we find our path to enlightenment and realize the truth of our existence.

Your Story: A Tapestry of Inherent Intelligence

Every individual's journey, including yours, is intrinsically interwoven with the grand tapestry of the universe. Your existence is not a mere coincidence or a random act of nature; it's a testament to the profound intelligence that courses through every facet of the universe. Every heartbeat, every breath, and every thought that flashes through your mind is a miracle orchestrated by a force far greater than our comprehension.

The very fabric of your being is a marvel of intricate design and unparalleled complexity. Imagine, within you, a vast universe operates: cells working in harmony, neurons firing in perfect synchrony, organs diligently performing their designated functions. This isn't just biology; this is the epitome of a sophisticated intelligence at work.

Yet, amidst this wonder, a common misconception often clouds our perspective—the illusion of separation. We often perceive ourselves as solitary entities, navigating the vast expanse of life in isolation.

This perceived detachment breeds the idea that we must control our environment, our circumstances, and even our own bodies. This urge to control is a manifestation of our disconnection from the innate wisdom of life.

However, embracing the understanding that we are not separate but rather integral components of this magnificent web of existence can shift our perspective. Recognizing and respecting the intelligence that sustains us can dissolve our compulsive need to control. By doing so, we open ourselves to the flow of life, the rhythm of the universe, and the dance of existence.

This realization is the pathway to higher consciousness. When you begin to see yourself not as an isolated entity but as a beautiful expression of the universe's intelligence, you align with its flow. You move in harmony with its rhythm. And in this alignment, the sheer joy of existence, the thrill of being part of this grandiose story, becomes evident.

Your story, thus, is not just about your individual journey, challenges, joys, or sorrows. It's a chapter in the vast narrative of the universe. And as you embrace this truth, you'll find yourself evolving, growing, and ascending to a realm of consciousness where you see, feel, and live in unison with the boundless intelligence of life.

How often do we recognize this profound intelligence within us and see its mirrored reflection in our daily lives?

The belief that life is a series of random, disconnected events is an illusion that stems from our ego, which often feels the need to control, to dictate, and to shape our reality. But what if, instead of being mere puppeteers of our lives, we acknowledged the maestro—the universe itself—and its incredible design?

Your life, in all its complexity, beauty, and challenges, isn't a mere coincidence. To some, this maestro is the universe—vast, enigmatic, and omnipotent. To others, like myself, this supreme conductor is God, the divine craftsman who molds our destinies with love, wisdom, and intention. Whomever or whatever you believe holds the baton, it's evident that our existence isn't accidental. There's an underlying rhythm, a melody that plays beneath the cacophony of everyday life.

This realization, this understanding of a higher power or a grand design, is both humbling and empowering. It suggests that our joys and sorrows, our triumphs and trials, are not mere happenstances. They are part of a larger narrative, a chapter in a story that has been written especially for us.

Beyond the tangible, beyond what we can touch, see, or hear, there's a force that binds us all—a cosmic energy, a divine blueprint. It's a force that stitches together the moments of serendipity, the unexpected blessings, and even the inexplicable challenges.

In recognizing this, we can find solace during turbulent times and gratitude in moments of bliss. For in this vast cosmos of countless stars and infinite mysteries, our individual stories have been penned with intention and care. The orchestration of our lives by God or the universe is a testament to the fact that we are not just fleeting specks in the vastness of space and time. We are cherished, we are significant, and every note of our existence resonates with purpose.

The very intelligence that orchestrates the movements of celestial bodies, that governs the changing seasons, and that breathes life into every living creature is deeply intertwined with your journey. Each moment, each challenge, and each joy you experience is meticulously designed to help you evolve, grow, and ascend.

This realization carries with it a profound sense of trust. Trust in the understanding that there's an intelligence far grander than our individual selves at play. Trust in the unfolding journey, in the experiences woven by the universe specifically for us. And, with this trust comes the freedom to let go—to relinquish our need to control and, instead, embrace the flow of life.

As you pause and gaze around, realize the beauty of this singular, unique moment. This exact moment, with its specific blend of feelings, surroundings, and sensations, will never recur. You're witnessing a once-in-a-lifetime event in the vast timeline of the universe. The privilege to experience, to bear witness, to be part of this grand cosmic story is indeed a testament to the magic of life and the profound intelligence that underpins it all.

When you begin to deeply trust life, every event, emotion, or circumstance becomes a chapter in the ever-unfolding narrative of your existence. Instead of walking through life with a preset map, you dance with spontaneity, allowing life to lead. This dance isn't always graceful; sometimes, it's a waltz of joy, and at times, it's a tango of challenges. Yet, every step, every twirl, and every stumble holds a purpose.

You might find yourself looking at the mundane differently. That mundane traffic jam isn't just an inconvenience but a moment of stillness, a pause, perhaps a reminder of the journey's importance over the destination. A disagreement with a loved one isn't just a rift but an invitation to deeper understanding, patience, and compassion.

The more you trust in this unseen choreography, the more you notice the subtle cues, the nudges, the synchronicities. The random stranger you met in a café who said just what you needed to hear, the unexpected rain shower that made you take shelter and inadvertently avoid an accident, the forgotten book that falls off a shelf, offering wisdom you've been seeking. These aren't mere coincidences but whispers from the universe, guiding notes in your dance of life.

When you operate from this realm of trust, you cultivate a deeper listening. Not just the listening of words but the listening of experiences, of emotions, and of the silent pulses of life. You begin to recognize that beneath the visible surface of events lies a bedrock of profound intelligence and intention.

Diving deeper, you begin to encounter the parts of yourself that had been buried under layers of conditioning, fear, and past hurts. In trusting life, you trust yourself. You give yourself permission to excavate, to explore, to heal, and to rediscover. The inner child that wants to play, the wounded teenager that seeks understanding, the wise elder that holds timeless truths—all these facets begin to emerge, reintegrating into your being.

To trust life is to live with your heart open, even when it aches because you understand that even pain has its purpose. It's about living with curiosity, wonder, and an unshakeable belief that every experience is a step closer to your higher self, to wisdom, to love, and ultimately, to awakening.

The Unfurling Journey Within

When you start living in the resonance that life is inherently for you, a transformative shift happens. This isn't a naive belief that negates the challenges and heartbreaks of existence but a profound understanding that even in the midst of turmoil, there's an underlying purpose designed to serve your evolution.

The external world, with all its chaos, distractions, and demands, often appears to be the source of our discontent. We point fingers at circumstances, at others, at the countless external variables, convinced they are the architects of our suffering. But as higher consciousness emerges, clarity dawns. You realize that while external situations can be challenging, the real suffering is the internal narrative you craft around them. It's not the rain but the complaint about the rain, not the wound but the story of the wound that intensifies our pain.

The spells or deeply ingrained patterns of behavior and belief are like old scripts running in the backdrop, influencing your actions, reactions, and interpretations of the world. These were formulated during the tender years when the psyche was malleable, absorbing every praise, criticism, and experience. These patterns, like tinted glasses, color every aspect of your perception.

But here's the magic of higher consciousness: it gifts you the ability to recognize these spells, these stories. You start seeing the illusory nature of these tales, and their grip on your reality starts loosening. Like a diligent gardener, you begin to weed out these outdated patterns, making space for fresh blossoms of insights and realizations.

Imagine a bottle filled with muddy water. Left undisturbed, the sediment settles at the bottom, and clarity emerges on top. In the same vein, when you stop agitating your internal world with resistance and instead bring gentle awareness to it, the muddiness of old wounds, traumas, and beliefs settles. The clear water of consciousness rises, and you start navigating life with lucidity.

The journey of awakening is a spiral. As you ascend higher, you might encounter familiar challenges, but with each loop, you face them with more wisdom and more grace. The fear of old spells diminishes, and what remains is a profound trust—trust in the process, trust in life's wisdom, and trust in the miraculous dance of existence. Life, you realize, isn't happening to you but is you, and in that realization lies the freedom to truly BE.

Embracing the Gift of Response-ability

The gift of "response-ability" is akin to possessing the keys to one's own prison. It's the key that unlocks the chains of victimhood, blame, and resentment. While our innate reaction might be to see challenges as barriers or as evidence of life's injustice, embracing our ability to respond paves the way for empowerment, freedom, and growth.

Our initial reaction to adversity is often resistance. The storyteller inside might weave narratives of blame, painting us as the perennial victims of circumstances or other people's actions. This stance, while momentarily comforting, robs us of our power. It places our joy, peace, and well-being in external hands.

However, recognizing our own "response-ability" in situations is like discovering an inner compass. Instead of feeling lost in the storm of challenges, this compass reminds us that we have the capacity to navigate, to choose our response, and to steer our ship in the direction of growth. It's about acknowledging that while we might not have control over external events, we have complete control over our reactions to them.

When we see every challenge as an opportunity, a teacher in disguise, we evolve. Instead of being knocked down by adversity, we develop resilience. Much like the inflatable doll, no matter how many times we're pushed over, we bounce back, standing taller and stronger each time. It's not about denying the pain or difficulty but about recognizing its transformative potential.

It's in these moments of challenge that the true essence of "response-ability" shines through. It whispers to us, "Look within. What can this teach you? How can you grow from this?" As we heed to this inner call, we find reservoirs of strength, wisdom, and resilience we never knew we possessed. We start seeing life not as a series of random events but as a perfectly orchestrated symphony guiding us toward our highest self.

In embracing our "response-ability," we reclaim our narrative. We become the authors of our life stories and are no longer mere characters acted upon by external forces. Every challenge becomes a plot twist, leading us to greater wisdom and deeper understanding.

And in this understanding, a profound joy emerges. It's the joy of knowing that life is inherently for us. The hurdles, the pains, the setbacks—they're all stepping stones, helping us bridge the gap between who we are and who we are meant to be. And as we walk this bridge, we discover a profound truth—all the joy, clarity, and aliveness we ever sought were never outside. They've always been within, waiting for us to simply tune in and listen.

Embracing higher consciousness means realizing that the external world, with all its ups and downs, is not the final reality. The final reality, the ever-present truth, is the essence of our being—vibrant, alive, and joyful. It is always with us, just waiting for us to pay attention.

So, every time you feel lost in the whirlwind of life, pause. Take a deep breath, say "hello" to whatever you're feeling, and remember you are life. With each acknowledgment, with each moment of awareness, you thin the cloud bank of illusion, stepping closer to the radiant truth of who you truly are.

With every level of consciousness, there's an invitation to evolve, to shed old patterns, and to embrace a richer, more profound understanding of existence. As your journey continues, may each stage illuminate a path toward greater wisdom and inner peace.

Navigating Consciousness: A Path to Freedom

My life had been haunted by an unmet need—the need to feel seen, to be acknowledged, to matter. The true transformation came when I decided to validate myself. The choice to believe that I mattered, irrespective of external circumstances or comparisons, was liberating. It was a conscious decision to reclaim my space, to affirm my existence, and to embrace every facet of my being.

Choosing to matter was not about seeking validation from others but about recognizing and honoring my intrinsic worth. It was about understanding that my existence, emotions, and experiences were valid and valuable. And in this newfound realization, I found not just acceptance and freedom but a profound sense of belonging—to myself, my family, and the world.

Throughout the pages of this book, we embarked on a transformative journey, one that took us through the intricate maze of human consciousness, guiding us from the very depths of our unaware states to the pinnacle of awakened realization. This journey is not just theoretical; it is deeply practical, deeply human, and profoundly transformative.

Given the inner geek in me who can't resist a well-crafted summary, let's encapsulate our journey as we approach the final leg of our time together.

The Pillar of Self-Awareness: Choice in the Midst of Challenge

Our journey began with the recognition of the first two phases: when life seems to be happening to you and by you. These phases encapsulate the foundational pillar of self-awareness. At this stage, we often perceive ourselves at the mercy of external circumstances or believe that we must take the reins of control to dictate our destiny. But within this pillar lies the profound gift of choice. With self-awareness comes the ability to recognize patterns, to see our habitual reactions, and, most importantly, to choose our responses. Even in the stormiest of situations, self-awareness illuminates the power we have in choice—a choice in perception, reaction, and action.

The Pillar of Self-Acceptance: Embracing Life With Love

Progressing further, we delve into the realm where life unfolds in you and for you. This represents the revered pillar of self-acceptance. Here, we start to recognize that our experiences, emotions, and thoughts are not merely random events but profound lessons tailored for our growth. With this realization comes the gift of love. We begin to embrace ourselves with compassion, understanding, and genuine acceptance. We see that every challenge and every joy has its purpose. In this pillar, love is not just an emotion; it becomes a way of being.

The Pillar of Self-Awakening: The Ultimate Freedom

As our journey culminates, we step into the realm where life happens through you and recognize that life is you. This is the pillar of self-awakening. Here, the boundaries between the self and the universe blur. The duality of existence melts away to reveal the interconnectedness of all. Within this pillar lies the ultimate gift of freedom. Freedom from the confines of limiting beliefs, freedom from the shackles of the ego, and freedom to truly be in sync with the cosmic dance of existence.

In summary, this book is not just about understanding concepts. It is a guide, a companion, and a tool to navigate the phases of consciousness. From the choices we make rooted in self-awareness to the unconditional love of self-acceptance, culminating in the boundless freedom of self-awakening, this journey is an invitation to witness and experience the profound beauty of existence in its entirety.

To my dear reader:

What does this tormented child inside me truly need to understand?

That it's okay to be silly, to be joyous, to be sad. Emotions are a spectrum, and each hue is crucial.

She needs the freedom to indulge in excitement without the fear of forgetfulness. She needs to know that spontaneity doesn't mean negligence.

Can we convince her that she isn't bound to a rigid regime? That she can bask in spontaneity, trust herself, and navigate through emotions without the looming threat of consequences? Can we show her the bliss of self-love, unmarred by societal standards or personal doubts? Can we show her she matters by "being" not by "doing"? And in this journey of self-discovery and acceptance, can we gently lead her to the profound realization that her worthiness is a divine birthright bestowed upon her by a higher power, perhaps God, as understood in her faith or spirituality? This worthiness is not something she has to earn or prove; it's an inherent gift. It's a testament to the idea that we are all created with an intrinsic value, a sacred essence that is not contingent on external validation or accomplishments. Can she feel, deep in her soul, that her worthiness is 100% and has nothing to do with her actions or achievements but is rather a grace given by God, a fundamental truth that exists simply because she does.

Can we remind her that on the other side of failure are her dreams. She is not limited by her current ability but rather by the capacity and the expansiveness within her. She doesn't have to do this alone. She can seek support, and that is not considered weak but rather wise. Can I remind her that there is room between resilience and grit and space to be cared for?

May she be open to the possibility that divine inspiration resides within her. She doesn't need validation, not even from a divine Post-it note. Loving herself is not selfish; rather, it is selfish to not show love for her and expect others to do it for her. Can we encourage her to break away from toxic beliefs, release pent-up guilt, and embrace her true self, and implore that those are her rights? Can we remind her that she is loved, that she is love, and that no one is coming to save her because no one ever needed to; everything she ever needed is within.

And so as it is written for me, may it be written for you.

The Unending Dance of Self-Discovery

And so, dear reader, as the pages of this book draw to a close, it is my hope that your own journey is just beginning—a dance that will continue to ebb and flow with the rhythms of your life.

In the passages of this book, we embarked on an exploration from awareness to acceptance to awakening, only to realize that this trajectory isn't linear. The path isn't a straight line from ignorance to enlightenment but rather a series of undulating waves, where, at times, we find ourselves deeply submerged in self-awareness, and at others, we float on the surface of awakening.

Our lives are not chapters to be completed but circles to be embraced, circling back and spiraling upward, ever-evolving. Just as a spiral staircase leads us higher with every turn, so does our journey, taking us deeper into ourselves even as we ascend to greater consciousness.

The universe, in its grand wisdom, serves us a perfect blend of light and shadow, day and night, joy and pain. This 50/50 balance isn't a glitch; it's a feature. It is a potent reminder that nothing is ever truly in discord. In the juxtaposition of the delightful and the distressing, we are offered ceaseless opportunities to grow, to understand, to accept, and ultimately, to awaken.

However, while the world around us will always throw challenges our way, it's our interpretation of these events that defines our experience. We oscillate between moments of sheer awareness and sudden sleepiness, from heart-opening acceptance to stubborn resistance, from the clarity of awakening to the fog of confusion.

But remember, nothing has gone awry. The universe doesn't expect us to be perennially joyous, nor does it want us to constantly seek perfection. The real invitation isn't to attain an uninterrupted state of happiness but to be conscious humans—humans who don't wait for a nod from the world to live or love. Humans who understand that their true essence is one of boundless curiosity, unwavering worth, and limitless love.

In this dance of life, as you waltz between awareness, acceptance, and awakening, remember you have always been and will always be a magnificent amalgamation of everything. You're the universe's way of experiencing itself, of celebrating its vastness and variety.

So, as you turn this page and step into the world with renewed understanding, know that there's no one coming to save you—because you were never lost to begin with. All along, you've been your savior, your guide, and your compass. Embrace your journey, for in its twists and turns lies the magic of becoming who it is that you have always been. Life itself.

Thank you for taking this journey with me. Wherever you are, whatever you're facing, know that within you lies an ocean of potential waiting to be explored. Dive in, dear reader, for the depths hold treasures unimaginable.

Final Notes

Crafting this book has been a journey spanning five years. As I approached its final stages, readying it for print, I was taken aback by the immense evolution I had undergone during this period. Many of the insights and perspectives that once felt groundbreaking to me seemed no longer sufficient, necessitating a re-evaluation and refinement. Please bear with me; the nature of our personal and collective growth means that some of these perspectives may seem outdated soon—perhaps within a year or even a mere moment after reading them. As we continually delve deeper into our boundless selves, always expanding and redefining our understanding, we realize our infinite potential. The essence of our being is in perpetual evolution, and the knowledge we accumulate is our gift to share freely with the world. So, thank you for joining me on this evolving journey.

Letter to My Younger Self

Dear Younger Me,

As I sit here, reflecting on the journey that has led to the creation of this book, my thoughts inevitably drift back to you—the hero of this story, the resilient spirit that has endured more than you ever should have. I see you with your broken flowers, each petal a symbol of the hardships and trials you've faced. You've hung on hooks of doubt, fear, and uncertainty, wondering if your grip would hold or if you'd fall into the abyss of despair.

I remember the dark highways you've navigated, the paths that seemed endless and shrouded in shadows. Those roads were winding and treacherous, filled with obstacles that tested your strength and resolve. Yet, here you stand, a testament to the unyielding power of the human spirit.

You, younger me, are the embodiment of strength and potential. Every step you took, every tear you shed, has been a stepping stone to the future you were building—a future I now live. Your experiences, as harrowing as they were, have been the raw materials for the wisdom and insights that fill the pages of this book.

Your journey has not been in vain. It has been a pilgrimage back to your true home—the home within yourself. You've discovered that the love, acceptance, and validation you sought were never hanging on someone else's hook; they were always nestled within the depths of your own heart.

As I acknowledge your role in this grand narrative of my life, I want you to know that every challenge you faced and every obstacle you overcame has been integral to shaping who I am today. You taught me resilience. You taught me that even in our darkest moments, there is a light within us that never dims. You showed me that our worth is not contingent on external circumstances but is an unassailable truth that lives within us.

Your legacy lives on in every word I write, in every life that this book touches. You are not just a character in a story; you are the soul of my story, the heart of my journey. Because of you, I have found my way home—to a place of self-acceptance, love, and boundless potential.

So, thank you, younger me. Thank you for your courage, for your tears, for your laughter, and for your undying hope. Thank you for enduring those broken flowers and dark highways. You are the unsung hero of this story, and I am forever grateful for the path you've walked.

With all my love and gratitude,

Me

Acknowledgments

To My Dearest Mom,

As I pen these words, my heart brims with gratitude, for it was your unwavering belief in me that made this journey and this book possible. Your faith in my potential was the guiding light that led me to recognize that I, too, mattered. That my story had significance and that love, indeed, conquers all.

You were the voice of truth that challenged me to see beyond the veil of my own narrative. I vividly recall the day you questioned my self-deceiving story of, "I don't love what I do, but I love that it enables me to do what I love." That moment was a turning point, a catalyst that propelled me towards authenticity.

Your subsequent battle with cancer was a period that redefined my life's priorities. Those two years spent caring for you, the person I cherished the most, were both heartbreakingly precious and profoundly transformative. In your courage, I found my own. In your love, I discovered a depth of compassion and resilience I never knew I possessed.

Your passing was not an end but a new beginning. It sparked the birth of my true calling—a journey I had been too apprehensive to embrace. But armed with your legacy, I stepped into the world of coaching, no longer lying to myself but living in alignment with my purpose every single day.

I write, I speak, I coach, and in every word, every piece of advice, every moment of connection, I carry a piece of you. Your spirit, your strength, and your love are intertwined in the very fabric of my work.

Thank you, Mom, for being the wind beneath my wings, the steady force that lifted me to soar to heights I once thought unreachable. Your belief in me was not just a gift but a sacred trust that I carry forward with honor and love.

In memory of you and in honor of the love that you so freely gave, this work continues. Every breakthrough and every moment of healing that happens through my coaching is a testament to the incredible person you are.

With all my love and endless gratitude,

Your adoring daughter—Leah

To My Beloved Boys,

In these pages and within the chapters of my life, there's an ever-present, glowing thread of love—a love so vast and deep, dedicated to the three of you. May you always feel the warmth and security of this love enveloping you in every step you take.

I want you all to know your worth, to feel it deep within your bones. Remember, the best of who you are has always been nestled inside you, like a precious gem waiting to be discovered and polished. Nothing more is required of you than to be your authentic selves, embracing the unique brilliance you each possess.

My faith in you is boundless, unwavering, and unconditional. It's a faith that sees your potential even when clouds obscure the sky, a belief that knows no limits, and a trust that endures through every challenge and triumph.

I am forever grateful for your belief in me and for the space, time, and understanding you've generously offered, allowing me to pursue this dream of writing. Your patience and support have been the quiet yet powerful forces that helped bring these words to life.

As you journey through life, may you always carry the knowledge of your worth, the strength of your character, and the endless love that surrounds you. May you stand tall, grounded in the truth that the best of who you are shines brightly from within. I love you more.

With all my love and deepest gratitude,

Mom, MORE

To My Dearest Husband,

In the symphony of my life, you are the steady rhythm that grounds each note, the harmony that enriches every melody. To call you my best friend, my life partner, feels like an understatement for the profound connection we share, a bond that transcends time and space. If love could be measured, know that my love for you would stretch a thousand years more, and even then, it would only just begin to touch the surface.

In the chapters of my next life, my only prayer is to find you sooner, to be granted the gift of navigating a longer journey together, treasuring each moment more deeply than the last. You are my steady force, my unwavering rock, the one who brings a sense of calm to the chaos of the world.

Your love is the foundation upon which I stand tall. It's a love that supports and strengthens me, giving me the courage to extend myself into the world in the biggest ways possible. In your eyes, I find the unwavering belief and understanding that fuels my spirit, reassuring me that no matter what life throws our way, no matter what others may say or think, you know the true essence of my heart and intentions.

Thank you for being there in every sense of the word. For your presence that is both a sanctuary and a source of endless strength. Thank you for being my forever, the constant in my ever-changing world. Knowing that you are there, that you will always be there, is the greatest assurance I could ever have.

With all my love, now and a thousand years more

Leah

To My Dear Sister and Brother,

This acknowledgment is a tribute to you both, the unsung heroes in the story of my life.

To my sister, who had to step into roles and responsibilities far beyond her years. Growing up, we navigated the complex dance of sisterhood, often finding ourselves out of step. But as the years have passed, those steps have synchronized, transforming us from siblings to forever friends. Your soul radiates a beauty that is both internal and external, a beauty that I consciously choose to have in my life, not just as family but as an integral part of my world.

To my brother, your unwavering faith in me has been a constant in my life. Your prayers for my tests, my races, and my struggles have been a source of strength, especially knowing the magnitude of your own challenges. Your life is a testament to what truly matters, a lesson in grace and resilience. You could have chosen the path of complaints and grievances, yet you chose gratitude and acceptance, teaching me more about life and its values than any book or lecture ever could.

Both of you, in your unique ways, have enriched my journey, helping shape the person I am and aspire to be. I am profoundly grateful for your love, your lessons, and the shared bond that continues to grow with each passing day.

With all my love and appreciation,

Sledge

To the Extraordinary Souls That Make Up My Tribe,

This acknowledgment is for you—my steadfast community of friends who have journeyed with me through the ebbs and flows of life. Your support, love, and unwavering presence have been the bedrock upon which I've built my courage to face the world.

In times of difficulty, your empathy and understanding have been my sanctuary. In moments of triumph and joy, your celebration and happiness for me have amplified the sweetness of those victories. Each of you, in your unique and special way, has contributed to the richness of my life.

I am immensely grateful for the laughter we've shared, the tears we've shed, and the countless memories we've created. This book and the journey it encapsulates is as much yours as it is mine. It is a dedication to our shared past, a celebration of the present, and an excited toast to the future that is yet to unfold.

Here's to the beauty of friendship, to the journey we've shared, and to the adventures that await us.

With deepest gratitude and love,

Leah

Made in the USA
Middletown, DE
02 February 2024